WITHDRAWN

The French Revolution
Debate in English
Literature and Culture

Recent Titles in
Contributions to the Study of World Literature

The French Revolution Debate in English Literature and Culture

Edited by
LISA PLUMMER CRAFTON

Contributions to the Study of World Literature, Number 87

GREENWOOD PRESS
Westport, Connecticut • London

PR
129
.F8
F74
1997

Library of Congress Cataloging-in-Publication Data

The French Revolution debate in English literature and culture /
   edited by Lisa Plummer Crafton.
      p.   cm.—(Contributions to the study of world literature,
  ISSN 0738-9345 ; no. 87)
   Includes bibliographical references and index.
   ISBN 0-313-30496-3 (alk. paper)
   1. English literature—French influences. 2. France—History—
Revolution, 1789–1799—Literature and the revolution. 3. France—
History—Revolution, 1789–1799—Foreign public opinion, British.
4. English literature—19th century—History and criticism.
5. English literature—18th century—History and criticism.
6. France—In literature. I. Crafton, Lisa Plummer, 1956– .
II. Series.
PR129.F8F74   1997
  820.9′358—dc21   97–13719

British Library Cataloguing in Publication Data is available.

Library of Congress Catalog Card Number: 97–13719
ISBN: 0-313-30496-3
ISSN: 0738-9345

First published in 1997

Greenwood Press, 88 Post Road West, Westport, CT 06881
An imprint of Greenwood Publishing Group, Inc.

Printed in the United States of America

The paper used in this book complies with the
Permanent Paper Standard issued by the National
Information Standards Organization (Z39.48–1984).

10 9 8 7 6 5 4 3 2 1

34398-5

Contents

vi   Contents

Representations of Revolutionary Women in Political
Caricature

Acknowledgments

The original works in this volume all owe debt to the National Endowment for the Humanities and to David Bromwich at Yale University, who directed the 1991 NEH Summer Seminar on "The Revolution Debate and English Literature of the 1790s." Like all the contributors, I thank the NEH and Professor Bromwich for this exciting intellectual endeavor.

My work on this volume was made easier by collegial advice from all the contributors and has been particularly aided by my colleagues in the English Department at the State University of West Georgia. I wish to especially thank my colleague and chair, Robert Snyder, for release time to complete and edit this collection and my graduate research assistants Amy Faulds and Mitzi McFarland for their assistance during various stages of this work.

As always, I thank my family and friends for support and encouragement.

Introduction

Lisa Plummer Crafton

It may not be exaggerated to say, as did the London Corresponding Society in 1789, that the debate in England over the French Revolution was the topic to which "all thinking minds were drawn" during the decade of the 1790s. Certainly, the effects of the French Revolution upon English culture in the last decade of the eighteenth century has been a topic to which many scholarly minds have been drawn in the late twentieth century, especially during the last ten years. Romantic studies in particular have served to interpret the alliance between the Romantic movement and the Revolution since at least M. H. Abrams 1963 essay "The Spirit of the Age." Abrams's thesis has had such impact that recently Abrams noted that his speculations have become attributed to him as almost a formula for defining Romanticism. Responding to such reductionism, Abrams reaffirmed his point by quoting from the original essay: "I do not propose the electrifying proposition that 'le romantisme, c'est la revolution.' Romanticism is no one thing. It is many very individual poets, who wrote poems manifesting a greater diversity of qualities it seems to me than those of any preceding era."[1] That being said, Abrams goes on to reaffirm his belief that the complexities of the Revolution of 1798 clearly shaped intellectual and imaginative discourse.

More recent evidence of the continuing interest in the interrelationships between this phenomenal historical event and a range of intellectual and cultural disciplines, literature in particular, came in the form of three scholarly meetings in the United States (as well as four significant bicentennial conferences in England in 1989–1990) in the past nine years: the Indiana Symposium on Romanticism, held in February 1988 in conjunction with "William Wordsworth and the Age of English Romanticism," a highly praised exhibit which emphasized "The Age of Revolutions"; the 1990 conference "Revolutionary Romanticism 1790–1990," a Bucknell University meeting sponsored by the Wordsworth Trust America; and the National Endowment for the Humanities

1991 Summer Seminar at Yale University, "The Revolution Debate and Literature in the 1790s." Directed by David Bromwich, this seminar went much further than the conferences in examining the phenomena of the Revolution debate as a network of cultural influences that affected and shaped not only history and literature but also philosophy, political theory, art, economics–in short, a vastly interdisciplinary cultural event.

The kind of investigations and analyses within the scope of the NEH seminar and of more interest in the last five years risks being undervalued because of the almost clichéd nature of the theory that the French Revolution— in its urge for democratic reform, its ideals of liberty, equality, and fraternity— represented the optimistic impulses of mankind in the *fin de siècle* of the eighteenth century. The alliance between the Romantic exaltation of this period—lines like Wordsworth's "Bliss was it in that dawn to be alive" exemplify—and the new hopes for political and economic equality (seen in Paine, Godwin, Wordsworth) ensure that both literature and political theory see the Revolution as a watershed date in their histories. But there is much danger in accepting the cliché without fully examining and understanding both what influenced and shaped the discourse of the debate and its effects, especially after the Revolution's violent turn of events and the declaration of war between England and France in February 1793. It still remains to be understood that the Revolution was not simply a background or an influence on cultural history but rather, as Raymond Williams said in 1958, "the mould in which general experience was cast."[2]

The French Revolution then is arguably the largest, most far-reaching and broadest "debate" in literary and cultural history, a war of ideas that encom- passes philosophy, theories of history, the study of language, the history of art, gender stereotypes, religion as well as a much broader spectrum of literature than might be thought, in terms of subject, genre, style, and chronology. In the introduction to her collection of excerpts from the debate, Marilyn Butler suggests that the formal parameters of the debate span about six years, from the enthusiastic first responses to the Revolution in 1789 to the active repression and censorship of radicalism through the printed and spoken word, actions that came to a climax in 1795.[3] While it is fair to isolate the debate's parameters in terms of the most specifically focused revolutionary tracts and counterrevolu- tionary responses, such a formal time line is an artificial narrowing of the debate, whose influences reach far into the nineteenth century.

The last decade has seen many solid individual studies of the effects of the Revolution upon a variety of genres, disciplines, themes, and styles of discourse. Some of the most notable include Olivia Smith's *The Politics of Language 1791–1819* on political/theoretical controversies over language; Lynn Hunt's *Politics, Culture, and Class in the French Revolution* on the sociocultural and political networks of the Revolution; Ronald Paulson's *Representations of Revolution 1789–1820* on aesthetic representations of revolution; Seamus Deane's *The French Revolution and the Enlightenment in England* on the influence of French Enlightenment philosophers on English radical writers; Chris Jones' *Radical Sensibility: Literature and Ideas in the 1790s* on the concept of sensibility as a "site of ideological conflict" in the Revolutionary decade; Gary Kelly's *Revolutionary Feminism: The Mind and Career of Mary Wollstonecraft* on Mary Wollstonecraft's formulation of a feminism shaped by revolutionary concerns; Gerald Izenberg's *Impossible Individuality: Romanticism, Revolution, and the Origins of Modern Selfhood, 1787–1802* on the ways in which modern selfhood emerged in the wake of political, sociocultural, and psychological forces in the 1790s; Barton Friedman's *Fabricating History: English Writers on the French Revolution* on the boundary between history and fiction in narrative strategies after the Revolution; Doris Kadish's *Politicizing Gender: Narrative Strategies in the Aftermath of the French Revolution* on how nineteenth- century narratives (French and British novels) retell the Revolution, politicizing gender through semiotic strategies; Stephen Prickett's *England and the French Revolution* on how English society assimilated ideas about the Revolution, especially in the radical Reform activities; and others that are named in the select bibliography at the end of this volume.

Also, readers should be aware of four recent collections of essays that have to do with revolution in some significant sense, each of which had its origin in conferences on the French Revolution: *Wordsworth in Context* (1992) offers six essays on William Wordsworth and two on Dorothy Wordsworth, each of which touches on the political, aesthetic, or philosophical revolutions inaugurated in Wordsworth's work; *Romantic Revolutions: Criticism and Theory* (1990) contains twenty-one essays on recent "revolutions" in Romantic criticism and theory; *Revolution and English Romanticism: Politics and Rhetoric* (1990) offers fourteen essays on figurative and linguistic modes of representation of the Revolution, emphasizing the indeterminacy that pervades Romantic discourse; finally, more relevant to this study is *Revolution in Writing: British Literary Responses to the French Revolution* (1991), a collection from the bicentennial conferences on the Revolution held in England in 1989–1990, which contains seven essays on some of the notable players in the Revolution debate— Wollstonecraft, Paine, Burke, Hannah More—but within a general framework of theoretical exploration. As the editor Kelvin Everest points out, the essays in this collection are all concerned with the negotiation between text, history, and theory.[4]

It is this purpose of this volume to explore a redefinition of the debate that acknowledges the far-reaching power and consequences of the Revolution that Matthew Arnold characterized as a "spiritual event" of "powerful and worldwide interest." Like Arnold, the authors of these essays acknowledge that this revolution appealed to "an order of ideas which are universal, certain, permanent" and believe it to be a remarkable thing, especially "when we consider how little of mind, or anything so worthy and quickening as mind, comes into the motives which alone, in general, impel great masses of men."[5] While it is true that Romantic poetry and prose offers a natural and fruitful example of the effects and manifestations of the "spirit of the age," (note that three of the four collections listed above emphasize Romantic studies) the Revolution debate in England transcended boundaries and margins of genre, style, and discipline. The aim of this volume is to represent inclusively within one collection explorations of the diverse effects of the Revolution in both verbal and visual art, poetry and prose, history and fiction, politics and religion, philosophy and language theory. By offering analyses of such a broad range of writers and artists who shaped and were shaped by the French Revolution, this volume dramatizes the broad scope and diversity of the debate, thus offering an interdisciplinary analysis of the debate as a whole and an emphasis on the extent to which "all thinking minds" were drawn to the debate on one level or another.

The essays here treat both old and new names (figures writing before, during, and after the 1790s), both traditional and nontraditional subjects. While Faulkner dissects what is perhaps the most compelling relationship in the pamphlet wars, that between Edmund Burke and Richard Price, other major figures are seen in conjunction with subjects not traditionally associated with them. Burke, Paine, and Wollstonecraft, for example, are contextualized in terms of religion; Blake's vision of universal harmony is seen in the context of the politics of language and language theory.

Appropriately, the first essay traces the complexities of the rhetorical and political relationship between Burke and his primary adversary Richard Price, figures identified now as primary agents of the Revolution debate. With attention to all of Burke's writing, not just *Reflections*, John Faulkner analyzes Burke's dialogic relationship with Price in many facets of the debate, especially the characterization of the English revolution of 1688, the notion of "rights," and the representation of the October Days incident. In noting Burke's specific representations of Price, Faulkner suggests the ways by which Burke attempts to deny authority to Price (e.g., satirical portrayals) and the subsequent reactions to a perceived misrepresentation of Price by contemporary Mary Wollstonecraft and by recent scholars, notably D. O. Thomas. Finally, Faulkner exposes the political lenses through which Burke perceived Price, by close historical and rhetorical analysis of the politics of toleration and the political maneuvering of figures like Shelburne, thus disclosing "strands of coherence not always recognized" between Burke as Whig and Burke as counterrevolutionary.

Next, Pat Michaelson takes up the marriage of religion and politics in the debate, focusing on Wollstonecraft, Paine, and Burke. She frames her discussion by questioning the effect of a writer's religion upon his or her audience and the extent to which it affects the power of argument, defining religion as a kind of "theory" in that it is a set of basic assumptions from which argument can begin. Thus, because "religious convictions necessarily have political implications," as Michaelson suggests, and because most forms of radicalism in England had religious origins, the major figures in the Revolution debate are contextualized here in terms of the critical heritage about their religious beliefs (Paine's Deism or Quakerism; Wollstonecraft's Anglicanism, and Burke's Anglicanism or Catholicism) and, more importantly, why, to what extent, and in what function these labels matter. Michaelson then focuses on the rhetorical role of religion in the debate, examining Paine's *Rights of Man*, Wollstonecraft's *Vindication of the Rights of Men*, and Burke's *Reflections*. Although religion functions differently in each text and in the scholarly debates about the authors, it functions to cement the bond of shared assumptions between author and reader that is essential in the art of persuasion.

In my essay on Blake, I examine Blake's participation in the Revolution debate in his rendering of the first stages of the Revolution in the prophetic poem *The French Revolution*. Emphasizing the poem's synthesis of historical and mythological realms and its place as an early text in the formation of Blake's later mythology, one can see the comparison between Blake's moral, spiritual interpretation of revolution and that of Richard Price's *Discourse on the Love of our Country*. While Price and Blake are both partisan writers in some sense, they subordinate political to moral or metaphysical discussion, especially in terms of imagery and in the author's emphasis upon an "eternal language." Given this characterization of language, both writers are seen in context of the political debates about language and linguistic theory that flourished in the last decades of the eighteenth century and which helped shape the parameters of the debate. Blake's *The French Revolution* is read in terms of its verbal warfare and emphasis on voicing, which urges the Blakean necessity of individual imaginative engagement that effects a revolution in any ultimate sense.

Figures traditionally associated with the debate are subjected to close analyses of their relationships with other pivotal figures and movements. One of the key figures of the polemical debates of the 1790s was William Godwin, whose progressive philosophy included rationalism, utilitarianism, and the idea of universal benevolence. Centering on Wordsworth's Revolutionary crisis as narrated in *The Prelude*, Evan Radcliffe analyzes Wordsworth's experience in context of his participation in the debate of the liberal philosophical tradition, especially his belief in the ideal of human benevolence. A belief widely debated in the 1790s, the ideal of benevolence—that benevolence and sympathy can be extended to all humanity—went through many permutations in the decade. While Godwinian philosophy appealed to many, the fact that his rationalist approach appeared to deny the value of individual human affections caused the ideal of benevolence to become tarred along with Godwin himself. Radcliffe examines the discussion of major figures in the debate (including Shaftesbury, Hutcheson, Hume, Smith, and Burke), suggesting that it is their discussions that in effect defined the terms of the debate. In pointing out the differences among various versions of the ideal, Radcliffe exposes how Wordsworth's final repudiation of Godwin disclaims only a particular, exclusive definition of benevolence and suggests that Wordsworth, in fact, uses that repudiation to strengthen his own ideals after the disappointment of the Revolution itself, so that what "Godwin finally provides Wordsworth in *The Prelude* is something to blame and cast out."

Suggestive of the broad chronological scope of the debate, Frye analyzes Carlyle's 1837 *French Revolution* and its continuing dialogue with the tenets of the debate of the 1790s. Frye contextualizes Carlyle among other interpretations of history in the 1830s and the use of the Revolution debate in the agitation for Parliamentary reform. Frye notes that Carlyle sought to achieve an "historical understanding of the French Revolution," not subordinated to Whig, Tory, or Radical political concerns, that would keep Britain from violence of revolution. Thus, Carlyle asserts his right to define and interpret for his age the significance of the Revolution. In form, Carlyle calls for a revolution in historiography and a revolution in narrative perspective that could adequately represent revolution. To exemplify, Frye analyzes the relationship between Burke and Carlyle as Carlyle attempts to displace Burkean ideas and rhetoric, specifically by, in Frye's metaphor, "dismembering" Burke's treatment of the October Days episode in the *Reflections*.

The extent to which the Revolution affected other genres and modes of discourse is explored in Trolander's analysis of the epistemic and discursive changes, especially in the "discourse of general nature," linked to the politics of the Revolution and in Kromm's analysis of visual artists' representations of Revolutionary women. Taking up the subject of the interrelationship between the political events and changes in discourse before and after the 1790s, Trolander points out that the political outcome of the French Revolution has rarely figured as a contributory factor in changes in discursive practice after 1790; rather it has been seen by most as a symptom of epistemological and ideological shifts already under way. Trolander, by contrast, suggests that the discursive changes that took place at the end of the eighteenth century *did* hinge upon the outcome of revolutionary political events, thus challenging the notion, outlined by Foucault and other critics of intellectual history, that discursive practices develop, mutate, or react upon each other according to inherent laws or principles. Using the development of and changes in the "discourse of general nature" that was so prominent in the eighteenth century, Trolander exposes how such changes were linked to political mediation as progressives positively valued such discourse and conservatives tried to negate it. Burke's *Reflections* is analyzed as a text that was "successful in linking the aims and methods of the discourse of general nature to the violent and chaotic events of the French Revolution."

Kromm explores the cultural, political, and aesthetic influences that supported the representation of French revolutionary women in British political caricature. The interrelationship between cultural/political forces and artistic representation allowed the practice to assume, Kromm argues, a kind of documentary accuracy which extended not only to revolutionary women but to all women in the public sphere. Kromm grounds the essay by discussing the market for political caricature in the 1780s–1790s, then explores both positive and negative representations of French events, especially the Bastille and October Days crowd scenes, positing a "representational trajectory" that begins with depictions of actual female participants whose seductive tendencies are rendered as documentary, then moves to an exaggerated, more abstract, allegorical representation, and comes full circle after 1793 when British caricaturists were motivated to return to the portrayal of actual women. Throughout, Kromm associates the political representations with the rising gender stereotypes of madness in women. Although imputations of madness were common in the debate, Kromm focuses on gendered constructions of madness, especially as used by Rowlandson and not common in visual stereotyped representations until the 1780s for reasons related to the social and political constructions of gender roles.

All of the essays contribute to the ongoing exchange of ideas about and interpretation of the relationship between English intellectual culture and the historical phenomenon of the Revolution. Thus, the debate in England of the 1790s continues to enliven the intellectual, literary, and critical debates of the 1990s and serves as a rich focal center for evolving ideas about rhetoric, politics, religion, art and literature.

NOTES

1. Abrams's essay, "Revolutionary Romanticism 1790–1990," appears in a collection of essays from the April 1990 conference at Bucknell University. *Wordsworth in Context*, ed. Pauline Fletcher and John Murphy (Lewisburg: Bucknell University Press, 1992), 19–34.

2. Raymond Williams, *Culture and Society: 1780–1950* (New York: Columbia University Press, 1960), 31.

3. See Marilyn Butler, *Burke, Paine, Godwin, and the Revolution Controversy* (Cambridge: Cambridge University Press, 1984).

4. The four collections of essays are *Wordsworth in Context*, cited in note 1 from the 1990 Bucknell University conference "Revolutionary Romanticism 1790–1990"; *Romantic Revolutions: Criticism and Theory*, ed. Kenneth Johnston et al. (Bloomington: Indiana University Press, 1990), from the 1988 Indiana Symposium on Romanticism; *Revolution and English Romanticism: Politics and Rhetoric*, ed. Keith Hanley and Raman Selden (London: Harvester Wheatsheaf and New York: St. Martin's, 1990), from the 1989 Lancaster University conference on "Revolution and English Romanticism"; and *Revolution in Writing: British Literary Responses to the French Revolution*, ed. Kelvin Everest (Milton Keynes: Open University Press, 1991), papers taken from five different bicentennial conferences in England in 1989.

5. See the "Function of Criticism at the Present Time," where Arnold characterizes the Revolution as "the most animating event in history." *The*

Complete Prose Works of Matthew Arnold, ed. R. H. Super, 10 vols. (Ann Arbor: The University of Michigan Press, 1962), 3:264–65.

Chronology

"September Massacres" in Paris
Newly elected National Convention meets for first time and abolishes
    the monarchy
Blake's *Marriage of Heaven and Hell*
Paine's *Rights of Man* (pt. 2)
Wollstonecraft's *Vindication of the Rights of Woman*
Wordsworth's *Letter to the Bishop of Llandaff*

1793   Execution of Louis XVI and Marie Antoinette
        French declaration of war on England and the Dutch Republic
        The "Terror" begins
        French Girondins executed
        Godwin's *Political Justice*
        Blake's *America*

1794   Habeas Corpus suspended
        State Treason Trials (Thomas Holcraft, John Thelwall, Horne Tooke,
            et al. acquitted)
        Robespierre executed
        Godwin's *Caleb Williams*
        Wollstonecraft's *An Historical and Moral View of the Origin and
            Progress of the French Revolution*

1795   "Two Acts" passed (against seditious meetings)

1796   Burke's *Letters on a Regicide Peace*

1798   Thomas Malthus' *Essay on the Principle of Population*
        Wordsworth and Coleridge's *Lyrical Ballads*

1799   Napoleon becomes first consul
        Wordsworth's *The Two-Part Prelude* (later publications in
            1805 and 1850)

1801   Wordsworth and Coleridge's two-volume edition of *Lyrical Ballads*
            (dated 1800) with Preface

1802   Peace of Amiens halts hostilities between England and France
        for fourteen months
        Cobbett's *Weekly Political Register* founded

1803   England declares war on France

1804   Napoleon is made emperor

1811   Prince of Wales becomes Prince Regent

1814   France invaded by allies of the Fourth Coalition
        Paris falls
        Napoleon abdicates, is exiled to Elba
        Bourbon monarchy restored

1815   Napoleon escapes from Elba and returns to France
        (The "Hundred Days")
        Allied armies defeat the French at Waterloo
        Napoleon surrenders and is exiled to St. Helena
        Louis XVIII restored to the French throne

1817   Habeas Corpus suspended
        Legal suppression of democratic societies

1818   Habeas Corpus restored

1819   Peterloo Massacre

1825   Hazlitt's *The Spirit of the Age*

1837   Carlyle's *The French Revolution*

Burke's Perception of Richard Price

John Faulkner

On November 11, 1789, Edmund Burke received a letter from Charles François Depont, the "very young gentleman at Paris" whom he would address in *Reflections on the Revolution in France*, requesting not so much his opinion as his approval of the French Revolution. Burke could not give Depont the assurances he desired. Burke's wary suspension of judgment on the Revolution, his correspondence suggests, had already ended in settled antipathy late in September. When news arrived of the forced removal of the royal family to Paris on October 6th with the Constituent Assembly in its train, he appears to have regarded it as a confirmation of earlier suspicions.[1] Still, by offering Depont criteria by which the Revolution might be evaluated—even possibly approved—and by keeping to a high level of generality, he was able to imply his disapproval in a tone more equable than that in any of the public writings he would later publish. This is probably a measure of the relatively low intensity of his opposition to what he could consider a while longer to be a French misfortune.[2]

Although for good rhetorical reasons Burke would address *Reflections* to Depont, there are no indications that he had intended to write or even speak publicly on the Revolution until he began to see it as a *British* issue. This occurred in mid-January 1790 when he read the sermon Dr. Richard Price had delivered on November 4th to the Society for Commemorating the Revolution [of 1688] in Great Britain, published as *A Discourse on the Love of Our Country*. Burke began taking notes for a reply, and the greater part of this essay will inquire into how he may have perceived Price as he read it. A month later he would issue his first published writing on the French Revolution, the "substance" of his *Speech on the Army Estimates* delivered in the House of Commons on February 9th, in which he does not mention Dr. Price. Even before its appearance, the London press had reported a second work under way.[3]

The title given for Burke's work-in-progress, *Reflections on Certain Proceedings of the Revolution Society of the Fourth of November, 1789*, amplified his concern in the *Speech on the Army Estimates* to differentiate the Revolution of 1688 in England from that of 1789 in France and indicated that his anxiety about the Revolution in France lay primarily in its consequences for Britain.[4] It also pointed to Price, and on March 2, 1790, he quoted from Price's *Discourse* when he opposed an attempt to repeal the Test and Corporation Acts.[5] Eight months, then, before publication of *Reflections*, public statements had disclosed to any who might be interested many of Burke's positions in the book, if little of the scope of its development or the range of its expression. When *Reflections* did appear on November 1st, "on the Revolution in France" had taken precedence in its title, and "the Proceedings of the Revolution Society" had been generalized to those "of Certain Societies in London relative to that Event." Neither shift in emphasis, however, had deterred Burke from casting Dr. Price as his primary adversary.

Since Burke had not been in London at the time of the Revolution Society's November meeting, Burke's attention may originally have been directed to Price's sermon by Depont (although we shall see that other, primarily British, associations were to influence his first reading of the *Discourse*). In a second letter to Burke dated December 29, 1789, Depont had incidentally mentioned that "*l'autorité de la Societé de La Revolution D'Angleterre me le fait esperer*" (*Correspondence*, 6:59). In any case once he had adopted the form of a letter to a young French correspondent, Burke had positioned himself to explain the occasion for the *Discourse* and to identify its preacher. His purpose was to discredit both the *Discourse* and Price as authorities of any sort.[6]

Burke's chief constitutional quarrel with Price centered on Price's apostrophe to George III as "almost the only lawful King in the world, because the only one who owes his crown to the choice of the people."[7] To Burke this account was both dangerously unconstitutional and meaningless. George III had been chosen by no one; like his grandfather who had preceded him, he assumed the crown by hereditary succession. If "by the choice of the people" Price referred merely to a tacit acquiescence in the succession revised in 1701 by Parliament when it had become apparent that Queen Anne would not have a surviving Protestant heir, "choice" signified little and could hardly distinguish George III from some other, "unlawful" kings. Though insignificant in its application, Price's characterization was not thereby innocuous. He had asserted that the only basis by which a king may reign lawfully is the choice of his people, a doctrine Burke considered subversive not only to monarchy, but to the monarchical component in a mixed government.[8] To Burke, who, in supporting the cause of the Prince of Wales a year earlier during the Regency Crisis, had persuaded himself that the hereditary principle was under attack, Price's exception of George III on such apparently spurious grounds looked suspicious. He may perhaps have attempted, in circumstances which would raise no alarm, to establish his assertion "as if it were a first principle admitted without dispute" by which the king or a successor might be deposed at a more opportune time.[9]

This suspicion was intensified by the way in which Price had formulated what he presented as principles of the Revolution of 1688. A year earlier the Revolution Society had adopted a declaration of political principles which it had acclaimed as those of the Revolution of 1688, the centennial of which it was celebrating.[10] Price, selecting and amplifying for his own purposes, identified three such principles:

First, the right to liberty of conscience in religious matters.
Secondly, the right to resist power when abused. And
Thirdly, the right to chuse our own governors, to cashier them for misconduct, and to frame a government for ourselves.

On these, "and more especially the last," he insisted, "was the Revolution founded."[11] To the extent that the Revolution of 1688 was founded on Price's assertions, the right to "cashier" a "governor" is that to depose a king or queen. Not contesting the first two, Burke listed separately the three components of the third assertion of right. Their exuberant language is vulnerable and perhaps revealing: "cashier" may be a Paineite phrasing meant to collapse any awe still attaching to the process in question, but merely quoting it, as Burke readily does, can make it sound frivolous. "Misconduct," Burke argues, will not do either because it is indefinite and open to conflicting interpretations. Burke agreed that, if no other resort remained to them, an oppressed people could overthrow its government. To choose to do so, however, was fraught with trag-edy—historically the tragedy of civil war which in England, at least, had not been easily distinguishable from revolution:

The ceremony of cashiering kings, of which these gentlemen talk so much at their ease, can rarely, if ever, be performed without force. It then becomes a case of war, and not of constitution. Laws are commanded to hold their tongues amongst arms; and tribunals fall to the ground with the peace they are no longer able to uphold. The Revolution of 1688 was obtained by a just war, in the only case in which any war, and much more a civil war, can be just. Justa bella quibus *necessaria*. The question of dethroning, or, if these gentlemen like the phrase better "cashiering kings," will always be, as it has always been, an extraordinary question of state, and wholly out of the law; a question (like all other questions of state) of dispositions, and of means, and of probable consequences, rather than of positive rights (116).[12]

So evil are these probable consequences that "with or without right," Burke judged, "a revolution will be the very last resort of the thinking and the good" (117).

The error of what Burke now called "the Society for Revolutions" in its proprietary expounding of the Revolution of 1688 was to "take the deviation from the principle for the principle" (107). He admitted that in the accession of King William there had occurred "a small and temporary deviation" in the order of hereditary succession (101). To Price this deviation was precedent for the exercise of rights to choose and cashier. To Burke it was an act of necessity to preserve an ancient constitution threatened by the king. It had certainly been an opportunity for members of the Convention Parliament to exercise whatever rights they believed they possessed, but so unwilling was the House of Commons to exercise a right of cashiering James II, even for conduct it agreed was unconstitutional, that it had adopted the fiction of his abdication. Neither did the Convention nor later Parliament in its Act of Settlement in 1701 make provisions according to any principle of election. The latter declared that "*succession*" in the Protestant line was "absolutely necessary 'for the peace, quiet, and security of the realm,'" and that it was urgent "to maintain a *certainty* in the succession thereof, to which the subjects may safely have recourse for their protection" (101). What a certain succession protects subjects from is civil war. Once Divine Right is dismissed—and Burke, a Whig, had always dismissed it—the point of hereditary succession is to ensure that there is no choice and thus no violent contest over pretensions to the throne. The Convention Parliament had, of course, "chosen" William and Mary, but since its only alternative had been not even Mary alone but James II and the variant of absolutism he pursued, its decision can be as readily described by Burke's necessity as Price's choice. Then, by reconstructing the hereditary succession, it removed the accession of subsequent monarchs from questions of choice. And in 1701, by further revising the succession, Parliament acted in advance to prevent another elective situation from arising.[13]

In his *Discourse* Price had attempted to assimilate certain political principles to the glorious deliverance of 1688 and to acclaim the French Revolution in the name of both. He did so in a sermon, not a disquisition—a circumstance which led understandably to assertion rather than argument. That sermon, moreover, was addressed to the already converted, and such addresses are usually at a disadvantage when read by more skeptical audiences. Price's Revolution Society audience viewed the Revolution from a Lockean perspective which had in some instances been rejected and in others sacrificed in the 1689 settlement. That settlement had itself been an interpretation of the events that preceded it, and Burke was merely orthodox when he replied in effect that, whatever the settlement had achieved, it had accomplished by disregarding assertions like Price's. Although Price's appropriation of the Revolution of 1688, however deeply felt, is historically disputable, the rights he asserted did not depend on his interpretation of it. When not elaborations of Locke's philosophy of right, they were often abstract political corollaries of Price's earlier, largely religious, definitions of humanity. These he had developed mainly in relation to America in writings published in the 1770s. Burke was conscious of these writings but in *Reflections* addressed primarily the assertions of the *Discourse*. Although he disputed some specific propositions, mainly he dismissed the abstract assertion of rights both by Price and his French counterparts as metaphysics and geometry. When Burke satirizes French revolutionaries or their British admirers as "metaphysicians" or "political geometricians," he refers to people who approach government deductively, reasoning from abstract notions of rights to institutions without regard for the historical circumstances which, he insisted, determined the moral character of those institutions. He was fully aware that his adversaries attempted to ground their arguments on "self-evident"—itself an adjective from geometry—principles (79).[14] When, more rarely, he described them as "mathematicians," he may have remembered a distinction drawn early in Aristotle's *Nicomachean Ethics*: "it is the mark of an educated man to look for precision in each class of things just so far as the nature of the subject admits; it is evidently equally foolish to accept probable reasoning from a mathematician and to demand from a rhetorician demonstrative proofs."[15] But when he deployed the characterization he was also recalling Jonathan Swift. Burke's political geometricians are direct descendants of the mathematicians Lemuel Gulliver observed on Laputa:

What I . . . thought altogether unaccountable, was the strong Disposition I observed in them toward News and Politicks; perpetually enquiring into publick Affairs, giving their Judgments in Matters of State; and passionately disputing every Inch of a Party Opinion. I have indeed observed the same Disposition among most of the mathematicians I have known in *Europe*: although I could never discover the least Analogy between the two Sciences.[16]

The judgment of Gulliver—not far at this point from that of Swift—upon these ineffectual theoreticians floating in the sky is implicit in Burke's characterization of the political geometricians of Paris and London in *Reflections*.[17] Gulliver:

I . . . take this quality to spring from a very common Infirmity of Human Nature, inclining us to be more curious and conceited in Matters where we have the least Concern, and for which we are least adapted either by Study or Nature.[18]

Burke:

Those who quit their proper character, to assume what does not belong to them, are, for the greater part, ignorant both of the character they leave, and of the character they assume. Wholly unacquainted with the world in which they are so fond of meddling, and inexperienced in all its affairs, on which they pronounce with so much confidence, they have nothing of politics but the passions they excite. (94)

In *Reflections*, however, Burke uses geometry and metaphysics more often to describe the thinking of the legislators of revolutionary France than of Price, though he clearly considers them to share the same intellectual misorientation and the same deficiency of sympathy. Against Dr. Price, Burke directs another of Swift's satiric characterizations.

As a dissenting minister who, Burke comments, "with the best intentions in the world . . . naturally *philipizes*" (94), Price was vulnerable to satiric casting as the fanatic dissenting preacher familiar from much post-Restoration satire and most memorably from Swift's *A Tale of a Tub*. (Two decades before, Burke had drawn on this type to caricature his Grenvilleite adversary in his *Observations on a Late State of the Nation*.) Although Burke is careful to concede the mixed character of a sermon that contained "some good moral and religious sentiments," those religious sentiments are not his subject. He characterizes its political assertions as fanatic by two comparisons between the Unitarian Price and the Puritan extremist, Rev. Hugh Peter, and by such figures as that in which Price "chaunts his prophetic song in exact unison" with the designs of "literary caballers" and "theological Politicians" (93–94, 157–58).

Prophecy, though it can suggest a singularity of judgment at odds with the commonly held assumptions that Burke wished to exalt as the wisdom of experience, has an ambiguity he had to face. It is not out of place in a pulpit, and the role of a prophet, recalling his hearers to the paths of righteousness, has an authority from which Burke was unwilling to let Price benefit. He thus characterized Price as "a sort of oracle" among his followers. Like Swift, he reduces his adversary's preaching to "prophetic song" (94). To the extent that Price appears as a prophet in *Reflections*, it is as the emitter of "delusive gypsy predictions" (101). Burke extends this impression by attributing the Revolution Society's address of congratulations "to the same Dr. Price, in whom the fumes of his oracular tripod were not entirely evaporated" (159). "Fumes" is nicely resonant, capable of suggesting an impotent resentment, and here certainly conveying a noxious obscurity. It has an earlier counterpart in Burke's reference to that address having been passed "by those who came reeking from the effect of the sermon" (93). Whether those enthusiasts are to be understood as reeking from the fumes of their oracle's tripod or from figurative drunkness—elsewhere Burke had referred to British republicans' "intoxication of their theories"—is ambiguous (155). Nor is clarification required: both readings imply a mechanical operation of the revolutionary spirit that has obscured their vision and dislodged restraint.

Dr. Price lent himself to Swiftian satire by his preaching and by a bland confidence in quantitative reforms, and Burke was not so obtuse as to miss the satiric opportunity presented him. He did not, however, reach for Swift's weapons merely because they were ready at hand; he used them to fight Swift's battle. This was not a political battle in any partisan sense. Swift had, after all, savagely treated Lord Somers and other Old Whigs whose wisdom Burke contrasted to the simplifications of the Revolution Society, and Burke regarded his mistreatment of them as a sad instance of partisan blindness.[19] Burke's affinity with Swift is political rather in that enlarged moral sense in which he always insisted that politics ought to be founded upon human nature comprehensively imagined. What deterministic Puritan preachers, myopic mathematicians, astrologers, and mechanists of all kinds represented to Swift, Price and his associates embodied for Burke. He perceived Price as an oracle of an inhuman order derived from extensive oversimplification of human experience. Of course this puts it too tepidly. The stakes were far higher in Burke's controversy than in any of Swift's, and he was rarely more than momentarily capable of the latter's resourceful detachment. He conceived *Reflections*, at least in part, as a dunciad to expose the inadequacy of Price's politics and the deficiency of imagination and feeling he thought Price shared with French revolutionaries. In a letter charged with outrage perhaps greater than that which burns in *Reflections*, he declared his purpose to a friend who had provocatively questioned it:

I mean to set in full View the danger from their wicked principles and their black hearts [those of Dr. Price, Lord Shelburne, and their set]. . . . If any one be the better for this exposition, well and good. I mean to do my best to expose them to the hatred, ridicule, and contempt of the whole world. (*Correspondence*, 6:91–92)

"Wicked principles" and "black hearts" go well beyond the discourses of constitutional dispute and intellectual satire into direct moral rebuke, and there are passages of such rebuke in *Reflections*. The most prominent of them occupies a central place in the book's development. Burke's account of the royal family's—and especially Marie Antoinette's—ordeal on October 6, 1789, rises from his judgment upon Price's apparent exultation in the events of that day. In the *Discourse* Price had begun his self-consciously prophetic peroration by identifying himself with Simeon, who in Luke 2 recognizes salvation in the infant Christ:

What an eventful period is this! I am thankful that I have lived to see it, and I could almost say, *Lord, now lettest thou thy servant depart in peace, for mine eyes have seen thy salvation.* I have lived to see a diffusion of knowledge which has undermined superstition and error. I have lived to see the rights of men better understood than ever, and nations panting for liberty, which seemed to have lost the idea of it. I have lived to see thirty millions of people, indignant and resolute, spurning at slavery, and demanding liberty with an irresistible voice, their king led in triumph, and an arbitrary monarch surrendering himself to his subjects.[20]

Burke italicized the last two phrases when he quoted the passage. In a comparison of Price to the Puritan enthusiast Hugh Peter, who had quoted the same prayer of Simeon upon the trial of Charles I, Burke sarcastically uses variants of the word "triumph" six times in six sentences. Implied in this repetition is another context in which Price's language has become unintendedly self-exposing.

The triumph Price had acclaimed is the French Revolution interpreted and imagined as a progress of liberty. "Their king led in triumph," however, imposes this vision upon a particular event, and most readers late in 1789 or early in 1790 would plausibly have assumed that event to be the removal of the king to Paris less than a month before Price's sermon. The marchers to Versailles on October 5th were not, however, clearly representative of thirty million people. Both their suspect instigation and their pointless savagery permitted very different perspectives on this event. To Burke it was nothing a morally sensitive observer could celebrate:

I find a preacher of the gospel prophaning the beautiful and prophetic ejaculation, commonly called "*nunc dimittis*," made on the first presentation of our Saviour in the Temple, and applying it, with an inhuman and unnatural rapture, to the most horrid, atrocious, and afflicting spectacle, that perhaps ever was exhibited to the pity and indignation of mankind. This "*leading in triumph*," a thing in its best form unmanly and irreligious, which fills our Preacher with such unhallowed transports, must shock, I believe, the moral taste of every well-born mind. (159)

More fitting than Dr. Price's response was that of several English spectators who, Burke writes, were left "stupefied and indignant" by that triumph. More than the "triumphal pomp" of a civilized nation, that spectacle had resembled "a procession of American savages . . . leading into hovels hung round with scalps, their captives, overpowered with the scoffs and buffets of women as ferocious as themselves" (159). (Begun as a protest march of women to Versailles, the removal of the royal family to Paris was conducted by a crowd bearing on pikes the heads of two Royal Guards.) Burke affects to regard the Constituent Assembly's failure to punish "the authors of this triumph" as humiliating evidence of its lack of power. In a way its weakness is an excuse, but one which does not apply to its British admirers: "the apology of that Assembly is found in their situation; but when we approve what they *must* bear, it is in us the degenerate choice of a vitiated mind" (159–60). Burke uses the first person plural merely to differentiate the freedom of British observers from the compulsion of French legislators; the only British approver of the events of October 5th and 6th whom he names in his discussion is Dr. Price. And in the course of his account of Marie Antoinette's ordeal which immediately follows, he twice returns to Price's unsuitable response.

To deny Dr. Price authority—rather than, for example to contest his assumptions—entailed characterizing him, something Burke readily undertook. In *Reflections* Price emerges as a well-intentioned enthusiast in whom abstract political speculation has suppressed natural sympathy. Not surprisingly, this characterization has been questioned by readers who consider him misrepresented.

Less than a month after he published *Reflections* on November 1, 1790, Burke was attacked for his treatment of Dr. Price by Mary Wollstonecraft in *A Vindication of the Rights of Men*. She revered Price whom she had come to know during her residence at Newington Green and whom she had suspected of contributing to financial help she had received from other hands.[21] Addressing Burke in an open letter, she suggests petty motives for his hostile characterization: "had Dr. Price's sermon not lighted some sparks very like envy in your bosom, I shrewdly suspect that he would have been treated with more candour."[22] The self-congratulatory "shrewdly" is only one of the signs that, within this uneven though interesting book, this is not Wollstonecraft at her best. She had already told Burke "had you been a Jew—you would have joined in the cry, crucify him!" and had erroneously accused him of accepting a pension—"the wages of falsehood" (14, 13). Her editors acknowledge that "Burke's attack on Price never stoops to the kind of personal abuse that Wollstonecraft levels at Burke,"[23] and her rebuke suffers from inconsistency both with her practice and with her scorn of Burke's sentimentality:

In reprobating Dr. Price's opinions you might have spared the man; and if you had had but half as much reverence for the grey hairs of virtue as for the accidental distinctions of rank, you would not have treated with such indecent familiarity and supercilious contempt, a member of the community whose talents and modest virtues place him high in the scale of moral excellence. . . . I should touch his errors with a tender hand when I made a parade of my sensibility. Granting, for a moment, that Dr. Price's political opinions are Utopian reveries, and that the world is not yet sufficiently civilized to adopt such a sublime system of morality; they could, however, only be the reveries of a benevolent mind. . . . I could almost fancy that I now see this respectable old man, in his pulpit, with hands clasped, and eyes devoutly fixed, praying with all the simple energy of unaffected piety; or, when more erect, inculcating the dignity of virtue, and enforcing the doctrines his life adorns; benevolence animated each feature, and persuasion attuned his accents; the preacher grew eloquent, who only labored to be clear; and the respect that he extorted, seemed the only respect due to personified virtue and matured wisdom. (18–19)

Still, Wollstonecraft's generalized portrayal of Dr. Price as a man of simplicity and benevolence seems to be widely corroborated and, with greater restraint, to be repeated by his recent biographers. Carl Cone, later author of a detailed, sound life of Burke, began his biography of Price with a character sketch titled "The Good Dr. Price," a phrase he could have culled from any number of Price's acquaintances but attributes to "orange women in the market stalls."[24] D. O. Thomas concludes *The Honest Mind*, his valuable study of Price's thought, with a chapter titled "Edmund Burke" attempting to free Price from the character Burke devised for him and from the dismissive image of the "unfortunate Dr. Price" which followed from Burke's partial success.

Thomas's last chapter deserves particular attention, and not only because it is the fullest available discussion of the differences between Price and Burke's representation of him. On the whole he succeeds in recovering Price from Burke's oversimplifications and occasionally from those of Price's own *Discourse*. His book accumulates critical readings of Price's earlier works to which, but for Burke, the *Discourse* would be only a pendant. In this last chapter he can draw upon those readings to represent Price far more extensively and adequately than Burke had—although his emphasis on moral and political philosophy slights Price's activity as a partisan controversialist. Thomas's conscientious effort to do justice to Burke's arguments, moreover, enables his extended account—though it is still partial to Price—to explore more fruitfully than any predecessor certain issues which divide the two. All this makes the chapter valuable as a point of departure to an inquiry into how Burke viewed Price both for its perceptions and for the problems its occasional inadequacies expose.

Given his primary concern to recover Price, Thomas is prudent merely to treat him as misrepresented by *Reflections*, as he does on most occasions when, after scrutiny, he rejects an element of Burke's portrayal. "Misrepresent" is relatively neutral, a word that commits him to no particular characterization of Burke. However, at the beginning of the chapter, the questions Thomas poses frame its inquiry problematically: "To what extent was Burke's portrait accurate? Was it a true representation or was it rather an invention cunningly contrived to distract attention from Price's real aims and purposes?"[25] A true representation and a cunning invention are not, of course, the only alternatives. It is possible, for example, that on some matters Burke was honestly mistaken about Price's position, and in the *Discourse* to which Burke responded, Price, himself, had made statements that were misleading about his intentions (something Thomas does recognize elsewhere). Thomas's second sentence may be an inverse compliment to Burke's literary skill, but it also raises questions about his use of satire at all. Satire's purpose *is* to misrepresent to a degree, in the manner perhaps of hyperbolic metaphor, though its conventions seem to require degrees of resemblance beyond which it appears merely scurrilous. Of course some portions of Burke's treatment of Price are inventions, cunning if you will, though I suspect Burke not to have agreed with Thomas on some of Price's real purposes and to have regarded his efforts to be exposing rather than concealing them. Readers *can* accommodate satire as a distinct form of discourse, identify its oblique representation, and draw appropriate distinctions when necessary, and in the British debate on the French Revolution, they should be prepared to do so. One further complication to Thomas's alternatives is that, depending on the nature of its subject, the perspectives of differing audiences, and the backgrounds against which it is understood, the language of an assertion—especially a political assertion—can be perceived in multiple contexts and bear different implications from those its speaker may have anticipated. Still, if misrepresentation has more sources than Thomas acknowledges, he identifies some instances which lead to a more adequately complicated understanding.

On November 4, 1790, exactly one year after the sermon that had provoked Burke, Dr. Price presided over the Revolution Society's annual dinner. In the course of the evening he proposed the widely publicized toast "The Parliament of Britain, may it become a National Assembly."[26] Using this language only three days after the publication of *Reflections*, he naturally seemed to many to have confirmed elements of Burke's characterization. Thomas explains:

It gave the impression that his reforming intentions were very much more extensive than they if fact were. In the fourth edition of the *Discourse* he tried to repair the damage done. . . . He explained that by their new constitution the French had obtained an adequate and free representation. By subdividing France into equal electoral districts (a) on a territorial basis, (b) on a demographic basis, and (c) on a fiscal basis, they had achieved a form of representation which allowed their assembly to be justly called a representation of the people. In wishing that the British Parliament should also become a National Assembly what Price maintained he intended was simply that the representation of the kingdom should be reformed so that "the Parliament consisting of Lords and Commons might justly be deemed a National Assembly." (308)

The words "National Assembly," capitalized, inevitably alluded to France's Constituent Assembly which was Price's standard. For most Britons its most prominent differences from Parliament were its being unicameral and republican as opposed to Parliament's mixed democratic, aristocratic, and monarchical character. In his reference to Lords and Commons Price tries to reassure his readers that he does not intend, for example, elimination of the House of Lords. He is also disclaiming republican aspirations but vaguely enough to make one wonder what his colleagues in the Revolution Society had understood by the toast. It was not the first time Price had denied being a republican,[27] and Thomas's insistence on his moderation may well be correct. However, his observation that Price had "made it easy for his critics to misrepresent his views" (308) is more questionable in appearing to hold those critics responsible for reading Price's mind. At least until he issued his clarification, the one who had misrepresented Price was Price. Since, as Thomas notes, Price explained his toast by referring to a speech he had prepared but not delivered (308), his imprudence had probably not been excited by the celebration. On the French Revolution he seems to have had trouble negotiating his way between audiences of convinced colleagues and skeptical readers.

Price's clarification of his meaning in the toast was not the only such explanation he had to make in the fourth edition of the *Discourse*. In its preface he accused Burke of a "horrid misrepresentation" in *Reflections* by applying his celebration of "their King led in triumph" to the forced removal of Louis and his family to Paris on October 6, 1789, rather than what he claimed to have meant, events "of the 14th of July and the subsequent days."[28] Whether, as Price implies, this was a deliberate misrepresentation is questionable. Many readers must have thought Price's phrasing referred to the shocking events of less than a month before which the words "led in triumph" described more closely than anything in July. F. P. Lock has noticed that Catharine Macaulay and William Belsham in their hostile replies to *Reflections* appear, like Burke, to have understood Price to refer to the October Days.[29] The grounds for Price's accusation are that, because Burke twice cites a letter from another dissenting clergyman visiting in France which uses similar language about the king's appearance in the National Assembly on July 15th (or possibly his visit to Paris on the 17th), he should have known that Price also referred to these July events. Those letters, Price points out, were dated in July and could not have any reference to events in October. Thomas, in an admirable investigation, has identified the other clergyman as Price's nephew, George Cadogan Morgan.[30] His letters, Thomas has found, were published in August in a newspaper, *The Gazetteer*, of which no copies of the crucial issues seem to have survived, and in an anonymous pamphlet, *A look to the last century: or the dissenters weighed in their own scales*, not published until 1790. Had Burke's source been the newspaper, he would have known at least that Morgan's language referred to events in July. Although it does not necessarily follow that Price's did also, it gives some support to his complaint, for Burke would have known Dissenters had used such language about July's events. Thomas, though, inclines to believe that the later pamphlet was Burke's source. That would have made it easier for him to assume "without malice" that Price had alluded to October 6th.[31]

Recently Steven Blakemore has pointed out that, in his complaint about Burke's "horrid misrepresentation," Price inaccurately quotes from his own sermon. In his *Discourse* he had written of a people "indignant and resolute spurning at slavery." In his preface to the fourth edition, he softens it to "a vast kingdom spurning at slavery," a phrasing Blakemore observes, "less likely to conjure up the people who participated in the King's forced removal on 6 October."[32] Whatever Price had originally had in mind, this silent editing probably betrays some embarrassment. The ambiguous passage had been no improvisation; it was the consciously allusive peroration to Price's address. Even had some in his Revolution Society audience assumed that he meant October 6th, they probably would not much have minded. In publishing the *Discourse* Price sought a broader audience. Still, although he must have expected some controversy over his provocative assertions about George III, in his reaction to *Reflections*, he seems shocked that any reader could have understood him to intend the more plausible of the passage's alternative readings. Why, one can only guess. His experience in political controversy was enough to rule out sheer innocence. He was, however, entirely persuaded that the future—and that God—was on his side. Except in the United States, humankind had not made much progress toward institutionalizing the conception of liberty he had propounded, but now, late in his life, an unexpected, unprecedented revolution had occurred in France—a *providential* event, as his identification with Simeon proclaims— which promised a greater advance toward universal moral independence than he had ever dared hope to see. Against the breakthrough of the summer of 1789, the October Days must have seemed insignificant, and how could anyone imagine that he had referred to them? One could rather easily, it turned out, if one did not share the context his vision imposed.

It is quite possible that Burke and Price each erred about the other's intentions. Misrepresentations did occur, but though it cannot be shown conclusively why, it seems at least doubtful that they were horrid ones.

In the context within which Burke observed the French Revolution and tried to determine its character, the fall of the Bastille had made many things possible but had itself been inconclusive. The October Days, though, had confirmed his accumulating suspicions, and they occupied a much more central position in his understanding of the Revolution than they had for Price and probably more than for many of his readers.

The context in which Burke perceived Price himself was similarly a rather special one. In his letter of January 31, 1792, to William Weddell, his colleague as M. P. for Malton, a letter written after his breach with Charles James Fox and intended to be shown to sympathetic Foxites, Burke explains the circumstances in which he first read Price's *Discourse*. Until he returned to London in mid-January 1790 for the resumption of Parliament he had not read it, although he had heard of it—perhaps in Depont's second letter.[33] It was not Price's rapture at the revolution in France, however, which provoked Burke to read it, but partisan British politics. Dining in a large company on the day of his return, he was told by a dissenter, a close and sympathetic but unnamed friend, that so great was the hostility to Fox among dissenters that they could never be reconciled to Burke's party so long as Fox led it. They spoke of him, Burke got the impression, in a manner that "one would not speak of some better sort of Highwayman." After defending Fox, Burke went home, where

late as it was, before I went to bed, I read Dr. Price's sermon and *in that very sermon* (in which were all the shocking Sentiments and seditious principles, which I have endeavoured to expose) the leading feature was a personal invective against Mr. Fox—very much in the Style and manner, (a trifle indeed less coarse) in which my worthy friend had represented the general conversation of the dissenters when Mr. Fox was the subject.[34]

Burke's identification of the *Discourse's* "leading feature" is remarkable not only because of his quite different criticisms in *Reflections*, but because Price's allusion omits Fox's name. Still most readers would have known Price's meaning. The allusion, a gratuitous insertion at the end of his discussion of the principles of the Revolution of 1688, appears to be an attempt to exclude Fox from leadership in the reform movement Price foresaw gathering strength from the example of France. The immorality Price mentions refers to Fox's association, now in its sixth year, with his mistress Elizabeth Armistead (they would marry in 1795), whom he already called his wife:[35]

Oh! that I could see in men who oppose tyranny in the state a disdain of the tyranny of low passions in themselves, or at least such a sense of shame and regard to public order and decency as would induce them to hide their irregularities and to avoid insulting the virtuous part of the community by an open exhibition of vice! I cannot reconcile myself to the idea of an immoral patriot, or to that separation of private from public virtue, which some think to be possible. Is it to be expected that—but I must forbear. I am afraid of applications which many are too ready to make and for which I should be sorry to give any just occasion.[36]

Price's sentiments are unquestionably sincere, even if his last sentence rings false. His editor, Thomas, speculates that "what appeared in print was toned down considerably from what was said in the sermon,"[37] and Burke likely surmised as much. He also knew that the earnest voice of the disapproving preacher was simultaneously that of a close associate of the Earl of Shelburne (more recently Marquess of Lansdowne), before Pitt, Fox's bitterest political enemy.

The attack on Fox restored to Price the factional character Burke had perceived in him during the American Revolution. This character is superimposed on another, Price's recognized leadership among Dissenters. Thus Burke describes him as "a man much connected with . . . political theologians and theological politicians" (93). The phrase perhaps reflects the frustration Burke felt at what he saw as inconsistent fluctuations between both characters. In his letter to Weddell, he refers to "the leading dissenters" as "unalliable with the Party," and reproaches them for deserting it in 1784 (*Correspondence,* 7:55–56). Many commentators have taken Burke's disappointment at his party's electoral disaster then to explain his coldness toward Dissenters, and it is one good explanation. There are, however, others.

Burke's reactions to various parliamentary efforts to relieve Dissenters from legal disabilities reflect his changing perception of Dissenters, some of whom, both in theology and politics, were themselves changing significantly. In April 1772 he supported a bill to relieve dissenting preachers from the seldom enforced statutory requirement of subscribing to the doctrinal articles of the Anglican Church. The bill passed in the House of Commons but was defeated in the House of Lords, the fate also of a slightly meeker version proposed the following year. Burke, who would not commit himself to toleration as an absolute principle, nevertheless believed in extending its protection very broadly. His speech in 1773, influenced by his recent visit to France, concludes with an attack on atheism. There a line is drawn, but, as he wrote to William Burgh in 1775, he favored conferring immunity "from all disturbance" of public worship and teaching to all reformed and unreformed Christian churches, and beyond them "to Jews, Mahometans and even Pagans."[38]

Price had worked on the committee that had drafted the bills. Their defeat, Thomas writes, left in him "a deep sense of grievance"—perhaps because he may have considered them already to have conceded too much. Although he and Burke agreed in supporting the bills, they characteristically differed in principle. Price was convinced that the state has no authority in matters of religion.[39] Such a position committed him to a general opposition of church establishments. While the constitutions of some American states would elate him in the 1780s, there was little mileage in such an opposition in Britain. He would thereafter concentrate most of his politician activity on secular issues such as parliamentary reform.

Burke shouldered on. Having played an important behind-the-scenes role in the drafting of the Savile Act—the legislation the Gordon rioters sought to repeal—which in 1778 had among other things removed the threat of life imprisonment from Catholic clerics and teachers, he spoke in support of a successful bill to relieve dissenting school masters and ministers the following year.[40] However, a decade later, when Dissenters sought to repeal the Test and Corporation Acts, he responded differently.

In March 1787 and again in May 1789 when Henry Beaufoy moved to repeal the Test and Corporation Acts, Burke absented himself from the House of Commons. In 1789 illness may have contributed to his absence, but when on March 2, 1790, Fox made a third attempt to repeal them, Burke acknowledged he had not formerly been able to decide how to vote.[41] Even though as recently as the preceding September he had gone to some trouble to try to improve Fox's standing with Dissenters associated with Joseph Priestley, in the circumstances of March 1790 he opposed repeal. Fox's attempts to minimize the damage done by Price's *Discourse* and statements by Priestley gave Burke the opportunity to introduce the French Revolution, but he for once subordinated it to a more immediate concern, that the ultimate goal of the Dissenters' leadership was not toleration but disestablishment of the Church of England. He still disapproved of the sacramental test and was willing to see it eliminated even now if another test could be substituted pledging the office holder to refrain from subverting the constitution of the Church of England "as is now by law established."[42] This expedient anticipated a similar declaration which would finally secure repeal of the two acts in 1828.

Burke retained enough friends who were Dissenters to know they were not politically monolithic. He distrusted their leadership, however, and certainly did not recognize them as the friends of British liberty they believed themselves to be. There was clearly some self-interest in their efforts to repeal the Test and Corporation Acts (and in their agitation for parliamentary reform), and Burke's experience had prepared him to consider it extensive. Had he attended the debates in 1787 and 1789, Burke would have heard Henry Beaufoy assure the House that ample securities remained after repeal to exclude Catholics, Jews, and—in 1789—Quakers from office and that the only persons empowered would be Presbyterians, Independents, and Baptists.[43] He might well have subsequently read these assurances, and if he did, they would have reinforced earlier impressions. As Conor Cruise O'Brien has explained, Burke's own commitment to toleration arose from his experience in Ireland of penal laws, more severe than the prohibition to power endured by Dissenters, to which the Catholic members of his family and a large majority of Irish people were subjected.[44] His support of toleration in 1772 and 1773 had made him popular with Bristol Dissenters when he was elected to Parliament there in 1774. In 1780, though, when he withdrew in defeat from Bristol, his support of Sir George Savile's Catholic Relief Act of 1778 in defiance of the Gordon Rioters was one of the matters most objected against him.[45] British anti-Catholicism could be found as often in the established church as in dissenting congregations; it was marbled throughout the society.[46] But, unless one shared the view that Catholics were uniquely treacherous, which Burke emphatically did not, it did place Dissenters' arguments for removing their political disabilities in an ironic though not invalidating context. As late as 1825–28 when the prospects of relief for Dissenters and Catholics became far more mutually dependent, the Dissenters, as Richard Davis concludes, "were not united on the crucial principle of religious liberty," and the eventual repeal of the Test and Corporation Acts required the outflanking of persistent dissenting opponents of Catholic Emancipation by the able parliamentary leader William Smith.[47] Burke, who was opposed for seeking to extend toleration to Catholic and Protestant Dissenters rather than to Protestants alone, may well have inferred that what unified the Dissenters was not so much principle as a desire for access to office and power. He had thought they should have this access, though on a principle of toleration rather than of right, but by 1790 he wished first to inquire how they were likely to use it.

If Burke's experiences in 1780 both in the Gordon Riots and in the Bristol election left him with a jaundiced view of the Dissenters' moral authority, it was likely a generalized view, held loosely as the realities of opposition for the Rockingham Whigs dictated continued—though often unsatisfactory—contact with the Dissenters. Having been identified to the mob as an adversary by Lord George Gordon, Burke had walked London streets with defiant courage concealing neither his identity nor his support for Savile's Catholic Relief Act. Although his home had been threatened with destruction, in the House of Commons he attacked this outrageous attempt to restore intolerant laws by intimidation.[48] In his circumstances most London radicals, among whom Dissenters were heavily represented, would have appeared contemptible for their political maneuvering during the riots. For the prudent distance most had kept from Gordon's Protestant Association, many had compensated by various signals of sympathy. They were slow in condemning attacks, of which some approved, on the homes and chapels of Catholics. Afterward, as Nicholas Rogers has summarized, they underplayed the strain of anti-Catholicism which informed the riots and overplayed the rioters' drunkenness. They preferred to shift blame from the Protestant Association to the government to avert if possible—in the end it wasn't—the discrediting of associations and mass petitioning in general.[49] In such a picture, however, Richard Price is not visible. From his public position that the state has no authority in matters of religion, one can infer without difficulty that he opposed the laws which the Catholic Relief Act had repealed, but I have found no specific comments by Price on the Gordon Riots. In his recently published correspondence, no letters at all survive for the month of the riots, June 1780.[50]

In the absence of better information, Burke was likely to have associated Price with the position of the Earl of Shelburne, whose loyal political "friend" Price remained. Since Shelburne's conduct situated him far from what we can infer of Price's position (one reason perhaps for Price's silence, if he had been silent), this association, though plausible, would not have been accurate. Price, while capable of derisive allusions to Catholicism, had assimilated his hostility to general notions of the separation of Church and State. Shelburne, for a time, as John Norris has described, was considered to have "played a part which the ministry and a good many other people regarded as treasonable."[51] This was not a just characterization, however much it might have seemed to confirm earlier impressions of the man; Shelburne had supported the Catholic Relief Act in 1778 when it had passed without opposition and, unlike certain other lords, did not call for its repeal as a concession to the rioters. To some extent his political allies implicated him with the Protestant Association. Frederick Bull, a former Lord Mayor of London, a Dissenter, and a Shelburnite, had seconded Gordon's motion to repeal the Catholic Relief Act in the House of Commons on June 2d, and, as late as June 20th had applauded the Protestant Association and threatened the House in a speech which Burke denounced for its "ignorance, falsehood, and fanaticism."[52] In his own speech in the House of Lords on June 3d, after the first night of rioting, Shelburne blamed Catholics and most of all the government while he declared the erroneous but sincere petitioners (who understandably had not threatened *him*) "objects rather of pity than resentment." Then he argued for repeal of the Quebec Act which, having replaced locally the Test Act by an oath Catholics could conscientiously take and thus enabled them to participate in the government of that almost entirely Catholic colony, had been duly attacked for establishing popery. Now it was a surrogate for the Catholic Relief Act, which could not be repealed without abject surrender to mob violence. It was the next best bone he could throw, enough to have made Gordon's campaign seem a compromised success. Norris, as he absolves Shelburne from suspicions of involvement in the riots, draws this conclusion: "Probably he intended no more than to take somewhat irresponsible advantage of the Ministry's desperate situation, or perhaps at most to use the Protestant association movement to alter the balance of power in opposition in his favour."[53] It was enough to damage his already strained relations with the Marquis of Rockingham. Though also critical of Lord North's administration's failure to prepare for the riots, the Rockingham Whigs had supported the government during the emergency. That Shelburne could for a time be widely suspected of more, of actual involvement in the riots themselves, was the consequence of his already being one of the least trusted persons in British politics.

From his twenties Shelbourne had acquired a reputation for intrigue in the service of Lord Bute. As early as 1767, he had been called "Malagrida" after an Italian Jesuit executed in Portugal, who, perhaps not accurately, had become proverbial in Britain for duplicity.[54] (Oliver Goldsmith, whose travel on the continent may have acquainted him with a differing view, once remarked to Shelburne: "I wonder they should call your Lordship *Malagrida*, for Malagrida was a very good man."[55]) Since Fox and Burke had partisan reasons to detest him, perhaps the most telling circumstance of how colleagues in office felt about working with him is the failure of the younger Pitt, who had received his first cabinet post from Shelburne, to find a place for him in his own talent-starved first cabinet.

The hostility to Shelburne which steams in *Reflections* dates, however, from the Second Rockingham administration in the spring of 1782 when he, as a leader of the surviving Chathamities, shared power with the Rockingham Whigs after the fall of Lord North. From the beginning the king had assured Shelburne of his preference for him to Lord Rockingham and especially to Charles Fox. Set up by the king as an alternative and preferred channel of patronage, Shelburne proceeded to undermine his colleagues' credibility. In the cabinet he seconded the resistance of Lord Chancellor Thurlow, the king's known agent, to provisions of Burke's bill on economical reform; outside he continued to charm reformers like Christopher Wyvill. As secretary of state he wanted to impose conditions before recognizing American independence (a course the king approved) and thwarted the intention of Fox, the other secretary of state, to recognize it immediately. To the embarrassment of the administration, each had representatives in Paris with different instructions. Before Rockingham's death on July 1, 1782, Shelburne and the king were planning a new cabinet; that night the king offered Shelburne the treasury with his support. The administration had come to power fighting the influence of the crown and, as L. G. Mitchell reports: "in Fox's eyes, Shelburne had not only surrendered to that corrupt power, but had clearly become its agent."[56] Burke wholly agreed. A year later, returned to office in the coalition with Lord North (a far more candid colleague), Burke wrote to his old friend Richard Shackleton:

We have demolished the Earl of Shelburne; but in his fall he has pulled down a large piece of the Building. He had indeed undermined it before. This wicked man, and no less weak and stupid, than false and hypocritical, has contrived to break to pieces the body of men, whose integrity, wisdom, and union, were alone capable of giving consistency to publick measures, and recovering the Kingdom from the miserable State into which it had fallen. (*Correspondence*, 5:72)

This is partial truth taking on the feel of myth, a myth which would be in place well before the fall of the coalition late in 1783 banished it into prolonged opposition. The Shelburne Burke describes does not very much resemble the Shelburne who emerges from his letters to Price, but since it is a portrayal recognized by people better situated than most to observe his behavior during the year of his greatest public responsibilities, it ought to count for a good deal.[57] What matters here, though, is that it gave Burke a perspective on Shelburne he retained for the rest of his life.

What made Price's attack on Fox's "licentious and immoral conduct" insufferable to Burke was that it came from the pen of one who had so long approved Shelburne, now Marquess of Lansdowne. From Burke's perspective, no one who could swallow Lansdowne was entitled to that sort of prudery. Price's attack also would have made Burke, if he had not been already, a hypercritical reader of subsequent passages. To see what that could entail, I wish to look closely at a single clause of Price's concluding vision: "And now, methinks, I see the ardor for liberty catching and spreading, a general amendment beginning in human affairs, the dominion of kings changed for the dominion of laws, and the dominion of priests giving way to the dominion of reason and conscience."[58] By January 1790 Burke had rejected this view of the French Revolution in its entirety, but the phrase I want to single out is the last. In his opposition of "priests" to "reason and conscience," Price depends on long-held associations for his rhetorical effect, associations that appear to have led many of its British admirers to have approved the French Revolution as what Conor Cruise O'Brien has called an "anti-Papist reformation."[59] To Price this opposition embodied a vision of moral progress he could be confident that his original audience shared. Its anti-Catholicism, moreover, was limited in his own mind by views on the separation of church and state which had permitted him eight years before to advocate civil rights for Catholics in Ireland.[60] Its formulation, however, would have appealed to many in his Revolution Society audience whose hostility to Catholicism greatly exceeded his own, and it is positioned—at the end of the paragraph which begins with his appropriation of the *Nunc Dimittis*—to acquire emphasis. In Burke, Price had a reader certain to be alienated by such rhetoric since he neither thought the "giving way" of the Catholic Church in France desirable, nor conceived reason or conscience to be embodied in French revolutionaries.[61]

One additional event contributed to Burke's perspective on Price. Later in the day of Price's sermon, the Revolution Society held a dinner at which Price moved a congratulatory address to the National Assembly, hailing the example of France in encouraging "a general reformation in the governments of Europe and to make the World free and happy."[62] In *Reflections* Burke considers this address inseparable from the *Discourse*, and he deployed much of his rhetoric to discredit Price as a voice representative of British values. This development includes his famous portrayal of Price and his associates as insects chinking amid thousands of silent cattle under the British oak (181) and his addressing the book to a young Parisian gentleman. Depont had, in fact, referred hopefully to the "authority" of the Revolution Society in his second letter (*Correspondence,* 6:59). Burke's portrayal of Price in *Reflections* attempts to destroy that authority which the Natural Assembly had sought in its cordial replies to nurture. Still, Burke would have had few grounds for taking Price's address so seriously had it not been for the intrusion of another correspondent in Paris.

On January 17, 1790, in the week Burke first read Price's *Discourse*, Thomas Paine wrote Burke from Paris to report on the progress of the Revolution. The editor of the recent Clarendon edition of *Reflections*, L. G. Mitchell, scolds Burke for "turning his back . . . on the first-hand intelligence" Paine offered and thereby badly misconstrues the significance of Paine's letter.[63] Paine misjudged his reader so far that he gleefully quotes a pun to Burke which links the word "aristocrat" with "Iscariot," but that does not mean that Burke disregarded his opinions. His assertion that "the Revolution in France [a phrasing Burke would use in his title in preference to "the French Revolution"] is certainly a Forerunner to other Revolutions in Europe" could not have been better calculated, had

Paine intended it, to confirm Burke's darkest suspicions. More important in relation to Price, Paine's reference to a "new mode of forming alliances affirmatively with Countries and negatively with Courts" placed the correspondence between the National Assembly and the Revolution Society in a lurid, if not very illuminating, light (*Correspondence,* 6:73, 71). In addressing the National Assembly, Price had spoken for a body that affected a special relation to the British constitution. Paine now unintentionally implied such a role had a part in larger French designs. To Burke, who perceived the French Revolution very differently from either, Price's address seemed a dangerous folly which he determined to expose.

To diminish Price's authority was one of Burke's rhetorical purposes in *Reflections*, but his unwillingness to "spare the man" for which Mary Wollstonecraft reproached him was also the consequence of his own perception of Price. He acknowledged some good religious sentiments in the *Discourse* and sarcastically admitted greater deference to his adversary on matters of demography than politics, but his view of Price is almost exclusively political, and it drew upon impressions of Price in contexts that preceded the French Revolution. (In these contexts, it may be worth noticing, his dissatisfactions were not necessarily conservative.) His impressions were not always accurate or immediately relevant. But reading the *Discourse* in these contexts, Burke found in its language—especially in its unnecessary warning against Fox—apparent confirmation of some of his suspicions. Although I think Price's rhetoric needs more wary attention than it has so far received, it should be clear that I am not inviting readers of this essay to adopt Burke's view of him, only to understand how that view could develop. Burke's perception of Price neither explains nor explains away his substantial disagreements with Price concerning the English Revolution of 1688, the French Revolution through the summer of 1790, and the nature of rights. Those disagreements greatly extended his view of Price but did not alter the direction in which the prospect faced. An awareness of the angles of observation on Price which the politics of toleration and the political maneuvering of Shelburne provided him can disclose strands of coherence not always recognized between Burke, the Rockingham Whig, and Burke, the counterrevolutionary. In Burke's gradually increasing isolation. after Rockingham's death, it may be that the most sturdy of these strands was the adversary relationship. To him Price represented—somewhat inaccurately—people who could attack him for having sought legal relief for Catholics while they claimed it as a right for themselves, people who now talked of cashiering kings, but who, when they had had the opportunity to correct a remediable abuse of royal power, had connived with George III. It was not only that he was sure that they were mistaken now about France; harsh experience would have seemed to characterize them as abstract, inconsistent, and irresponsible in their political reasonings.

Acknowledgments

I wish to thank Steven Blakemore and George Bretherton for steering me to helpful scholarship on the settlement of 1689 and on later phases of the struggle to repeal the Test and Corporation Acts. Neither, of course, bears any responsibility for the ways I've applied that scholarship. More general thanks are due to my colleagues in our seminar, Professor Bromwich, and the NEH.

NOTES

1. *The Correspondence of Edmund Burke*, ed. Thomas W. Copeland, 10 vols. (Chicago: University of Chicago Press; Cambridge: Cambridge University Press, 1958–1978), 6:25–26, 30. Hereafter abridged to *Correspondence*.

2. Burke was a long way from embarking on a crusade. To Earl Fitzwilliam about this time he referred to France as "undone." *Correspondence,* 6:36.

3. Carl Cone, *Burke and the Nature of Politics*, 2 vols. (Lexington: University of Kentucky Press, 1957), 2:301–2.

4. William B. Todd, *A Bibliography of Edmund Burke* (London: Rupert Hart-Davis, 1964), 143.

5. *The Parliamentary History of England* (London: Hansard,1817), 28:439.

6. Burke's intention would be greatly reinforced by a remark of Thomas Paine discussed later in this essay.

7. Richard Price, *Political Writings*, ed. D. O. Thomas (Cambridge: Cambridge University Press, 1991), 186.

8. Although he had written "*almost* the only lawful king in the world" [my emphasis]—and Burke quotes him accurately—Price conceded no other basis for lawfulness in the *Discourse*.

9. Edmund Burke, *Reflections on the Revolution in France*, ed. Conor Cruise O'Brien (Harmondsworth: Penguin, 1986), 89. Subsequent references to this edition will be made parenthetically in the text.

10. The Revolution Society's annual meeting commemorated the birthday of William III, November 4th. The statement adopted in its centennial observance declared

1. That all civil and political authority is derived from the people.
2. That the abuse of power justifies resistance.
3. That the right of private judgment, liberty of conscience, trial by jury, the freedom of the press and the freedom of election ought ever to be held sacred and inviolable.

Albert Goodwin, *The Friends of Liberty: The English Democratic Movement in the Age of the French Revolution* (Cambridge, Mass.: Harvard University Press, 1979), 87. Price's own three-part statement is an acknowledged abridgment, but his third proposition, on which he places special emphasis and to which Burke pays exclusive attention, goes somewhat beyond the Society's principles, which are closer to those of the Bill of Rights of 1689.

11. *Political Writings,* 189–90.

12. J.G.A. Pocock explains some of the implications of Burke's arresting characterization of the Revolution of 1688 as a civil war in his striking speculative essay "The Fourth English Civil War: Dissolution, Desertion, and Alternative Histories in the Glorious Revolution," *The Revolution of 1688–1689: Changing Perspectives,* ed. Lois Schwoerer (Cambridge: Cambridge University Press, 1992), 52–64.

13. J. R. Jones, who, like Burke, finds "the essence of the Revolution" in the Declaration of Rights, attributes the success of the Convention "to the fact that it confirmed, protected, and perpetuated the existing rights and liberties" and to its "conscious preoccupation with the need to preserve the constitution from change." *The Revolution of 1688 in England* (N.Y.: Norton, 1972), 316–17, 327. Historians like Jones eventually part company from Burke in his admiration of the settlement of 1689 as conclusive, complete, and all but lithified.

14. In the American Declaration of Independence the phrase "self-evident" appears, inconveniently for anyone seeking its source, to have been added to Jefferson's draft in committee.

15. Aristotle, *The Nicomachean Ethics,* trans. David Ross, rev. J. L. Ackrill and J. O. Urmson, The World's Classics (Oxford: Oxford University Press, 1980), 3.

16. Jonathan Swift, *Gulliver's Travels,* pt. 3, ch. 2. *The Prose Works of Jonathan Swift,* ed. Herbert Davis (Oxford: Blackwell, 1941), 11:148.

17. In a recent unpublished paper, "The Academy and Politics: The Engine of Broken Sentences, The Method of Discovering Plots," James Engell considers the "overarching theme" of Gulliver's Third Voyage to be "intellectual pride." He examines within the voyage abuses of interpretation and their implications in both the academy and politics.

18. *Gulliver's Travels,* pt. 3, ch. 2. *Prose Works,* 11:148.

19. *The Annual Register for 1758,* 256–57.

20. *Political Writings,* 195.

21. Eleanor Flexner, *Mary Wollstonecraft, A Biography* (Harmondsworth: Penguin, 1976), 47, 53.

22. *A Vindication of the Rights of Men, The Works of Mary Wollstonecraft,* eds. Janet Todd and Marilyn Butler, 7 vols. (N.Y.: New York University Press, 1989), 5:44. All subsequent quotations taken from this edition.

23. *A Vindication of the Rights of Men,* 44nb.

24. *Torchbearer of Freedom: The Influence of Richard Price on Eighteenth Century Thought* (Lexington: University of Kentucky Press, 1952), 3.

25. D.O. Thomas, *The Honest Mind: The Thought and Work of Richard Price* (Oxford: Clarendon, 1977), 309. All subsequent quotations taken from this edition.

26. Quoted in *The Honest Mind,* 308.

27. See, for example, *Political Writings,* 164–65.

28. *Political Writings,* 177.

29. *Burke's Reflections on the Revolution in France,* Unwin Critical Library (London: Allen & Unwin, 1985), 204n19.

30. "Edmund Burke and the Reverend Dissenting Gentlemen," *Notes and Queries* 29 (June 1982): 202–4.

31. "Dissenting Gentlemen," 204.

32. "Misrepresenting the Text: Price, Burke, and the 'October Days' of 1789," *The Friend: Comment on Romanticism* 1, no.4 (Oct. 1992): 1–9. The quotation is taken from page 2.

33. Burke came to London sometime between January 12, 1790, when he dated a letter written at Beaconsfield, and the 23d, when he endorsed a note with his London address, *Correspondence,* 6:67, 76. Depont's second letter is dated December 29, 1789; if Burke received it only upon his return to London, it is possible that he read it earlier the same day he read Price's *Discourse.*

34. *Correspondence,* 7:56; the letter to Weddell in its entirety, 7:50–63.

35. See John W. Derry, *Charles James Fox* (N.Y.: St. Martin's, 1972), 122–24. Price may, in addition, have referred to the "tyranny" of Fox's notorious gambling.

36. *Political Writings,* 193.

37. *Political Writings,* 193n. Thomas also writes that the passage "was intended to be and was generally understood as an attack" on Fox.

38. *Correspondence,* 3:112; *The Writings and Speeches of Edmund Burke,* 12 vols. (Boston: Little Brown, 1901), 7:23–38.

39. *The Honest Mind,* 175, 180–82.

40. *Parliamentary History,* 20:306, 309.

41. On 1789, see Burke's letter to Richard Bright, a Dissenter from Bristol who had solicited his support for Beaufoy's measure, *Correspondence,* 5:470–72. On his indecision, see *Parliamentary History,* 28:432.

42. *Parliamentary History,* 28:441–42; *Writings and Speeches,* 7:58.

43. *Parliamentary History,* 26:804–5; 28:8–9. Beaufoy presumably included Rational Dissenters under his "Presbyterians."

44. *The Great Melody: A Thematic Biography and Commented Anthology of Edmund Burke* (Chicago: University of Chicago Press, 1992), 3–86, esp. 19–23. See also Louis Cullen's speculative, sometimes dubious, but often suggestive "Burke, Ireland and Revolution," *Eighteenth-Century Life* 16 (Feb. 1992): 21–42.

45. Conor Cruise O'Brien has called attention to the disproportionate space Burke gave the issue in his "Speech at Bristol, in the Guildhall, Previous to the Election." *The Great Melody* 79; *Writings and Speeches,* 2: 367–423. An anonymous correspondent, in an account of the Bristol election very hostile to Burke, considered his "support of the Roman Catholic bill" the determining factor in Burke's defeat. *Gentleman's Magazine* 50 (1780) 619.

46. Linda Colley considers anti-Catholicism to have been a crucial component of British national identity in the period she studies between the Act of Union and the First Reform Act. *Britons: Forging the Nation 1707–1837* (New Haven: Yale University Press, 1992), 18–36.

47. *Dissent in Politics 1780–1830: The Political Life of William Smith, MP* (London: Epworth, 1971), 217–47. My quotation is from 223.

48. *Correspondence*, 4:245–47; *Parliamentary History* 21:655–62; *The Historical and Posthumous Memories of Sir Nathaniel William Wraxall 1772–1784*, ed. Henry B. Wheatley, 5 vols. (London: Bickers, 1884), 1:248–49.

49. "Crowd and People in the Gordon Riots," *The Transformation of Political Culture: England and Germany in the Late Eighteenth Century*, ed. Eckhart Hellmuth (Oxford: Oxford University Press, 1990), 42, 50–52.

50. *The Correspondence of Richard Price*, eds. W. Bernard Peach and D. O. Thomas. 3 vols. projected. (Durham: Duke University Press; Cardiff, Wales: University of Wales Press, 1983–), 2:60–61.

51. *Shelburne and Reform* (London: Macmillan, 1963), 133.

52. *Parliamentary History*, 21:707–10; *Shelburne and Reform*, 133.

53. *Shelburne and Reform*, 134; *Parliamentary History*, 21:677–82.

54. Hester Piozzi annotated her copy of Wraxall's *Memoirs* concerning Shelburne: "A man remarkable for his duplicity will be always suspected whether deserving suspicion or no." *Autobiography, Letters and Literary Remains of Mrs. Piozzi (Thrale)*, ed. A. Hayward, 2 vols. (London: Longman, 1861), 1:338. On Malagrida: *Boswell's Life of Johnson*, ed. George Birkbeck Hill, rev. L. F. Powell, 6 vols. (1934; Oxford: Clarendon, 1971), 4: 174–75n5.

55. James Boswell, *Boswell: The Applause of the Jury 1782–1785*, eds. Irma S. Lustig and Frederick A. Pottle (N.Y.: McGraw-Hill, 1981), 82. Most of Goldsmith's friends construed his remark as serious and a blunder, but Sir Joshua Reynolds appears to have believed it an attempt at humor. *Portraits by Sir Joshua Reynolds*, ed. Frederick W. Hilles (London: Heinemann, 1952), 49n2.

56. *Charles James Fox and the Disintegration of the Whig Party, 1782–1794* (Oxford: Oxford University Press, 1971), 16. In this paragraph I have drawn on both this book and Mitchell's recent biography, *Charles James Fox* (Oxford: Oxford University Press, 1992).

57. An outsider, at this time no admirer of Burke, Horace Walpole, wrote eight months after Burke's letter to Shackleton: "I saw a moment (which I had long despaired of seeing arrive) thrown away by the treachery of Lord Shelburne." *Horace Walpole's Correspondence with William Mason*, eds. W. S. Lewis and Grover Cronin Jr. (New Haven: Yale University Press, 1955), 2:314. Another outsider, Adam Smith, wrote to Burke of his warm approval of his and two Rockingham colleagues' resignations after Shelburne's accession to the treasury, *Correspondence*, 5:9–10.

58. *Political Writings*, 195.

59. "Introduction" to *Reflections*, 33.

60. *Correspondence of Price,* 2:190. Price published the letter to Lt. Colonel Sharman in which he advocated these rights in September 1783. When it appeared in London, Burke seems to have been traveling with his family in the west of England and South Wales; I have found no evidence that he read it.

61. My account does not examine one important early phase of the Burke-Price contention: their muted dispute in 1777–1778, which requires an essay of its own. The dispute was quiet because both were in an overwhelmed minority opposed to the war in America, and public bickering would have had the appearance of sheer folly. In his "Letter to the Sheriffs of Bristol" [*Writings and Speeches,* 222–23, 229], Burke without mentioning Price, criticized recent abstract speculations on civil freedom, dismissing them in terms familiar to readers of *Reflections* as geometry and metaphysics. How much of this language refers to Price is not clear, though Price was sure that some did; some clearly applies also to government apologists, such as William Markham, Archbishop of York, whose arguments both Burke and Price rejected. Concerning Price, Burke was responding to what he regarded as a divisive attack on the Declaratory Act in Price's *Observations on the Nature of Civil Liberty* (1776). In his General Introduction to the 1778 printing of *Observations* and its successor, *Additional Observations,* Price repelled Burke's veiled criticism, mentioning him by name. (*Political Writings,* 15–16. This is an abridged edition. Bernard Peach's fully annotated edition, *Richard Price and the Ethical Foundations of the American Revolution* [Durham: Duke University Press, 1979] is preferable for Price's American writings. See 47–50). Two points can be made briefly about how this fencing affected Burke's view of Price. First, his distaste for Price's deductive speculations is evident in the "Letter." Second, Price concluded *Observations* by commending Lord Shelburne's peace proposals of November 10,1775. This, along with his attack on the Declaratory Act, would have made *Observations* appear to any Rockingham Whig less the philosophical treatise that recent scholars have for the most part rightly considered it and more a Chathamite political pamphlet. To Burke it would have still more firmly identified Price as one of Shelburne's "set."

62. *The Honest Mind,* 303.

63. "Introduction," *The French Revolution 1790–1794, The Writings and Speeches of Edmund Burke,* ed. Paul Langford (Oxford: Clarendon, 1981–), 7:12.

Religion and Politics in the Revolution Debate: Burke, Wollstonecraft, Paine

Patricia Howell Michaelson

On January 19, 1793, after Louis XVI had been found guilty of treason by the National Convention, Thomas Paine spoke to that body, through a translator, urging that Louis be imprisoned and exiled, but not executed. He argued that Louis had been a friend to America, and that the French should not "bestow upon the English tyrant the satisfaction of learning that the man who helped America . . . has died on the scaffold."[1] Paine's speech hints at the curious triangulation of alliances and enmities between America, England, and France, and it foreshadows his own imminent imprisonment, rationalized partly by the ambiguity as to whether his citizenship was American or British. But even more ominous are the interruptions the speech suffered, by the powerful Jacobin Marat. At one point, Marat denounces the translator: "Such opinions are not Thomas Paine's. The translation is incorrect" (557). But twice, at the beginning and end, Marat rejects Paine's authority because of his supposed religion: "I deny the right of Thomas Paine to vote on such a subject; as he is a Quaker, of course his religious views run counter to the infliction of capital punishment" (556), and "Paine's reason for voting against the death penalty is that he is a Quaker" (558). On one level, Marat's "accusation" seems harmless enough; on another, it is frightening primarily because Marat was a person no one would want as an enemy. But what does it mean, really, to be "accused" of being a Quaker (or any other religion)? In what sense does it diminish the power of one's argument?

Religion and politics are, of all things, the most difficult to talk about dispassionately. Together banned from the dinner table, they all too often drive people to spout hot-headed, strongly felt nonsense. Here in America, we still cling to the myth that they can be separated: that government belongs in a secular space shared by all, while religion is a matter of only private or local interest. That myth, of course, does not hold up under scrutiny; given the evidence of the peace and justice movements (including the civil rights leadership of the black churches, liberation theology, and so on) and the dramatic revitalization of the religious right, it is a wonder the myth survives at all.   Religious convictions necessarily have political implications.   Yet Americans often agree with Marat that an argument doesn't "count" as political if it is rooted in religious belief. Paine's vote doesn't "count" if he believes we are led by God to oppose all executions, because he isn't looking at the specifics of the individual case. Marat's "of course" ("of course his religious views run counter to . . . capital punishment") implies that views based on religion are predictable, prejudged. His claim that religion is "Paine's *reason* for voting against the death penalty" points to the supposed irrationality, hence invalidity, of judgments based on faith.

Of course, Marat's accusation gained additional force from the context of the French Revolution, whose anticlericalism was important to its sense of radical change and new beginnings. The arguments supporting the Revolution were predominantly secular. In England, by contrast, most political beliefs had a religious component.   Indeed, according to J.C.D. Clark, "all forms of radicalism in early-modern England had a religious origin."[2] In his brilliant, if cranky, book, Clark rejects the view of scholars like Alfred Cobban that Locke somehow "freed" politics from religion (257). He argues that, on the contrary, English political and social life in the eighteenth century was dominated by what he calls the "political theology" of Anglicanism, and that indeed the agency of the State was not, in everyday life, the Parliament, but rather the Church (277). In Clark's judgment, the majority view was Tory in fact if not in name, while the Commonwealthmen were a tiny minority who have gotten more than enough scholarly attention (279).   In his rebuttal of historians' dominant secularism, and his pronounced hostility to anyone critical of the ancien regime, Clark can sound extreme, but his reassertion of the religious underpinnings of virtually all political and philosophical issues of the period is compelling. Certainly the links between the reform movements and the Dissenting community are well established in the literature.[3]   Given these clear alliances, it is surprising that there should be disagreement about the religion of major figures in the Revolution debate. The question underlying Marat's accusation— what religion was Thomas Paine—has still not been answered to everyone's satisfaction, though it no longer holds such dramatic consequences. Similarly, the old accusations about Burke's religion still resonate: recent works on Burke argue that he was a Latitudinarian, a high-church Anglican, and (as contemporaries suspected) a Catholic. But what is at stake in these arguments? Why do these religious labels matter? To address these questions, I will first argue that much of the scholarly disagreement arises from different senses of what it means to be "of" a religion; what is at stake in the differences that remain, I believe, is largely rhetorical. I will then focus on the rhetorical role of religion in the political debate by briefly considering the use of religion in three major texts—Burke's *Reflections on the Revolution in France*, Wollstonecraft's

Vindication of the Rights of Men, and Paine's *Rights of Man*. Religion functions differently in each of these texts, as it does in the scholarly disagreements about their authors' faith. But to the extent that rhetoric, the art of persuasion, depends on the sharing of assumptions by individual authors and individual readers, and to the extent that naming one's religion makes basic assumptions explicit, religion plays a large role in the rhetoric of the debate.

While religion was important in the Revolution debate, few authors clarified what they meant by the religious labels they used. It was enough to call someone a Catholic or an atheist, without needing to specify further details. Modern historians, too, tend to assume that religious labels are unambiguous. But we can distinguish at least three ways in which a person may be said to be of a certain religion. Someone might consider herself Jewish, for example, if she was born of a Jewish mother; she may or may not be "culturally" Jewish; and she may or may not be Jewish by faith or practice. Heritage, culture, and faith can be independent variables. Moreover, each of these variables can be widened in definition so as to include much of the scholarly discussion. For example, heritage, or the focus on origins, could include the heritage of an idea. Culture can be broadly defined as membership in a community, and could include the partisan or factional aspects of religion that were so important in the 1790s. And finally, faith can be widened to include personal beliefs of all kind. Most discussions of religion focus on some combination of the heritage of belief, the faith community, and the individual's convictions.

For many people, these three variables coincide, and there is no question as to their religion: in Richard Price's *Discourse on the Love of Our Country*, we can clearly see a heritage of Commonwealth ideas, a sense of community backing a partisan political agenda, and the individual faith that undergirds the rest. But when there is some dispute about a person's religion, it is often because different people are considering different variables. Thomas Paine is a good example. Putting aside statements like Theodore Roosevelt's that he was "a filthy little atheist," the generally accepted view for a long time was that Paine was a Quaker; this view is epitomized in Moncure Daniel Conway's influential biography (1892). But, with some exceptions, more recent scholars describe Paine as a Deist. The difference, I believe, is that these later scholars focus on Paine's personal belief, especially the explicit Deism of *The Age of Reason* and the implicit rejection of the more mystical Inner Light of Quaker belief. Conway, on the other hand, sees Paine's religion in terms of some mixture of heritage and community. Yet even that is complicated. Since Paine never joined the Society of Friends or participated in its worship or business, he was clearly not a member of the sect in their terms. In his writings, Paine's attitude towards the Quakers is ambivalent: he saw his father's Quakerism as the source of his own "good moral education," praised the Quakers as being closest to Deism and "the only sect that has not persecuted," and finally asked to be buried in a Quaker cemetery, yet he was infuriated by the pacifism/passivity of the Pennsylvania Quakers before the Revolution.[4] Paine was not a "factional" Quaker, and he did not in any way participate in the limited Quaker political agenda. Scholars like Conway, then, refer partly to heritage and partly to community in the broadest sense of "culture" or "sensibility." For example, a much more recent work considers Paine Quaker because he had many Quaker friends and because his writing reflects the Quaker testimonies of equality, simplicity, and peace.[5] But arguing that Paine was Quaker in this sense does not really conflict with idea that his personal theology was Deist.

The question of Mary Wollstonecraft's religion is at least equally vexed, but for different reasons. In this case, there is no debate over her heritage (Anglican), nor over the partisan aspects of religion: as a friend and defender of Richard Price, Wollstonecraft's partisan loyalties are unambiguous. In Wollstonecraft's case, the issue is rather one of belief—and the value of belief. An early biographer, Emma Rauschenbusch-Clough, delineated three phases of Wollstonecraft's belief: although Wollstonecraft was always nominally an Anglican, we can see an early evangelical strain, then the influence of rational Dissent, and finally a silence about religion.[6] This schema is evidenced, in part, by the frequent mentions of the consolations of the Holy Spirit in early letters; the emphasis on rational religion in the two *Vindications*; then the disillusionment expressed in the "Letter on the Present Character of the French Nation."

But many recent scholars, while recognizing the partisan agenda, are unconcerned with Wollstonecraft's personal belief. American scholars, especially, and those who came to Wollstonecraft via liberal feminism, place Wollstonecraft in a secular framework dominated by the language of rights. For example, in his recent book, Gary Kelly downplays the religious subtexts in Wollstonecraft's writings. He explains the revised ending of the *Vindication of the Rights of Men*, in which Wollstonecraft rested her case on the "immutable attributes of God," as strategic: the second edition, unlike the first, had Wollstonecraft's name on the title page along with "As a 'mere' woman author writing on politics she had need to invoke divine validation."[7] Like many writers on early feminists, Kelly apparently believes that religious references must be explained away—that the argument is stronger without them. Secular notions of fairness and equality are privileged over those based on ideas about the nature of God. Because Wollstonecraft has entered the canon in the context of twentieth-century liberal feminism, her religious beliefs have received much less attention than those of figures who were studied by earlier generations of scholars. In the attention she has received, though, we can see the modern idea that views based on religion are predictable or irrational; that a religious argument does not "count" as political.

The historiography of Edmund Burke's religion is different yet again. Unlike Wollstonecraft's, Burke's religion has been the subject of centuries of discussion. Although Burke insisted he had always been and would always be faithful to the established church, he was dogged by accusations that he was, in fact, Catholic. As an Irishman, son and husband of Catholics, Burke was a likely "suspect," and political cartoons routinely portrayed him as a Jesuit. Burke could not dispute his heritage, and his personal beliefs were not, I believe, the issue: rather, what contemporaries feared was a Catholic cabal, a fear rather akin to the "Jewish conspiracy" theories that still resonate in some circles today. It was the partisan aspect of religion that worried Burke's detractors.

In the recent scholarship about Burke's religion, some of the disagreement stems from the different aspects of religion under consideration. Clark's emphasis on Burke's Anglicanism, besides fitting into Clark's overall thesis, is really an emphasis on the heritage of Burke's ideas. For Clark, "Burke's achievement in his later works was to give eloquent but unoriginal expression to a theoretical position largely devised by Anglican churchmen" (249); Clark traces decades of writings by Anglicans whose confessional state strongly resembled Burke's ideal. Frederick Dreyer's focus is on personal belief: he argues that as Burke was tolerant in matters of orthodoxy, liturgy, and church authority, he must be considered a Latitudinarian. And finally, a third position, argued most recently by Conor Cruise O'Brien, holds that Burke was indeed Catholic, or close enough: that he was baptized Catholic, attended Mass as a child, may have converted as a young man, and so on. O'Brien thinks the date (and hence, sincerity) of Burke's father's conversion is "absolutely crucial for Burke's biography,"[8] and he emphasizes the fearsome, secret ambivalence of Burke's feelings about Catholics. While considering many aspects of religion, O'Brien stresses the Catholic community.

Can Burke have been a Latitudinarian, a High Churchman, *and* a Catholic? While it is possible that each view illuminates aspects of Burke's thought, and certainly possible that at times he sounds like one, at times another, I do not believe we can reconcile views that he "was" all of these. In some sense, these arguments echo the partisan concerns of Burke's contemporaries. One gets the uncomfortable feeling that each scholar is trying to claim Burke for his own camp; or, to put it more positively, that each brings special knowledge of his own religion and sees that highlighted in Burke.[9] To define someone's religion is to specify his fundamental assumptions about how the world is and ought to be; those readers who find Burke's argument convincing are motivated to discover shared assumptions. This is not unlike what happens when Wollstonecraft scholars try to "explain away" religious statements: they are also seeking the assumptions they share with an author they admire. While some of these scholarly disagreements can be traced to different senses of what we mean by religion, then, much must also go back to the rhetorical situation: an individual author attempting to persuade an individual reader.

Religion has great power as a rhetorical tool: it can move those readers who accept the assumptions three giant steps forward in the argument, or it can stop the skeptics from proceeding. In the Revolution debate as a whole, religious differences were never very far below the surface. If Burke's pamphlet was answered by one declaring *Rights of Swine*, Paine's was answered by at least two called *The Rights of God*.[10] "Church and King," presumably in that order, motivated the Birmingham rioters, and on through the decade; in his *Essay on Population*, at the end of the debate proper, Malthus defends government inaction about feeding its people in an expression of traditional Christian apologetics. Still, the religious underpinning of an argument must be handled carefully; authors are unwilling to eliminate from their audience those who do not share all aspects of their faith, even while tracing the political consequences of their belief.

Even in the text that can be called the beginning of the Revolution debate, Price's *Discourse on the Love of Our Country*, there is a delicacy about mixing religion and politics. When Burke criticized Price on the grounds that "politics and the pulpit are terms that have little agreement,"[11] he was only repeating Price's own reservation. The *Discourse* began by noting that since this was the "anniversary of our deliverance at the Revolution from the dangers of Popery and arbitrary power," he hoped to be excused "should I, on such an occasion, be led to touch more on political subjects than would at any other time be proper in the pulpit."[12]

After this disclaimer, however, Price's sermon shows that religion and politics are inseparable: the point of the whole is to distinguish the kinds of patriotic duties to which Christians are called. Patriotism does not, according to Price, commit us to prejudices against other nations, but rather calls us to further in our own country the "chief blessings of human nature . . . : truth, virtue, and liberty" (181). And these are described in religious terms: truth includes knowledge of the Deity, while virtue is defined by religion and includes "the public duties of religion" (183); later in the essay, liberty is associated with the fruit of the Revolution, "the liberty of worshipping God in the manner we think most acceptable to him" (189). On the other hand, the partisan agenda alluded to throughout can become primarily secular. Price notes that the toleration gained at the Revolution was imperfect, but feels another issue is even more pressing: "the most important instance of the imperfect state in which the Revolution left our constitution, is the inequality of our representation" (191–92). This is "our fundamental grievance," (192) and it is clearly both partisan and secular.

Price's sermon, as answered by Burke, places the entire Revolution debate in a religious context. Burke did not, after all, *have* to retain his comments on Price as an important part of the *Reflections*; although he began to write soon after he had read the sermon, the *Reflections* were not published for another year. Keeping Price's *Discourse* as the "occasion" for the debate retains the strong link between religion and politics.[13] And while Burke lambastes Price for politicizing the pulpit, he is surely not prepared to argue that religion *should not* have a political agenda. The *Reflections* can easily be read as primarily a defense of the church establishment; Clark, for one, finds that here, as elsewhere, the constitutional arguments permitting 1688 but no future revolutions were less compelling than "the religious element, the assertion of the centrality of the Church, its validation of the Hanoverian dynasty, and its political message of subordination, loyalty and obedience" (261). Certainly some who responded to the *Reflections* read it as a treatise on the established church. In his response, for example, Priestley sets out to consider "whether it be right, and wise, to connect the business of *religion* with that of the *state*."[14] He accuses Burke of defending the Tory notions of "passive obedience and non-resistance" (vii) and argues strenuously against the civil establishment of religion.

Yet for all Burke's defense of the clergy and pronouncements that "religion is the basis of civil society" (186) and "man is by his constitution a religious animal" (187), and for all his mourning the confiscation of church property in France, there is still some reticence in talking about religion. O'Brien also sees defensive tactics here: he believes that what hurt Burke most about the French Revolution was its attack on Catholicism, and that Burke only redefined the problem as the Revolution's atheism because it was politically impossible to promote Catholicism (411). Whether or not this was the reason, it does seem that Burke discusses religion rather *less* than he might have done. In this brief essay, let me note just two quirks in the text of the *Reflections* that hint at Burke's ambivalence about discussing matters of faith.

First, and strangest, is his avoidance of the issue in a significant misquotation of Price. According to Burke, Price asserts that by the principles of the Revolution, the people of England have acquired three fundamental rights, including a right

1. To choose our own governors.
2. To cashier them for misconduct.
3. To frame a government for ourselves. (99)

Burke discusses each in detail, arguing strenuously against a contractual government. But while Price did indeed list three of the principles of the Revolution, they were not in fact those three. They were, rather these:

First, the right to liberty of conscience in religious matters.
Secondly, the right to resist power when abused. And
Thirdly, the right to chuse our own governors, to cashier them for misconduct, and to frame a government for ourselves. (189–90)

By giving only the last of Price's principles, and removing it from context, Burke has inappropriately secularized Price's argument. Perhaps he sensed that linking Price with liberty of conscience would have protected Price in the eyes of many readers.

Another textual quirk also indicates ambivalence about discussing religion. Although the *Reflections* is famously loose in structure, Burke does occasionally guide us through the argument by setting out lists of points to be discussed. For example, in the last third of the book, Burke says he will, and in fact proceeds to, discuss in order the French assembly's actions regarding the legislature, the executive, the judicature, the army, and the system of finance (284 ff.). But Burke's discussion of English government is much less orderly. He tells us he will cover the established church, monarchy, aristocracy, and democracy, and begins with the established church, "which is the first of our prejudices" (188). Eighty-six pages later, he abandons his plan for lack of time, having stayed focused (more or, perhaps, less) on his first topic, the church. These are, of course, details, but they point to some considerable ambivalence about linking religion and politics. The reader senses that Burke was trying to, but could not, keep religion from dominating the political debate.

In this context, Wollstonecraft's *Vindication of the Rights of Men*, the very first published response to the *Reflections*, appears to be a straightforward iteration of a partisan agenda. Wollstonecraft had become close to Price when they both lived in Newington Green, and she had reviewed his *Discourse* for the *Analytical Review*. One strong theme in the *Vindication* is a defense of Price as a person and a corresponding attack on Burke; the reader clearly senses the depth of Wollstonecraft's loyalty. But the *Vindication* is not only about individuals; as G. J. Barker-Benfield has shown, it is composed largely of pieces of the Commonwealth agenda. Wollstonecraft covers nearly all the points of the reform movement: the desire to open politics up to talent; the inequities of the penal laws, press gangs, and game laws; the preference for "manly" reason and civic virtue over weak, "effeminate" luxury; and so on.[15] Barker-Benfield says little about Wollstonecraft's specific use of religion, emphasizing rather the heritage of this partisan cluster of concerns.

In its partisanship, the *Vindication* is not so much a response to Burke as a restatement of a separate agenda, the Republican party platform "answered" by the Democratic one. Yet in other ways, Wollstonecraft's text is fascinating precisely as a reading—and a terrific one—of the *Reflections*. We see that what Wollstonecraft thought was important was not at the level of politics in the usual sense—she almost ignores the French, and says even less about the Glorious Revolution. Rather, Wollstonecraft goes after the cultural assumptions, like Burke's preference for theatricality, underlying the politics. And ultimately, nearly every criticism of Burke or Burke's text goes back explicitly to their disagreement about the nature of God.

In the Advertisement to the text, Wollstonecraft remarks that her argument remained focused on the "grand principles" that Burke had attacked. Towards the beginning of her essay, she provides the first of these: "The birthright of man . . . is such a degree of liberty, civil and religious, as is compatible with the liberty of every other individual with whom he is united in a social compact, and the continued existence of that compact."[16] So far, this sounds like a secular political statement. She goes on to note that "the demon of property" has limited this "sacred right." "But that it results from the eternal foundation of right—from immutable truth—who will presume to deny, that pretends to rationality—if reason has led them to build their morality and religion on an everlasting foundation—the attributes of God?" (9). In contrast to her own, Burke's first principles are expressed in secular terms: "that we are to reverence the rust of antiquity . . . that we ought cautiously to remain for ever in frozen inactivity" (10). Wollstonecraft critizes Burke's acceptance of the status quo in several examples, including religious ones: had he been there, Burke would not have justified the Reformation; had he been a Jew, he would have wanted Christ crucified. Even in matters of religion, we cannot worship the old only because it is old; and as for natural rights, "in receiving these, not from their forefathers but, from God, prescription can never undermine" them (14).

Probably the bulk of Wollstonecraft's essay attacks inequality of property and Burke as its defender. Wollstonecraft devotes much attention to the abuses suffered by the poor and to customs like primogeniture that protect wealth. But her humane impulse is generally expressed in religious terms. In her early letters, Wollstonecraft had frequently mentioned the consolation that religion could offer in hard times. Here, her emphasis is not so much on the sufferer but rather on others' duty to relieve suffering: "a conviction that there is much unavoidable wretchedness, appointed by the grand Disposer of all events, should not slacken [one's] exertions: the extent of what is possible can only be discerned by God" (52). Wollstonecraft cites a passage from Burke in which he offers the poor only the consolation of eternal justice. But, she retorts, this is "contemptible hard-hearted sophistry, in the specious form of humility, and submission to the will of Heaven.—It is, Sir, *possible* to render the poor happier in this world, without depriving them of the consolation which you gratuitously grant them in the next" (55). Moreover, Wollstonecraft takes care to distinguish her notion of proper treatment of the poor from a mere sympathetic emotion that doesn't lead to action: "We ought to beware of confounding mechanical instinctive sensations with emotions that reason deepens, and justly terms the feelings of *humanity*. This word discriminates the active exertions of virtue from the vague declamation of sensibility" (53).

The discussions of property that run throughout the *Vindication* are tied by this notion of religious duty to the central section of the text, the passages on instinct and reason (31–34). Here the target is Burke's reliance on "untaught feelings." Borrowing from the rational Dissenters, Wollstonecraft emphatically places reason as the central foundation for all morality. The cultivation of reason separates us from the brute creation; only reason gives us the ability to discern and choose virtue, and to improve in virtue so as to earn eternal rewards. Indeed, "If virtue be an instinct, I renounce all hope of immortality" (33). God is defined as the supreme exemplar of reason: "I fear that sublime power, whose motive for creating me must have been wise and good; and I submit to the moral laws which my reason deduces from this view of my dependence on him.—It is not his power that I fear—it is not to an arbitrary will, but to unerring *reason* I submit" (34).

Fundamentally, then, Wollstonecraft's disagreement with Burke is over the nature of God; all of her critiques—of sentiment, of property, even of Burke's aesthetics—come back to this. Where Burke's God created a hierarchical world in which suffering is inevitable, Wollstonecraft's God judges us by the extent to which we use the gift of reason to improve our lot and that of others. Wollstonecraft could have expressed the Commonwealth agenda without relying so heavily on theology, and she chose not to; to this reader, the revised ending is a straightforward summary of her text: "But neither open enmity nor hollow homage destroys the intrinsic value of those principles which rest on an eternal foundation, and revert for a standard to the immutable attributes of God" (60). Wollstonecraft had promised us she would "attack the foundation of [Burke's] opinions" (9); she does this by making explicit their religious differences. Yet Wollstonecraft's willingness to state her assumptions explicitly undoubtedly cost her readers: no one who believed in Burke's God would have been convinced by Wollstonecraft's essay. Moreover, the assumptions Wollstonecraft articulates were those shared by one faction in the debate. Contemporary readers would have understood Wollstonecraft's text as belonging to the Dissenting community, and their reactions to it would have been colored by whether they situated themselves in or outside that community.

While Wollstonecraft's pamphlet had a limited readership, Paine's *Rights of Man* was one of the great bestsellers of the century. Paine avoids expressing religious assumptions that would limit his audience to those of one faith. The argument of *Rights of Man* depends heavily on a faith in reason; where Burke relied on inherited wisdom exactly because each individual's stock of reason is small (183), Paine is confident that each generation has fully enough reason to address its own needs. But unlike Wollstonecraft, Paine does not explicitly trace reason back to God as first principle. In the context of this debate, Paine's text is remarkable for its apparent secularism. Eric Foner even claims that "Paine was one of the creators of this secular language of revolution."[17] Certainly Paine avoids the package of concerns that would categorize his text as a partisan Dissenter's document: he writes relatively little on the Test and Corporation Acts, parliamentary reform, the game laws, the press gangs, and so on. The text is dominated, rather, by recapitulations of recent French history, evaluations of government and, of course, the detailed scheme for progressive taxation and social programs of Part 2.

Yet in important ways, *Rights of Man* does exhibit a "sensibility" that is religious (Quaker) in origin. For example, Paine's critique of Burke's gaudy aesthetics—his utter lack of interest in physical beauty—is typically Quaker. So, too, is the extremism: in their confidence that they follow Divine leadings, Quakers frequently exhibit a fearlessness that can turn into a disinclination for subtleties. Also typically Quaker is the peculiar combination of libertarian and communitarian impulses, the insistence on individual rights mixed with organized social welfare. Paine has been criticized for being a capitalist who did not have the sense to know that the classes have conflicting interests.[18] But again, this is typically Quaker: many eighteenth-century Quakers were in business, and often very successful, yet their communitarian beliefs simply did not recognize adversarial relationships.

The Quaker vestiges in Paine's text go far beyond the generalized "simplicity" or "humanitarian impulses" that are often noticed. Some of his asides touch on issues at the heart of Quaker difficulties with the mainstream, such as his critiques of swearing oaths and of hereditary titles.[19] And he often uses phrases that resonate for Quakers. For example, when he says of the abolition of titles that "France has not levelled; it has exalted" (80), he transforms the common Quaker explanation that they had not eliminated the clergy, but raised everyone into it.

Finally, the text of *Rights of Man* is remarkable for the number of references to war, "the" Quaker issue. Paine himself was not a pacifist and, as noted above, he had criticized American Quakers who did not fight the British. But Paine's harping on war in this text is *not* explicable as a response to Burke. Burke had said almost nothing about war; Paine begins and ends his text with it. His major objection to war was economic. Wars, he says, are sponsored to justify big government: any unprejudiced person "would declare, that taxes were not raised to carry on wars, but that wars were raised to carry on taxes" (77). Paine's argument that war and commerce are mutually exclusive derives from Adam Smith and was (obviously) not the argument Quakers made.[20] Yet at the end of Part II, he relates war and religion in a paragraph that could easily have come from a Quaker:

Why may we not suppose, that the great Father of all is pleased with variety of devotion; and that the greatest offence we can act, is that by which we seek to torment and render each other miserable. For my own part, I am fully satisfied that what I am now doing, with an endeavour to conciliate mankind, to render their condition happy, to unite nations that have hitherto been enemies, and to extirpate the horrid practice of war, and break the chains of slavery and oppression, is acceptable in his sight, and being the best service I can perform, I act it cheerfully.[21]

Rights of Man is anything but an expression in politics of Quaker belief. Paine is the champion of representative government and majority rule; this is far from the Quaker "theocracy" in which action is taken only when all agree that a certain choice is God's will.[22] The text is not explicitly Quaker, and Paine was explicitly *not* Quaker in his personal belief. Then what is at stake in my effort to reveal this text's Quaker "sensibility"? Again, I believe it is a matter of individual readers matching their basic assumptions with those of individual writers. To say a particular text is "Quaker-like" is to define its orientation towards a cluster of specific issues. A reader who shares that orientation accepts basic assumptions made by the author, and listens to the argument differently.

I began this essay by asking, in part, what is at stake in our disagreements about the religion of political figures. In an age so much more openly confessional than our own, it seems unlikely for there to be so much ambiguity about the beliefs of major figures. We are invited to wonder, then, why these authors were not more explicit about their most basic assumptions. For although both the *Reflections* and *Rights of Man* reflect a strong religious culture, Burke and Paine were both more reticent about religion than they needed to be. Wollstonecraft, on the other hand, explicitly articulated the theology and political agenda of rational Dissent and emphasized the reliance of her argument on notions of God. In her reading of the *Reflections*, she points to the religious assumptions at the heart of Burke's argument—and indeed, of most eighteenth-century thought. These texts, and the Revolution debate as a whole, were largely shaped by the expression in political terms of religious belief and by the coalitions formed among faith communities.

All political argument rests on fundamental assumptions about human nature and the world's possibilities—leaps of faith, if you will. Arguments that link religion and politics simply make those assumptions explicit. The modern corollary is, perhaps, the painfully detailed confession of one's theoretical assumptions that must now preface works of literary scholarship. Religion is a "theory" in this sense—not a method of automatically reaching prejudiced or illogical conclusions, but a set of basic assumptions from which argument can begin. Our knowledge of an author's religion, whether we mean personal conviction or inherited culture, helps us situate ourselves as we begin to listen.

Acknowledgments
One sign of good teaching comes when a student honestly cannot determine which ideas are her own and which her teacher's. There is much in this essay that David Bromwich, the director of the 1991 NEH Summer Seminar, would not agree with, but I would like to thank him in advance for any readings I have borrowed without acknowledgement.

NOTES

1. "Shall Louis XVI Be Respited?" *The Complete Writings of Thomas Paine*, ed. Philip S. Foner, 2 vols. (N.Y.: Citadel, 1945), 1:558. Further references are to this edition. I should note that in the following I am not concerned with the actual motivation of the real-life Marat, but rather with his comments as rhetorical gestures.

2. J.C.D. Clark, *English Society 1688–1832: Ideology, Social Structure and Political Practice During the Ancien Regime* (Cambridge: Cambridge University Press, 1985), 277.

3. See, for example, Anthony Lincoln, *Some Political & Social Ideas of English Dissent 1763–1800* (Cambridge: Cambridge University Press, 1938); Michael R. Watts, *The Dissenters from the Reformation to the French Revolution* (Oxford: Clarendon, 1978); and James E. Bradley, *Religion, Revolution, and English Radicalism* (Cambridge: Cambridge University Press,

1990). In *Pulpits, Politics, and Public Order in England 1760–1832* (Cambridge: Cambridge University Press, 1989), Robert Hole examines religious arguments about politics as espoused by members of all the major denominations.

4. Paine criticizes Pennsylvania Quakers in "Thoughts on Defensive War," the "Epistle to Quakers," and *The American Crisis,* no. 3. Quotations are from *The Age of Reason* in *Complete Writings,* 1:496 and 1:597.

5. William C. Kashatus III, "Thomas Paine: A Quaker Revolutionary," *Quaker History* 74 (1984): 38–61. Conway's book is *The Life of Thomas Paine,* 2 vols. (N.Y.: Putnam, 1892). For a recent summary of opinions on Paine's religion, see Gregory Claeys, *Thomas Paine: Social and Political Thought* (Boston: Unwin Hyman, 1989), 101–04; Claeys cites Roosevelt, 177. For Paine as a deist, see Harry Hayden Clark, "A Historical Interpretation of Thomas Paine's Religion," *University of California Chronicle* 35 (1933): 56–87; also Robert Falk, "Thomas Paine: Deist or Quaker?" *Pennsylvania Magazine of History and Biography* 62 (1938): 52–63. Quakers and Deists were often confused in the eighteenth century. Though Quakers believe in a much more active God than do Deists, they are similar in that neither group has an ordained ministry, performs formalized rituals, nor emphasizes biblically revealed religion.

6. Emma Rauschenbusch-Clough, *A Study of Mary Wollstonecraft and the Rights of Woman* (London: Longmans, Green, 1898), 46–66. Other works that treat Wollstonecraft's religious belief include Melissa Butler, "Wollstonecraft versus Rousseau: Natural Religion and the Sex of Virtue and Reason," *Man, God, and Nature in the Enlightenment,* eds. Donald C. Mell Jr., E. D. Braun, and Lucia M. Palmer (East Lansing, Mich.: Colleagues Press, 1988), 65–73; Mervyn Nicholson, "The Eleventh Commandment: Sex and Spirit in Wollstonecraft and Malthus," *Journal of the History of Ideas* 51 (1990): 401–21; and my own "Religious Bases of Eighteenth-Century Feminism: Mary Wollstonecraft and the Quakers," *Women's Studies* 22 (1993): 281–95. See also Moira Ferguson and Janet Todd, *Mary Wollstonecraft* (Boston: Twayne, 1984).

7. Gary Kelly, *Revolutionary Feminism: The Mind and Career of Mary Wollstonecraft* (N.Y.: St. Martin's, 1992), 100. I single Kelly out only because his book is the most recent; in his preference for secular explanations he is in the mainstream. Other discussions of *A Vindication of the Rights of Men* that deemphasize religion include James T. Boulton, *The Language of Politics in the Age of Wilkes and Burke* (London: Routledge, 1963), 167–76; and Mitzi Meyers, "Politics from the Outside: Mary Wollstonecraft's First *Vindication,*" *Studies in Eighteenth-Century Culture* 6 (1977): 113–31. The second *Vindication* has, of course, received much more attention from feminist scholars.

8. Conor Cruise O'Brien, *The Great Melody: A Thematic Biography and Commented Anthology of Edmund Burke* (Chicago: University of Chicago Press, 1992), 4. Dreyer writes in "Burke's Religion," *Studies in Burke and His Time*

76 (1976): 199–212.

9. I make no apology about participating in this phenomenon myself: the issue of Paine's Quakerism undoubtedly catches my fancy because I am Quaker.

10. Gayle Trusdel Pendleton, "Towards a Bibliography of the *Reflections* and *Rights of Man* Controversy," *Bulletin of Research in the Humanities* 85 (1982): 65–103.

11. Edmund Burke, *Reflections on the Revolution in France*, ed. Conor Cruise O'Brien (London: Penguin, 1986), 94. Further references are to this edition.

12. Richard Price, *Political Writings*, ed. D. O. Thomas (Cambridge: Cambridge University Press, 1991), 178. Subsequent page references are to this edition. D. O. Thomas discusses the *Discourse* and Burke's response in *The Honest Mind: The Thought and Work of Richard Price* (Oxford: Clarendon, 1977), 297–339.

13. Frederick Dreyer offers another explanation: he points out the many long-standing and secular disagreements between Price and Burke in "The Genesis of Burke's *Reflections*," *Journal of Modern History* 50 (1978): 462–79.

14. Joseph Priestley, *Letters to the Right Honourable Edmund Burke occasioned by his Reflections on the Revolution in France*, 2d ed. (Birmingham: Pearson, 1791), vi.

15. G. J. Barker-Benfield, "Mary Wollstonecraft: Eighteenth-Century Commonwealthwoman," *Journal of the History of Ideas* 50 (1989): 95–115.

16. *A Vindication of the Rights of Men*, in *The Works of Mary Wollstonecraft*, eds. Janet Todd and Marilyn Butler, 7 vols. (London: Pickering, 1989), 5:9. Further references are to this volume.

17. Eric Foner, *Tom Paine and Revolutionary America* (N.Y.: Oxford University Press, 1976), xv.

18. For this gentle criticism, see E. Foner, *Tom Paine* xix, and E. P. Thompson, *The Making of the English Working Class* (N.Y.: Random House, 1963), 96.

19. *Rights of Man*, ed. Eric Foner (N.Y.: Viking Penguin, 1985), 207, 80. Further references are to this edition.

20. On the reception and extension of Smith's point, see J. E. Cookson, *The Friends of Peace: Anti-War Liberalism in England, 1793–1815* (Cambridge: Cambridge University Press, 1982), 54–73. Paine adapts this argument on 212 and elsewhere.

21. *Rights of Man,* 271. "Cheerfully" is another loaded word for Quakers, who are frequently reminded of George Fox's admonition to "walk cheerfully over the earth, answering that of God in every one."

22. I borrow this word from Conway, though I strongly disagree with his claim that "[Paine's] whole political system is explicable only by this theocratic Quakerism." *Life of Thomas Paine,* 2:231.

The "Ancient Voices" of Blake's *The French Revolution*

Lisa Plummer Crafton

William Blake and revolution have long been linked—Blake's depiction of the fiery rebel Orc in *America*, his revolutionary style in both narrative and visual art, and his radical redefinitions of religion and denuniations of religious, social, sexual, and political tyranny are enough to warrant him consideration in any discussion of revolution, but most especially the French Revolution, the event greeted by radicals in England as a new dawn, a time for potential regeneration of the world, and with which Blake is linked by associations with the publisher Joseph Johnson's circle of radical thinkers and artists.[1] Yet he was not a paying or even a listed member of any of the radical societies of the 1790s, and his emphasis consistently stays on the universal questions of humanity, even while directly critiquing the society he lived in. In the Revolution debate of the 1790s, Blake participates most directly through his poetic rendering of events in *The French Revolution,* 1791. After being virtually neglected for years or disparaged for inconsistency or obscurity of mythic vision, the poem has received much deserved attention in the past few years. At least three scholars have recently argued for its inclusion as a significant text in the debate, a text offering a poetic, visionary interpretation endorsing the radical events of the Revolution.[2] However, the poem does more than contribute to the historical debate by countering Burke or engaging the terms of the debate over "nature," as has been argued; its strength lies in its synthesis of historical and mythological realms, for in that synthesis, we see the poem not as an anomaly (as Bloom and others contend) but as an important early text in the formation of Blake's mythology, the central tenet of which is that it is through individual imaginative vision and one's own recognition of it that the ideals of liberty, equality, and fraternity can be gained. The poem, thus, should be viewed in both its historical and cultural context and within the framework of Blake's own mythmaking, a nexus of meaning that offers full appreciation of the poem.

To see Blake in context of the debate, let us go back to what might be considered the impetus for the debate as a whole, Richard Price's *Discourse on the Love of Our Country*. In that sermon delivered at the Old Jewry in November 1789, Dissenting minister Dr. Richard Price exhorted his English audience to behold the dawn of a new day. His rhetoric is apocalyptic, cosmic, linking the events of the very new French Revolution to millennial images of peace and the abstractions of liberty. His perspective on the Revolution is also, of course, in some sense partisan—urging radical support of change not only in France but in England—as are the perspectives of his decidedly political respondents Edmund Burke (whose *Reflections* begins with a response to Price) and the radical Thomas Paine whose *Rights of Man* is an overt response to Burke's *Reflections*. Yet Price's *Discourse* is qualitatively different in substance. As Marilyn Butler and others have noted, Price's Dissenting polemics are distinct from the rationalism of Paine and Godwin; it is a "quality of feeling," according to Butler, that defines his vision.[3] The most comparable poetic rendering of this kind of moral, apocalyptic representation of revolution is William Blake's *The French Revolution*. Although other Romantic poets treat the revolution as a larger than life, cataclysmic event—for example, Wordsworth's accounts in *The Prelude*—Blake is distinct in consistently representing revolution in moral mythological terms. There is no Blakean political statement comparable to Wordsworth's *Letter to the Bishop of Llandaff*; in fact, there are very few statements on any historical/political events. Rather, it is part of Blake's poetic program to depict historical events in light of his own vision.

Thus, Blake, the visionary prophet-poet, treats the Revolution exactly as one might suspect, not as a political event but as myth, the same way that he treats slavery and the subjection of women in *Visions of the Daughters of Albion* and the inspirational American revolution in *America*, both works in which the political and social subjects are enveloped within a mythological dimension. Yet nowhere is Blake's skill in the transformation of history into myth more distinct than in *The French Revolution,* which offers not only that synthesis but also presents early prototypes of what will become a few of Blake's permanent cast of mythological characters, Los and Urizen. Most significantly, the poem depicts Blake's abiding vision that the Revolution is a revolution in the largest sense of that word—a natural cycle or rotation that will restore France (and the world) to its original liberty. Blake's concern with rediscovering what Price calls the "words of the eternal language" links Blake's poem with Price's sermon in significant and revealing ways.[4]

The similarities, in fact, between Price's *Discourse* of 1789 and Blake's *The French Revolution* of 1791 speak emphatically of the kind of revolutionary discourse that subordinated political discussion to moral and metaphysical reflection. While in some sense always partisan, they differ from their contemporaries in their persistent prophetic and Protestant strain, as is evident from the pattern of images, the rhetoric, and the basis from which both Price and Blake view the revolution as a potentially revivifying, sacred event. As they both take up the mantle of the prophetic orator, it is not surprising that both use rhetoric about language itself as a component of their own revolutionary discourse. In fact, both revolutionary and counterrevolutionary writers recognized the centrality of language to their political arguments. For the revolutionaries, words like "freedom" and "nation" and "the people" had to be redefined, for it was the traditional definition of such terms that allowed maintenance of the status quo and preservation of prevailing social systems. Both revolutionary and counterrevolutionary writers argue in terms of either "traditional" or "democratic" language.[5] On a much more metaphorical and spiritual plane, both Price and Blake suggest that the authentic language of revolution—in Price's word, the "eternal language," and in Blake's poem the "ancient voices"—is one that gets lost in the morass of rhetoric on both sides. Their emphasis on an eternal or ancient language devalues contemporary debates about language and serves to supersede both the contemporary linguistic controversies about correct language and the political debates of the pamphlet wars of the 1790s. Examining the contexts of the political debate about language and of the debates about linguistic theory that in many ways informed and molded the parameters of the political debate helps to illuminate a reading of Blake's *The French Revolution*.

That the French Revolution was a momentous public event is clearly evidenced not only by the multitude of arguments for and against but also simply by the greatest proliferation of periodicals and pamphlets in history. The number of journals and newspapers in England rose from 90 in 1750 to 264 in 1800; in France, where there had been only a dozen or so periodicals circulating in Paris in the 1780s, more than 500 appeared between 1789 and 1792.[6] E. P. Thompson and Olivia Smith suggest that the debate in general and Paine's *Rights of Man* in particular did more to stimulate the reading public and, indeed, increase literacy, than any other event. Language was, however, not merely a medium but a topic in revolutionary and counterrevolutionary discourse. The most notorious and simplest example of the extent to which language became the impetus for fierce debate is the outcry over Burke's now infamous "swinish multitude" epithet. The phrase became a catalyst for many radical responses, for by vividly defining the populace as brutish, Burke provoked them into speech they might otherwise have deferred. In fact, the Revolutionary Society toasted Burke for having "provoked the great discussion that occupies all thinking people."[7] Radical pamphleteers helped give voice to the silent "swine" in various allegories, like *Politics for the People: A Salmagunday for Swine* and Eaton's *Pig's Meat: A Lesson for the Swinish Multitude*, in which Burke is ridiculed by such memorables as Gregory Grunter, Porculus, Old Bristle Back, and Spare Rib. Yet, such comic distortions of Burke reflect the larger and more significant debates occurring on both the levels of linguistic and political theory.

The political debates about language were informed and molded, in part, by debates among linguists that flourished in the last three decades of the eighteenth century.[8] Marilyn Butler points to these decades as an era of genuine debate over the belief in an aristocratic, hegemonic language versus the acceptance of a language more democratic, the language of the lower class, the vulgar, something akin to that which Wordsworth outlines for poetry in the "Preface."[9] On the whole, eighteenth-century linguists were largely prescriptive, defining a linguistic terrain that separated the refined from the vulgar. The tradition was set by those whom Olivia Smith calls the "Linguistic Trinity": Bishop Lowth's comprehensive grammar of 1762, Johnson's *Dictionary* of 1755, and James Harris's *Hermes* of 1751, a universal grammar. Harris is significant politically because in his belief that words themselves were "COMPREHENSIVE AND PERMANENT IDEAS," he denounced necessarily specific political language as immoral. Thus, words like "king" or "Constitution" are to be seen as forms not subject to historical change, a theory ideologically if not ontologically consistent with Burke. So the radicals, in their efforts on behalf of democracy, had not only to justify the abilities of the poor but also to redefine the nature of language. The revolt against or defense of hegemonic language theories that informed much of the linguistic debates became a politically charged issue. The radicals fought to delineate an "intellectual vernacular language" to fight the hegemonic theory that consistently eliminated the lower classes.[10] As Smith points out, the political and social effectiveness of ideas about language derived from the belief that language revealed the mind; thus, a distinction between refined/vulgar language helped maintain status quo social roles.

Those radical figures who influenced efforts to democratize language include Paine, Cobbett, Spence, Hone, and Tooke. Paine, whose *Rights of Man* had more impact on the mass of the reading public than any other single text, was an agent for change not only through his subject matter but also his plain style.[11] He combines a plainness of diction with symmetry and balance which, according to Butler, works as a legitimate feature of style "designed to hold the attention, and secure the trust of, an audience which was accustomed to being governed but not to being written for."[12] Cobbett, who believed that differences in language, especially grammar, were a means of class manipulation and, like Paine, believed that mystery and authority reinforce each other to oppress the majority of the population, offered a grammar to teach the self-educated how to participate in public life. Similarly, Thomas Spence, self-educated writer, compiled a phonetic alphabet and dictionary for the uneducated. John Horne Tooke, involved in almost all the major reform movements of the late-eighteenth century, argued for acceptance of evolutionary language change, his major work *The Diversions of Purley* pointed most directly against Harris whose linguistic precepts he saw as ideological devices used to uphold the status quo. All these representative figures, along with William Hone's brilliant self-defense against treason (a defense argued on the basis of language) and along with advances in printing, provide the context in which language itself informs and in many ways is the pivotal force behind the English radical movement.[13]

Nowhere is the marriage between the linguistic, theoretical debate and the political debate made more clear than in the work of Edmund Burke. Burke's well-known arguments against revolutionary change include the fear that change will abolish the traditional language of religion and monarchy. He condemns, for instance, Dr. Price's sermons as "philipizing," encouraging new congregations with many voices. Referring to an actual debate over what to call the king, he denounces the revolutionary stand toward "the French King, or the King of the French, (or by whatever name he is known in the new vocabulary)" and proudly asserts that he and other conservatives still call the king "our Sovereign Lord the King . . . [we] on our parts, have learned to speak only the primitive language of the law, and not the confused jargon of their Babylonian pulpits."[14]

Blake responds from the pulpit, treating the French king with a "new vocabulary," promoting a vision of democratic, apocalyptic peace, depicted by a war between voices and an eventual harmony. *The French Revolution* suggests the existence of a primitive or ancient language, but one far different from the "primitive language of the law" that Burke defends. It is surprising, then, that the emphasis on language or voices in *The French Revolution* has been unexplored, for it is the element that clearly unifies this poem. The subject is revolution, rendered in terms of verbal warfare; the structure is determined by voices contending against one another. Speakers are characterized by their language; symbolism is rendered in auditory terms; one of the most important scenes in the poem, the representatation of the seven prisoners of the tower, is developed in terms of how prisoners are deprived of their rights of speech and, concomitantly, of imagination; and language and deed become joined in several narrative instances, suggesting the power and effects of utterance. By examining the poem with attention to voice or language, we hear echoes of other voices, like those of Burke and Wordsworth, but most notably of Richard Price and his *Discourse*. In such a context between Blake and Price, we find that Blake's poetic representation of the potentially expansive quality of the Revolution and Price's prose exhortations against the narrow and blinding circle of one's self argue for the Revolution as moral renewal, not just political event.

After the poem opens with Blake's characteristic apocalyptic imagery of mist and clouds, the first voice in the poem is one of renewal, calling the narrator away from monarchy: "the ancient dawn calls us / To awake from slumbers of five thousand years."[15] Blake's vision is revolution in the sense of a cyclical rotation, a return to a former state, not a direct,violent overthrow.[16] Significantly, the calling voice is the "ancient dawn" or Eden, a kind of lost paradise. Blake's stress of "ancient" here (used seven times in the poem) is similar to Paine's strategy, in *Rights of Man*, of giving validation and authority to an authentic origin of rights, only to Adam and Eve's God-given, original liberties, not to any man-made ones. Directed primarily at Burke, Paine explains, "The error of those who reason by precedents drawn from antiquity, respecting the rights of man, is that they do not go far enough into antiquity. They do not go the whole way . . . to the divine origin of the rights of man at his creation."[17]

The poem's opening also sets up the transformation of history into myth, using a variety of techniques. Blake condenses the events of months in one day, breaking temporal and spatial bounds to achieve a cosmic dimension. He offers both fictional and historical characters, mixing well-known names of the Revolution—Orleans, Abbe de Sieyes, Lafayette, Mirabeau—with his own mythical characters—an "aged form hovering in mist" who is an early portrait of Nobodaddy; a Duke of Burgundy, whom I believe to be an echo of Burke; the ghost of Henry IV, used as a symbol of France's earlier dedication to republicanism; and a cast of reptiles who close the poem in a unique and effective reversal of the monster imagery commonly used to portray revolutionaries. Finally, Blake offers a setting in which the ominous, failing world of nature ["Sick the mountains, and all their vineyards weep" (6)] comments on the political and, ultimately, the imaginative events in the story.

Blake's interest in the representation of voices goes beyond the mythical "ancient" voice of the opening; he depicts metaphorically the actual tyranny over the voices of the people, historically prevalent at the time in the form of government censorship and repression. The antirevolutionary hysteria, including Paine's indictment for libel in 1792 and the 1794 treason trials for Hardy, Thelwall, and Tooke, is enough to confirm, as has been argued, Blake's (or Johnson's) probable anxiety about publishing his poem.[18] The repression of free speech was, then, a concrete reality, not just a debate among linguists about what speech should be allowable. Political arguments were referred to and dismissed on the basis of their language; radical politicians then found themselves defeated before they began. Many petitions to Parliament for suffrage and equal rights, for example, were denied because they did not meet Wilberforce's standard for "decent and respectable language" of petitions.[19] Decent language can not include such words as "rights," "liberty," and "the nation," whose very use suggested to those in power that the radicals planned complete overthrow of government. Thus, it is with historical validity that Paine, in *Rights of Man,* cautions against becoming "immured in the Bastille of a word" (2:320).[20]

Blake takes Paine's metaphor and literalizes it, through his depiction of the prisoners "immured" in the Bastille *for* a word, that is, prisoners whose offenses may be characterized in some way by their relationship to language, either explicitly in terms of the repression of free speech or metaphorically, in terms of the repression of creativity, of imagination, a matter linked to the explicit repression of speech, the loss of language being the loss of a medium in which to imagine. Either way, Blake's seven prisoners of the tower represent instances of oppression by the French monarchy.[21] Blake's use of the Bastille in this way becomes a metaphor of the prison or tyranny of language.

Blake's prisoners then are more than sociopolitical victims. In the tower named Horror, actual manacles around the neck silence the voice of the inhabitant. His crime is appropriate: "And the man was confin'd for a writing prophetic" (29). Blake himself comes to mind in terms of his reluctance either to publish or finish (depending on whether we see *The French Revolution* as finished or as fragment) his own seditious writing. Similar to the first, the tower named Bloody also houses one imprisoned for the crime of language. His refusal "to sign papers of abhorrence" (34) represents his refusal to submit, in words, to a system of oppression. Furthermore, imprisoned in the seventh tower named God, is a creative madman, pining for liberty, confined for his own act of free speech: "a letter of advice to a King" (51).

Not all captives have been imprisoned for overt crimes of language or speech; however, all in some way define Blake's view of the loss of imaginative freedom. In tower five, Order, lies a prisoner who is a victim of actual repression but whose description points to something more significant. The tower imprisons a creative voice in a space "as narrow as a grave" (40) whose crime was free speech: "he, by conscience urg'd, in the city of Paris rais'd a pulpit, / And taught wonders to darken'd souls" (42–43). This prisoner who "taught wonders to darken'd souls" resembles Price, whose revolutionary rhetoric was supported strongly by images of darkness and enlightenment, as in the following example from the *Discourse*: "Behold, the light you have struck out, after setting AMERICA free, reflected to FRANCE, and there kindled into a blaze that lays despotism in ashes, and warms and illuminates EUROPE" (32). In this tower, Blake uses the ironic associations of the word "grave" not only as loss or death in the sense of grave as burial place, but also as a a place of potential rebirth. In Blake's mythology, the grave is not just a place of death, but the place where Los, the zoa of imagination, works for creativity and the expansion of humankind through language, a place of renewal.[22]

Other prisoners whose metaphorical depictions point to the repression of imagination include towers two and four. The prisoner with "a mask of iron on his face" (31) in the second tower, Darkness, is silenced and hidden from the world. The allusion to the wrongly imprisoned royal heir of the seventeenth century (the man in the iron mask) is important in the fact that authentic royalty lay behind that iron mask, reminding of a line of nobility older, more ancient, than the Bourbons. Blake very specifically describes the prisoner's mask as hiding the "lineaments / Of ancient Kings, and the frown of the eternal lion" (31–32). The words "ancient" and "eternal" ally this prisoner with the "ancient voice," a voice that displaces the present monarchy. Finally, tower four encases Religion who refuses to submit to the minister of state and "with a knife smote him" (37). Here the true emblem of Religion resists the power of the state. Also, the weapon of knife is figurally a tool for etching as well as a violent means for revenge, an image supported, of course, by the fact of Blake as an engraver. In sum, Blake's depictions of the prisoners underscores his belief that the repression of human imagination and creative power, rendered by synecdoche as loss of speech or language, is the true crime of any tyrannical government.

As more demonstrative of how seriously Blake takes the effects of language, language and action are often conflated in the poem, as a voice or natural sound actually causes or engenders actions: "The voice ceas'd: the Nation sat:

And the triple forg'd fetters of times were unloos'd" (62). In these lines, language and action are linked in one single moment. Correspondent to the cessation of voice is the loosening of fetters, which refers not only to the breaking of chains within the tower but also more metaphorically to the spiritual freedom that the poem's finale depicts. This apocalyptic language is very similar to the closing declamation of Richard Price's sermon, which suggests that the people's calls for action enable the loosing of fetters: "Behold kingdoms admonished by you, rousing from sleep, breaking their fetters, and claiming justice from their oppressors" (32).

Conversely, just as language causes action, external events also affect the language of characters. The first turning point in the revolution causes the king to lose control of his own language. He "glow'd" (68), his heart "flam'd" (69), and "these words burst forth" (69). No longer confidently uttered by the king, his words escape from him. He hears a prophecy from counselors of "ancient Kings" (72), and he becomes a mere medium of their words. These counselors, bringing insight from the "ancient" voice, a word already designated as holy, rise from the *graves* of kings to bring words of warning. Again, the voices of the old order are unable to continue, as the king "ceas'd." Blake's manipulation of their progressive silence reveals his representation of defeat of the old order's tyranny.

The actual verbal warfare occurs most clearly in the council's debate. Burgundy, the conservative duke, speaks for war and is introduced and characterized in terms of his garments, which is an apt metaphor for language: "an odor of war . . . rose from his garments" (84); "Cloth'd in flames of crimson" (86); "burning robe" (87). Burgundy argues against the revolutionaries' vision and for maintenance of a traditional hierarchy in France. As such, he is an implicit parody of his phonologically similar historical counterpart, Burke. As he juxtaposes monarchy/democracy, he recalls Burke's lament for the death of Marie Antoinette, as Blake here joins Paine in satirizing Burke's pity for the "plumage" instead of the "dying bird." Burgundy worries that all "plumage" of aristocracy will be destroyed:

Shall this marble built heaven become a clay cottage, this earth an oak stool, and these mowers
From the Atlantic mountains, mow down all this great starry harvest of six thousand years?
Till our purple and crimson is faded to russet. (89–92)

Burgundy mourns what Burke termed the "decent drapery," using rhetorical questions, also like Burke, to call for assent.[23]

As Burgundy's defense strengthens the king's resolve, the king refuses to hear the voice of the ancients which had been trying to mediate through him. As the king's nobles fold close around "like the sun of old time quench'd in clouds" (68), the king sees that this system, these nobles, symbolically represented as mist, obscure his "true" knowledge "and blot the writing of God /

Written in my bosom" (108–9). Recalling Price's admonitions to hear the "words of the eternal language," Blake also provides an interesting twist to the eighteenth-century linguistic theory held by Bishop Lowth and others that refined, aristocratic language was the gift of God and that all other is perversion. Ironically, Blake's king knows that he should listen to the "writing of God," which tells him that his monarchical, hierarchical system, including his language, is wrong. The "writing of God" then represents the authentic voice that the king opposes. He knows that he is not in touch with the ancient or eternal, but he cannot change. He dismisses the liberal noble, Necker, who might have compromised the two sides; in fact, Necker's exodus allies him with Christ as the women and children "Kneel'd round him and kissed his garments and wept" (123).

Blake reserves as the final voice for hierarchy the archbishop, who enters "In the rushing of scales and hissing of flames" (127).[24] This Satanic description of the archbishop sets up the context of his sermon; he supposedly brings a "heaven utter'd counsel," but Blake uses him as a false prophet, a mere image of religion, and one only interested in preserving traditional practice. The archbishop's vision of "An aged form, white as snow, hov'ring in mist, weeping in the uncertain light" (131) provides a foil to the holy word. This white, weeping figure can be seen as an early prototype of Blake's Nobodaddy figure, also known later as Urizen. The characteristic white garments, the shivering and weeping, and the association with mist are all used later in depictions of Blake's abstract sky gods who separate themselves from the people and write laws from their exalted state.[25] Certainly, this visionary form represents the conventions of separation and hierarchy. He laments that God has departed from lives of people; specifically, he laments the change in language, similar to Burke's lament over the "confused jargon" of the "Babylonian pulpits" (Burke 115) created by revolutionary and evolutionary language. First, prayer has failed as has the "holy hymn from the thicken'd tongues" (140). The archbishop fears that the leveling process whereby the mitre turns to black and the crown vanishes is complete, and as sign of this transformation, he hears the language of the high turned into the words of the low: "And the sound of the bell, and voice of the sabbath, and singing of the holy choir, / Is turn'd into songs of the harlot in day, and cries of the virgin in night" (146–47). While the archbishop bemoans this fact, Blake sees it as the inevitable fate for a society whose priorities are so confused. Like the harlot of the last lines of Blake's "London," these songs of the harlot are a cry against the physical and social repression of freedom. Immediately following these lines, the archbishop unconsciously betrays that his true problem with the notion of democracy is the leveling of social roles; he is offended most by the thought that if all were equal, the priest would be forced, in death, to lie beside the "lawless lover," the "holy beside the accursed," and, most disturbingly, the king "beside the grey plowman, and their worms embrace together" (150). Blake here masterfully has the archbishop undercut his own point. His fear of worms embracing in the grave exhibits just how far his horror at equality goes while in the same image Blake emphasizes the common lot to which the king as well as the plowman must go, thus their common humanity.

The archbishop's vision and warning against change is then countered by a series of speakers representative of Blake's ancient voices. The ancient sign returns to France first through the liberal Orleans. His messenger, Aumont, is said to be "like a man that returns from hollow graves" (161), returning from a grave with words of rebirth. The archbishop attempts to break in, but by now his language, like Satan's in Book X of *Paradise Lost*, is totally perverted and distorted: "instead of words harsh hissings / Shook the chamber" (177–78) and "he ceas'd abash'd" (178). The liberal noble Orleans takes up the cause for the democratic revolution here, arguing that the nobility accept the leveling that is inevitable. In keeping with the garment imagery, Orleans "unfolded his robe" (175), in direct contrast to the specific description of the nobles' folding around the king (68) and the weeping souls enfolded in the burning robe of Burgundy (87–88). We hear echoes of the Revolution debate in general as Orleans uses one of the archbishop's earlier metaphors for his own purposes. The archbishop had complained of the revolutionaries' actions in terms of the body politic metaphor, denouncing revolutionaries who bathed "their feet / In the blood of Nobility; trampling the heart and the head" (155–56). Orleans responds in the same metaphorical terms, by emphasizing the metaphor of the full body politic. Strengthened by allusions to Biblical injunctions, Orleans asks: "Is the body diseas'd when the members are healthful? . . . can the soul whose brain and heart / Cast their rivers in equal tides thro' the great Paradise, languish because the feet / Hands, head, bosom, and parts of love, follow their high breathing joy?" (182–85).

These questions, reminiscent in tone of the motto to *Thel*, resemble parables that reveal Blake's democratic, visionary faith. All must be equal if any can be: "Learn to consider all men as thy equals, / Thy brethren, and not as thy foot or hand" (193–94). Blake, through Orleans, goes on to argue specifically against the solipsistic writing of laws, the use of language that comes from and applies only to *one*—individual, class, or gender.[26] In such a spirit, Orleans challenges the king to recognize the full, individual effects of his language instead of sending hierarchical epistles from his abstract sky-god position: "Go, thou cold recluse, into the fires / Of another's high-flaming rich bosom, and return unconsum'd, and write laws" (191–92). And he continues, "if thou canst not do this, doubt thy theories" (294). Orleans' answer further strengthens the idea that the archbishop's vision of the aged form is a precursor of Urizen in Blake's later myth. In *The Book of Urizen*, the sky god, sitting in the solitary void, delights in making laws from his secret position: "Here alone I in books formd of metals / Have written the secrets of wisdom . . . One command, one joy, one desire . . . One King, one God, one Law" (24–25, 38, 40). For Blake, who writes in *The Marriage of Heaven and Hell* that "One Law for the Lion & Ox is Oppression," Orleans' indictment denounces the narcissistic assumptions of superiority which are preserved only by separation and a lack of sympathy and of identification with the whole of humanity.

More than any other single element in the poem, this condemning speech finds echo in Price's *Discourse* and in the context of the revolutionary response to hierarchy. It is at the heart of what Price has to say about the love of country that we ought to cultivate versus a selfish egocentrism founded on "error and delusion" (25). Price takes up the issue of the "noble passion" of patriotism but warns that until one sees that every human being is equal and that "in other families there may be as much worth as in our own," one cannot indulge in patriotic feelings without becoming what Blake would call a "cold recluse." Price applies this assumption of superiority of country to individual pride as well: "We are too apt to confine wisdom and virtue within the circle of our own acquaintance and party" (25). In *The French Revolution*, Blake uses this image of the self-enclosing circle as well, as Orleans commands the nobility: "But go, merciless man! enter into the infinite labyrinth of another's brain / Ere thou measure the circle that he shall run" (190–91). Where a spirit of tolerance and acceptance is not followed, the result is desire for conquest and domination. Price asks of this kind of self "love": "What has it been but a love of domination; a desire for conquest, and a thirst for grandeur and glory . . . What has it been but a blind and narrow principle" (25).[27]

This climactic speech is the turning point of the poem's "war." Finally, the Abbe de Sieyes brings the Holy Word the poem has anticipated all along. He is the "voice of the people" (204) who stands before the noble council [the "mountains to be renewed" (205)], but, more importantly, he is "like a voice of God following a storm" (202). His word is that the word must be re-created; he speaks from the "valleys," not the mountains with a style that is highly repetitive and emphatic. In a passage that anticipates Blake's opening to *Europe*, Sieyes allegorizes man's cavernous existence in wait for redemption: "Till man raise his darken'd limbs out of the caves of night, his eyes and his heart / Expand: where is space! where O sun is thy dwelling! where thy tent, O faint slumb'rous Moon" (218–19).[28]

Sieyes calls for an internal expansion, an imaginative awakening and indeed a recreation of space and time. Continuing the garment metaphor, the Abbe prophecies that the "red robe of terror" will be put off as the meek embrace the strong. Further, the clergy will literally reverse its language toward the peasant: "no more I curse thee; but now I will bless thee" (225). This internal apocalypse will create peace as all voices are harmonized: the "wild raging millions" who "howl in law blasted wastes" (227) will "sing in the village, and shout in the harvest" (229). Finally, the Abbe marks the culmination of the hints of Los that have appeared throughout the poem, for it is through a creative revolution, through language and art, that the revolution will be effected. The Abbe teaches that the expansion of the minds of men is to be achieved through "the saw, and the hammer, the chisel, the pencil, the pen, and the instruments / Of heavenly song" (231–32). Here then is the complete alliance of the Losian character—

striking with hammer in his workshop, inscribing with chisel—with poet, man of new voice—pen, pencil, song. And because Los's instruments are used underground in his creative furnace, it is appropriate that the first to be taught this new harmony will be "the laborious plowman / And shepherd" (232–33), the one who tills the earth and the one most associated with pastoral piping.

The remaining narrative is informed by the coincidence of language and action, this time a fulfillment of the earlier parallels between voicing and freedom. Nature responds to Abbe's speech, not with a loud thunder but with a quiet "murmur": "the low voice of the labouring man, instead of the shout of joy" (245), not a voice of the winepress, like that of Burgundy, but rather as when "grapes are shaken on grass" (244), more like a Communion than a war. This sound, the peaceful voice of revolutionaries, then conflates with the blood of revolution, language and action intimately connected. As the voice sounds, "blood ran down the ancient pillars" (246), these lines another powerful precursor to later lines in "London" in which word and deed become powerfully connected and utterance actually makes or marks a visible change in the symbols of oppression: "And the hapless Soldiers sigh / Runs in blood down Palace walls" (11–12).[29] Clearly, the revolutionary language now has the power to effect change as Mirabeau's mere order of removal "smote the palace walls with a blast" (293), the word effecting the event. Renewal begins as the "aged sun rises appall'd from dark mountains" (270). The clearing of mists is associated with Voltaire and Rousseau who drive out superstitious, abstract sky gods: Blake sees "frequent spectres of religious men weeping / In winds driven out of the abbeys . . . by the fiery cloud of Voltaire, and the thund'rous rocks of Rousseau" (274–76).[30]

The poem presents a prophetic, optimistic ending, with Blake's hopes that the new voices will be triumphant. The fact that history did not bear out his hopes is no negation of the creative spirit with which Blake infused his history. The narrative ends, like Price's rhetoric at the end of his sermon, with a victory for the new voices and for creativity: "And the bottoms of the world were open'd and the graves of arch-angels unseal'd" (301). For this renaissance, the morning revives, and the king is now subject to follow the voice that has forsaken him and his nobles:

> Awful up rose the king, him the peers follow'd, they saw the courts of the Palace
> Forsaken, and Paris without a soldier, silent, for the noise was gone up
> And follow'd the army, and the Senate in peace, sat beneath morning's beam.
> (304–6)

Of course, little did Blake know that actual regicide would result and that Burke's fears would literally be fulfilled. For the world of the poem, political oppression as well as the repression of language and creativity has been lifted. A new voice has been established; mourning has been transformed into morning. The revolution in its natural sense is complete for the world of the poem as the ending fulfills the prophetic beginning. Clearly, Blake's poem belongs in the historical context of the Revolution debate but with the acknowledgment that his mythological powers are not, as has been argued, subordinated, constrained, or dictated by history; quite the converse, Blake's interpretation of history is subordinated to the espousal of his central myth—the absolute necessity of individual imaginative engagement with the world, an engagement that includes a belief that we live in a moral universe and since, as Blake says in *Visions of the Daughters of Albion*, "every thing that lives is holy," every being has a role to play in consummating any revolution.

NOTES

1. While he was not a paying member of the London Corresponding Society, run by the shoemaker Thomas Hardy, nor the more urbane Society for Constitutional Information led by John Horne Tooke, Blake was friends with many of the members and was part of the circle of writers and intellectuals that was associated with his publisher Joseph Johnson and included Fuseli, Paine, Godwin, and Wollstonecraft. For speculation of Blake's participation in radical activities and connection to the Johnson circle, see David Erdman, *Prophet Against Empire*, 3d ed. (Princeton: Princeton University Press, 1977), esp. 153–58, and Marilyn Butler, *Romantics, Rebels, and Reactionaries: English Literature and its Background 1760–1830* (Oxford: Oxford University Press, 1981), esp. 43–44. For general historical readings of Blake and the French Revolution, see also Jacob Bronowski, *William Blake 1757–1827: A Man Without a Mask* (1944; N.Y.: Penguin, 1954), esp. 67–85. Many scholars have treated Blake and revolution in less historical, more mythological terms, including most seminally Northrop Frye, *Fearful Symmetry: A Study of William Blake* (Princeton: Princeton University Press, 1947), and Harold Bloom, *Blake's Apocalypse: A Study in Poetic Argument* (Garden City, N.J.: Doubleday, 1963).

2. See Glen Brewster, "'Out of Nature': Blake and the French Revolution," *South Atlantic Review* 56, no.4 (Nov. 1991): 7–22; William Richie, "*The French Revolution*: Blake's Epic Dialogue With Edmund Burke," *ELH* 59 (1992): 817–37; Lisa Crafton, "Blake's Swinish Multitude: The Response to Burke in Blake's *The French Revolution*," *The Friend: Comment on Romanticism* 2, no.1 (April 1993): 1–12.

3. Marilyn Butler, *Romantics,* 44. For fuller disussion of Price, see D. O. Thomas, *The Honest Mind: The Thought and Work of Richard Price* (Oxford: Clarendon, 1977). The arguments and counterarguments between Price and Burke continue to be subjects of scholarly discussion; for the most recent, see Steven Blakemore's "Misrepresenting the Text: Price, Burke, and the 'October Days' of 1789," *The Friend: Comment on Romanticism* 1, no.4 (Oct. 1992): 1–9, and John Faulkner's essay in this collection.

4. Richard Price, *Political Writings*, ed. D. O. Thomas (Cambridge: Cambridge University Press, 1991). All quotations from Price are taken from this volume.

5. Consider, for example, Burke's "We have learned to speak only the traditional language of the law." Edmund Burke, *Reflections on the Revolution in France*, ed. Conor Cruise O'Brien (N.Y.: Penguin, 1986), 115. Part of the intensity of the focus on language stemmed from the French radicals' very real efforts to produce a new lexicon for the new republic with, for example, the creation of a new calendar, dated from Year One and featuring renamed months and the renaming of streets, towns, even people. See Ronald Paulson, *Representations of Revolution 1789–1820* (New Haven: Yale University Press, 1983), esp. 15–20, and Lynn Hunt, *Politics, Culture, and Class in the French Revolution* (Berkeley: University of California Press, 1984), esp. 19–21.

6. For the rise of periodicals in England, see Butler, *Romantics* 15, and E. P. Thompson's *The Making of the English Working Class*, (N.Y.: Random House, 1963), *passim*. For analysis of this rise in France, see Hunt, esp. 19–20.

7. James Chandler, *Wordsworth's Second Nature* (Chicago: University of Chicago Press, 1984), 18. See also Olivia Smith, *The Politics of Language 1791–1819* (Oxford: Oxford University Press, 1984) for solid historical interpretation of the radical societies and their relationship to Burke.

8. Murray Cohen's *Sensible Words: Linguistic Practice in England 1640–1785* (Baltimore: Johns Hopkins University Press, 1977) analyzes the early background to this controversy, and Smith's *The Politics of Language* interprets the revolutionary and postrevolutionary debate.

9. See Butler's *Burke, Paine, Godwin, and the Revolution Controversy*, (Cambridge: Cambridge University Press, 1984), esp. 14.

10. Smith, x.

11. The unprecedented sales of Burke's *Reflections*, 30,000 copies in two years, became a precedent when *Rights of Man* sold 50,000 copies in 1791.

12. Butler, *Burke,* 109.

13. In *The Politics of Language*, Smith, after a thorough introduction to the issue as a whole, offers detailed chapters on Cobbett, Paine, Tooke, and Hone.

14. Burke, *Reflections*, 178, 115.

15. William Blake, *The Complete Poetry and Prose of William Blake*, ed. David V. Erdman, rev. ed. (N.Y.: Doubleday, 1988), lines 7–8. All subsequent quotations are taken from this edition and are cited by line number. The opening is similar in tone and language to the "Introduction" to *Songs of Experience* in which a Bard who has heard the "Holy Word" from the "ancient trees" calls the lapsed soul to awake.

16. This view of revolution as natural cycle is supported by Blake's persistent tempest imagery. Characteristic of Blake's prophecies, the poem often uses storms, eclipses, and clouds to represent the tremendous upheaval. The poem opens with clouds and mist and ends with calm and sun. See Paulson, esp. 1–5, 44, for analysis of this complex of images in revolutionary art.

17. Thomas Paine, *Rights of Man, The Writings of Thomas Paine*, ed. M. Daniel Conway, 4 vols. (N.Y.: AMS Press, 1967), 2:303–04. Similarly, social criticism also used the contrast between modern and ancient in arguments for change, as in Rousseau's "state of nature" and in Priestley's and Price's claims for the unfettered liberty of Anglo-Saxon England. See Butler, *Romantics,* 23, and Thompson, esp. 86.

18. The title page of Blake's poem promised it to be a "Poem in seven books," and the advertisement read "The remaining Books of this Poem are finished and will be published in their order." However, only one set of page proofs (no manuscript, no illustrations) for Book I is extant.

19. In 1793, petitions from Nottingham and Sheffield explicitly stated the class of "general tradesmen and artificers" on whose behalf the petition was written. The petition ends by asserting that these people "though they may not be freeholders they are men and do not think themselves fairly used in being excluded the rights of citizens." The petition was rejected because of such "highly indecent and disrespectful language." These quotations are taken from Hansard's *Parliamentary Debates*, quoted in Smith, 30–32, where she points out that the distinctions between decent and indecent language obviously depended on who was speaking.

20. Paine's metaphor of the Bastille as language would have been widely understood, for as David Bindman points out, it was a commonplace in England at this time to refer to any place of unjust confinement as a Bastille. See David Bindman, *The Shadow of the Guillotine: Britain and the French Revolution* (London: British Museum, 1989), 37–38.

21. Bindman labels the entire poem a "Bastille poem," since it depends heavily upon a contrast between despotic, cruel rulers and innocent victims within. See "'My mind is my own church': Blake, Paine, and the French Revolution," *Reflections of Revolution: Images of Romanticism*, ed. Alison Yarington and Kelvin Everest (London: Routledge, 1993). Richie contrasts Blake's portrait of the abused prisoners with Burke's "tragic paintings" of royalty abused; see 835 n.15. Erdman speaks of them generally as "types of oppression to be removed by the people in their progressive opening up of a new heaven and earth" (67); Bloom sees them, as a group, manifesting the "tyranny of being a natural man" and sees the inner binding as figuratively revealed by the outward; see esp. 63–65; Victor Paananen, *William Blake* (Boston: Twayne, 1977) calls them "unwilling victims of the perceptual and physical tyranny of the old order" (63). No critic has explicitly linked them together by any specific basis nor treated them in very detailed form.

22. In Blake's *The Four Zoas*, Los, with his hammer, re-creates the word, stimulating Deen's theory of the derivation of the word Los from Logos, the original word: "Then Los built the stubborn structure of the language lest Albion be a dumb despair" (36:59). See Leonard Deen, *Conversing in Paradise* (Columbia: University of Missouri Press, 1983). It is fair to look for early signs of Blake's mythological system here because Blake has used this association

earlier than this text, especially in *Thel* where the grave over which Thel reflects is both end and beginning, determined by one's perspective and imaginative vision. While Morton Paley is right in cautioning against seeing Blake's myth evolve "with teleological certainty from his early lyrics to his later period" (vii), such intertextual analyses do help interpret Blake's symbolic world. In discussion of Blake's myth, I concur with Leo Damrosch that myth is "not an arbitrary way of manipulating symbols, but the conceptual framework in which they make sense" and functions as "a mode of organizing experience rather than as a code for describing it" (81). See Morton Paley, *Energy and the Imagination: A Study in the Development of Blake's Thought* (Oxford: Clarendon, 1970), and Leo Damrosch, *Symbol and Truth in Blake's Myth* (Princeton: Princeton University Press, 1980).

23. For discussion of the specific parallels between Burgundy and Burke and of the ways in which Blake's poem is a direct response to Burke's *Reflections*, see Crafton 1–12 and for discussion of how Blake uses the epic form in this poem as counterattack on Burke, see Richie, 817–37.

24. The description of the archbishop specifically resembles Milton's Satan in *Paradise Lost*. Several critics have noted the parallels between the council scene and Milton's council of Fallen Angels. See Richie, esp. 824; Crafton, 6. The resemblance is also briefly noted in Mark Schorer, *The Politics of Vision* (1946; N.Y.: Vintage, 1959), 258, and Halloran, 39–40.

25. In the book of *Urizen* (1794), the pale, self-enclosed abstract god is exiled to a shadowy "void" solitary "place in the North" (3). For a discussion of Blake's general use of this sky-god convention, see Frye, *passim*. Frye says that Blake specifically depicts the monarchy of France with the "god of empty space and blind will" (Nobodaddy/Urizen); see 62–63, 203, 208. Bloom points to the parallel between this unnamed Urizenic figure and the specifically named Urizen "who sat above all heavens" in *America*; see 126.

26. In the context of the debates in the late eighteenth century, this critique represents the challenge to hegemonic language theories and the call for more tolerant, evolutionary attitudes as evinced by Cobbett, Tooke, and others.

27. In a much more pointedly political accusation but with a similar moral conviction, Wordsworth, in his *Letter to the Bishop of Llandaff*, instructs the Bishop on the true function of representative government: " to be qualified for the office of legislation you should have felt like the bulk of mankind; their sorrows should be familiar to you, of which, if you are ignorant, how can you redress them?" See *Prose Works of William Wordsworth*, ed. Alexander Grosart, 3 vols. (1876; N.Y.: AMS Press, 1967), 1:20.

28. Compare lines 1–6 of *Europe* which also exhort an internal, perceptual change: "Five windows light the cavern'd Man."

29. Like the lyric, *The French Revolution* inscribes a world of political and social repression but offers a method of redemption through the voices that not only cry out for reform, but actually effect it through their cries. For discussion

of the essentially auditory nature of "London," see John Brenkman, *Culture and Domination* (Ithaca, N.Y.: Cornell University Press, 1987), esp. 124, 133.

30. Blake did not agree with Voltaire and Rousseau in their Enlightenment reliance on Reason and subordination of Imagination (as evidenced in his satirical "Mock on Mock on Voltaire Rousseau") but heralded them for their efforts against the superstition and mystery of orthodox religion. It is part of the paradox of Blake's role in the Revolution debate that he finds himself in the camps of the rationalists Wollstonecraft, Godwin, and especially Paine whose *Age of Reason* he will counter later and whom he attacks for refusing to see the Bible as poem of "probable impossibilities." Blake's unusual and absolute belief in the energy and divinity of Imagination places him, as usual, outside most identifiable groups of revolutionary radical activities.

Arguing Benevolence: Wordsworth, Godwin, and the 1790s

Evan Radcliffe

When Wordsworth describes in *The Prelude* the "errors" and "reasonings false" (10:882–83)[1] that helped lead him into, and deepen, his Revolutionary crisis, he includes among them the philosophy of William Godwin. For Wordsworth, as for many young intellectuals shaken in their support of the French Revolution, Godwin had initially represented a progressive alternative to French revolutionary ideology. In Godwin's philosophy, as set forth in *An Enquiry Concerning Political Justice* (1793), the individual mind makes purely rational moral choices, without reference to any emotional or contractual ties that might compromise its absolute independence; as Wordsworth puts it, for Godwin moral choice depends on "One guide—the light of circumstances, flashed / Upon an independent intellect" (10:825–29). Feeling betrayed by both Britain and France, and having what he calls a "young ingenuous mind" (10:815), Wordsworth at first sought to justify his allegiances by way of "evidence / . . . of universal application, such / As could not be impeached" (10:788–90), and consequently embraced Godwin's approach. Eventually, however, he learned not to trust this austere vision which, "with a resolute mastery shaking off / The accidents of nature, time, and place" (10:821–22), "promised to abstract the hopes of man / Out of his feelings" (10:807–8)—a vision, that is, which would base ideas of human possibility on the "purer element" (10:809) of reason and thus remove it from human contingency. As even Hazlitt, whose politics (unlike Wordsworth's) remained liberal and republican, and who portrayed Godwin sympathetically, said in *The Spirit of the Age* (1825), "in his [Godwin's] system . . . [m]an was indeed screwed up into a logical machine."[2]

But Wordsworth's views and uses of Godwin in *The Prelude*—even setting aside the vexed relation between the poem's account and the actual events of the 1790s—are more complex than his brief comments in the poem suggest. Although in the poem Wordsworth rejects the radical rationalism, individualism, and utilitarianism of Godwin's thought, he maintains his faith in an ideal of human generosity and benevolence for which Godwin also stood. In particular, Wordsworth was drawn to a belief widely held, throughout the 1790s and thereafter, by British liberals and radicals: the ideal of "universal bene-volence"—that is, the idea that benevolence and sympathy can be extended to all humanity. As Wordsworth acknowledges when he describes the attraction of *Political Justice* in *The Prelude*, his adoption of Godwinian philosophy was the result of a "noble aspiration"; even after his disenchantment with Godwin, Wordsworth (unlike conservatives who held that believing in ideals was destructive) retains a desire for a "higher" state of humanity (10:830–40).

In the polemics of the 1790s, the "noble" side of Godwin tended to be overshadowed by the way his intellectualist approach seemed to deny the value of individual human connections and affections. Opponents of Godwin and of the French Revolution fastened on one example in particular from *Political Justice*.[3] In his discussion of the actions dictated by "pure unadulterated justice," Godwin imagines the case of a fire at the palace of Fénelon, late archbishop of Cambray. If both Fénelon and his chambermaid were inside but only one could be saved, Godwin argues that we should save Fénelon; Fénelon's personal qualities as well as the widespread beneficial effects of his writing make him "of more worth" than his chambermaid. Rational but apparently heartless, still this choice might have avoided controversy had Godwin rested his case there. But he was always unafraid to follow up the implications of his arguments—Hazlitt writes that Godwin carried his "view of morality to the utmost extent with unflinching spirit" (*Works,* 16:404)—and he presses the case further: "the truth of the proposition" that "[t]he life of Fénelon . . . would be more valuable" than the chambermaid's would remain unchanged even if "the chambermaid had been my wife, my mother or my benefactor."

This example (like Burke's use of "swinish multitude" in his *Reflections on the Revolution in France*) became a 1790s version of today's sound bites.[4] Godwin's denial of any ties of family (or indeed ties of any affectional kind) developed into a standard feature of the conservative demonizing of Godwin. And since the denial of such ties was for Godwin the consequence of believing we should judge actions by the standard of universal benevolence—"the general good," the interests of "the whole family of mankind" (1:82 [sec.2, art. 2])—the ideal of universal benevolence in general became tarred along with Godwin himself: conservatives came to take universal benevolence as inevitably involving the dwindling of affections.

(In subsequent editions of *Political Justice* Godwin made changes, but he never retreated far from his principle. He changed the chambermaid [who might be his wife or mother] to a valet [who might be his father or brother], and he wrote in the preface to *St. Leon* [1799], "I apprehend domestic and private affections inseparable from the nature of man, . . . and am persuaded that they are not incompatible with a profound and active sense of justice in the mind of him that cherishes them."[5] But in replying to his critics in 1801, he returned to the example of Fénelon—an example "so often attacked with all the weapons of argument and ridicule"—and admitted only that he was wrong to choose a writer as an illustration: "The benefit to accrue from the writing of books is too remote an idea, to strike and fill the imagination." He insists that had he put the case of Brutus, who sacrificed his own sons to preserve "Roman freedom and Roman virtue," few would have disagreed with him: "It would easily have been seen, that to have sacrificed any life, rather than suffer the destruction of a man who could alone preserve his contemporaries and future ages from barbarism and slavery, was a proper theme for . . . godlike philanthropy."[6])

Some radicals did join Godwin in the thoroughgoing application of his idea of universal benevolence. Godwin's close friend Thomas Holcroft, for example, looked forward to an ideal society in which patriotism and "family attachment would . . . be weakened or lost in the general principle of benevolence," and in which "[e]xclusive friendships could no longer be formed, because they would interfere with the claims of justice and humanity, and because . . . the stream of affections . . . would be continually refreshed, invigorated, and would overflow with the diffusive soul of mutual philanthropy, and generous undivided sympathy with all men."[7] But for most supporters of the French Revolution, universal benevolence did not necessarily exclude or dominate other affections or attachments; it could coexist with them, as its sources in the British moral philosophy of the eighteenth century suggest. While a few eighteenth-century thinkers (such as Jonathan Edwards) foreshadowed Godwin's position,[8] most advocates of universal benevolence understood it as working together with other allegiances such as familial or national love. Indeed, it was those philosophers, the first to explore systematically the idea of universal benevolence,[9] who in effect defined the terms in which the debate during the 1790s was conducted. Examining the discussions of these philosophers can illuminate the debates of the 1790s, especially their concentration on the relation between universal benevolence and less extensive attachments.[10] The differences among various versions of universal benevolence can in turn help show that when Wordsworth disclaims Godwin, he is disclaiming only his exclusive and unqualified view of benevolence. Further, I will suggest that Wordsworth uses his repudiation of Godwin as a way to keep alive his own ideal of universal benevolence after the disappointments of the Revolution.

Despite their many disagreements, one of the great shared aims of eighteenth-century moral philosophers in Britain was to refute recent atomistic and egoistic theories of human behavior, theories set forth most prominently by Hobbes and then followed up by Mandeville. A chief point in this refutation was the existence of sympathy; sympathy and benevolence become central topics in the influential writings of Shaftesbury, Butler, Hutcheson, Hume, Hartley, Kames, Richard Price, Adam Smith, Jonathan Edwards,[11] and others. Indeed, their analyses of the concepts of sympathy and benevolence extend beyond what a refutation of egoism would require in itself, leading them to address a number of questions. Can sympathy and benevolence be powerful motives? What is the relation between benevolence (or sentiments in general) and conscience and duty? Can benevolence constitute the greatest part of virtue? Of all the more particular questions, however, the one that became predominant during the 1790s and after was the issue of extensiveness: How *far* can (or should) sympathy and benevolence be taken to apply? Is there such a thing as universal benevolence, and how much should we weigh the claims of universal benevolence against those of less extensive benevolence such as patriotism or family affection?

Eighteenth-century philosophers of benevolence occupied a range of positions that were later to be taken up in the debates on the Revolution. The most consistent advocates for universal benevolence were Shaftesbury, Francis Hutcheson, and Jonathan Edwards. The most rigorous of these was Edwards, whose uncompromising approach would be followed by Godwin and Holcroft. For Edwards, "true virtue" resides only in "general benevolence," which he defines as love to "being in general" and which he takes to be "in effect the same thing" as love for God. In Edwards's view, true virtue does *not* exist whenever "persons have a benevolent affection limited to a party, or to the nation in general of which they are a part, or the public community to which they belong, though it be as large as the Roman empire was of old"; indeed, Edwards goes so far as to insist that "private affections, if they do not arise from general benevolence, and they are not connected with it in their first existence, have no tendency to produce it."[12]

The most prominent opponent of the idea of universal benevolence was Hume, who simply believes that it does not exist. Since we feel for "any object" more deeply "the stronger the relation is betwixt [it and] ourselves," Hume argues, "there is no such passion in human minds, as love of mankind, merely as such."[13] A less absolute position on the existence of universal benevolence was stated by writers such as Butler or Kames, who argue not that universal benevolence is nonexistent but rather that it is too weak to affect our behavior.[14] Kames criticizes Shaftesbury, who "goes as far as not to admit of any thing like partial benevolence; holding, that if it is not entire, and directed to the whole species, it is not benevolence at all"; and he employs the image of the sun, whose heat touches all but diminishes with distance, to support the point that "The general good is an object too sublime, and too remote," to motivate us.[15] (Later Coleridge was to adopt the image of the sun's heat, but in order to stress the power of universal benevolence.)[16]

It is Hutcheson who explains most fully how universal benevolence can be important in human behavior.[17] Although some aspects of his outlook, such as his comment that "general benevolence" is a "weak motive" (*Inquiry,* 260 [sec. 7, art. 8]), would have seemed commonplace to his contemporaries, Hutcheson makes a number of arguments that strengthen the claims of universal benevolence. To the suggestion that "general benevolence" is a "weak motive" (*Inquiry,* 260 [sec. 7, art. 8]), for example, he in effect replies that universal benevolence works not alone but in conjunction with more powerful (though less extensive) appeals to our particular feelings of benevolence. When those appeals move us in different directions, universal benevolence helps us choose the best action, and thus a main purpose of universal benevolence is less to motivate us than to help us choose among actions to which we are already motivated (*Essay*, 32 [sec. 2, art. 2]). Hutcheson adumbrates what supporters of the Revolution will later assert about the proper relation between universal benevolence and other affections. For him, universal benevolence often functions as a kind of governor: the "general benevolence [of mankind] should continually direct and limit, not only their selfish affections, but even their nearer attachments to others." (*Illustrations*, 181 [sec. 6, art. 4]).

Moreover, Hutcheson believes that we can strengthen our originally weak feelings of general benevolence by "frequent Meditation and Reflection" (*Essay*, 168–69 [sec. 6, art. 1]; see also *System*, 1: 77 [bk. 1, ch. 4]) and by allying our benevolence with other "stronger affections" (*Illustrations*, 176 [sec. 6, art. 2]; see also *Inquiry*, 235 [sec. 6, art. 5]). (The dissenting minister Richard Price, who helped spark the Revolution debate and who wrote a well-known book of moral philosophy, resembles Hutcheson here; although unlike Hutcheson he is a rationalist, like Hutcheson he thinks that despite our "deficiencies and weaknesses" we should and can "cultivate to the utmost the principle of benevolence" to include even the entire species, and he sees that universal benevolence can be supported by particular affections.)[18]

But even if universal benevolence can really exist, as Hutcheson argues, objections to it remain. What happens *after* one learns to feel universally? How is one to select the proper objects for benevolent action—how can one possibly encompass all the possibilities and make the correct choice? As Hume puts it, if all we have is "loose indeterminate views to the good of the species, . . . no beneficial actions could ever result, for want of a duly limited object, on which they could exert themselves."[19] Similarly, Adam Smith says that "our effectual good offices can very seldom be extended to any wider society than that of our own country. "[20]

Hume, Smith, and other "moral writers" (to use Butler's term) were not using this point about our limited capacities to deny that benevolence can ever operate; rather, they were making the argument that we should direct our benevolence to those close to us, and that when we do so we are in effect serving the ends of universal benevolence (even if we are unaware of those ends, and even if, as Butler argues in criticism of Hutcheson, benevolence does not constitute the whole of virtue). Thus, unlike Hutcheson and supporters of the Revolution, they argue that the more extensive forms of benevolence are not the governors of local affections, but the result of those affections.[21] Often what these writers invoke is the Biblical love of neighbor: Butler preaches on that topic, showing the fitness of our neighbor (who "comes under our immediate notice, acquaintance, and influence, and with which we have to do") as the "less general and nearer object of benevolence" that we need (*Sermons*, 67). (In

Political Justice, by contrast, Godwin was to note that the "comprehensive maxim 'that we should love our neighbour as ourselves', . . . though possessing considerable merit as a popular principle, is not modelled with the strictness of philosophical accuracy" [1: 81 (2. 2)]; Hazlitt noted in 1816 that "[t]he whole of the *modern* philosophy"—"the doctrine of universal benevolence"—developed from giving to "the question, 'Who is our neighbour' the answer, 'He who most wants our assistance'" [*Life of Holcroft*; *Works*, 3:134 (4, 1)].)

In one way, the argument made by Hume, Smith, and others for the primacy of our closer connections is not much different from Hutcheson's. Yet there is still an important difference between views that give an important role to universal benevolence (like that of Hutcheson) and views that do not (like those of Hume, or Smith, or a number of others). Limited affections such as gratitude or family feeling may be convenient avenues for benevolence, but they can also disrupt, or at least not cooperate with, general benevolence, for if these affections link persons together within a small group, that group will also necessarily be distinct from and potentially in conflict with other groups. Hutcheson raises just such a possibility, explicitly following Shaftesbury, who notes that "the very Spirit of *Faction*"—what we see in seditious cabals and even war—stems from "*social Love*, and *common* Affection."[22]

This is where universal benevolence proves particularly useful as a concept. Its great virtue is its social function, for it provides a principle by which one can limit or govern selfish or narrow attachments. Although Hutcheson is no proto-Benthamite, for him universal benevolence suggests the utilitarian doctrine that he first stated: "that action is best, which procures the greatest happiness for the greatest numbers" (*Inquiry*, 166 [3. 3]). And he thus uses universal benevolence to help generate a number of guidelines or "maxims" by which, when we are pulled in different directions by "different inclinations of benevolence," we not only should choose but will naturally *want to* choose—for example, we should choose that action "which occasions most good" (*Inquiry*, 267 [7. 9. 14]; see also generally 265–68 [7. 9. 11–15], and *Essay*, 40–43 [2. 4]).

Of these several maxims, the most important from the perspective of the 1790s is the one stating that we should choose the action that benefits the person of greatest "*Moral Excellence*" (*Essay*, 43 [2. 4]), for it reveals an aspect of Hutcheson's approach that became central to many radical arguments. Hutcheson's emphasis on moral excellence can lead not only to an Edwardsean but also to a Godwinian devaluation of local, personal, and even family ties. Hutcheson advises us to attach ourselves "to Persons of real Goodness, good Offices toward whom are useful to the world," and argues for the value of this advice even when it conflicts with connections of kinship: "The Ties of *Blood* are generally very strong, especially toward *Offspring*; they need rather the Bridle than the Spur, in all Cases wherein the Object is not recommended to a singular Love by his good Qualities. We may, in a considerable manner, restrain our *natural Affection* toward a worthless Offspring, by setting our *publick Affections* and our *moral Sense* against it" (*Essay*, 108 [4. 4]). And

Hutcheson also applies a similar argument to national feeling: "our Attachment to a *Country* may be fixed by something else than the *Chance of our Nativity*"; "tyranny, faction, a neglect of justice, a corruption of manners, or any thing which occasions the misery of the subjects, destroys this national love, and the dear idea of a country" (*Essay,* 159 [5. 10. 3]; *Inquiry,* 149–50 [2. 12]).[23]

Hutcheson thus uses universal benevolence to provide a number of ways to deal with the antisocial possibilities of local attachments and affections. An outlook that does not appeal to universal benevolence needs to find some other counterweight to these disruptive forces. Both Hume and Smith recognize that our partiality toward those with whom we have ties—our "confin'd generosity"—is "contrary" to "large societies" (Hume, *Treatise,* 499, 487 [3. 2. 2]), and that "this partiality . . . may sometimes be unjust" in being opposed to the greater good (Smith, *TMS,* 231 [6. 2. 2. 10]).

Few eighteenth-century moral writers take up Hutcheson's suggestion that universal benevolence can be used to limit family affections, although Smith notes that parental affection is naturally "so strong" that "moralists . . . teach us . . . generally how to restrain . . . the unjust preference which we are disposed to give to our own children" (*TMS,* 142 [3. 3. 15. 13]). In contrast to the enormous attention given it during the debate over the Revolution, generally family affection does not occupy much space in these writers' discussions (although Hume does stress parental affection as a natural virtue); since they do not feel family affection to be challenged, they take it for granted and treat it as congruent with universal benevolence, as the place where benevolence or social feeling tends to begin.[24] What is more likely than family affection to be contrasted to universal benevolence is love of country.

Among moral philosophers love of country and universal benevolence are not placed in diametric opposition, as they sometimes are during the debate over the Revolution. Nevertheless, love of country is treated as an alternative to love of humanity, one that is proper and attainable: the nation is broader than a small group, yet within our limited human comprehension and abilities. To the rule that our affections diminish with distance, Kames makes love of country a particular exception (*Elements,* 75–76 [1. 5]; *Essays,* 381–82 ["Conclusion"]). Smith, though as usual aware of complications—here, the "mean principle of national prejudice," which disposes us to view other nations "with the most malignant jealousy and envy"—nevertheless asserts that love of country ought to prevail over love of mankind (*TMS,* 227–29 [6. 2. 2. 2–4]).

A final indication of the difference in views between writers who are thoroughgoing advocates of universal benevolence and those who treat it as a weak ideal is furnished by a disagreement between Hume and Hutcheson on our feelings about nations. In Hume's view, "as nature has implanted in every one a superior affection to his own country, we never expect any regard to distant nations, where a competition arises" (*Enquiry,* 225n [5. 2. 182]). But Hutcheson states a more cosmopolitan outlook. He proposes a case in which two groups of people help two different countries, one of which is our own. The first group, composed of foreigners who have come to our country because of persecution, adds greatly to our own country's wealth and power. The second group, composed of foreigners who have stayed in their own country despite severe oppression, is full of love and compassion, and through courage and diligence establishes a country whose power rivals our own. Hutcheson says that we will have "the most agreeable idea" of the second group, "by whose love to [their] own country, we have often suffered in our interests" (*Inquiry*, 106–7 [1. 3]).

These cases, though drawn from observation and experience, were primarily hypothetical. By the end of the century, however, they had been almost completely realized, in the debate over the French Revolution.

The pursuit of this argument about benevolence during the Revolution controversy was sparked not by Godwin but by Richard Price's speech of late 1789 to the Revolution Society, which spoke enthusiastically of the recent events in France. The Revolution controversy is usually taken to begin with Edmund Burke's *Reflections on the Revolution in France* (1790), his reply to Price, and it was significant to Burke that one of Price's chief concerns was the relation of love of country to universal benevolence. Titled *A Discourse on the Love of Our Country*, Price's speech criticized exclusive patriotism, arguing that it should be limited and governed by universal benevolence.[25] Burke, seeing the centrality of this issue to Price, and foreseeing (as well as helping to establish) its importance to the impending debate, attacked the whole notion of universal benevolence, insisting on the priority of local attachments. He returned to this theme throughout the 1790s, and opponents of the Revolution took up similar positions. In contrast, nearly every supporter of the Revolution spoke in favor of universal benevolence.

All the controversialists knew that ideas were at the center of the Revolution and of whatever might take place in Britain. To a supporter of the changes in France, such as Price, the Revolution was not only the result of French Enlightenment but also potentially the cause of British Enlightenment (*Discourse,* 11–14), while to an opponent such as Hannah More, it was "not so much the force of French bayonets, as the contamination of French principles, that ought to excite our apprehensions."[26] When one also remembers that many of the participants in the debate were well-versed in the moral philosophy of the century, it is unsurprising that in a number of ways the debate over universal benevolence and the Revolution recapitulates—though with important differences—earlier discussion.

The idea of universal benevolence was also particularly well-suited to the situation of British citizens who sympathized with French principles, since they faced—and needed a way to argue against—fellow citizens who both mistrusted anything French and worried about how events in France might harm their own welfare.[27] In an early pamphlet Samuel Romilly, noting British lack of "enthusiasm" about the Revolution, urged his fellow citizens not to reflect that

France "had been once their enemy," a reflection which might lead them to "check their admiration"; he advised them to take a universalist perspective and relinquish their kind of patriotism, which was false because "the true interests of a nation never yet stood in opposition to the general interests of mankind."[28] Romilly is true here to earlier (and later) views of universal benevolence, which asserted that universal benevolence and limited affections could cooperate, but which also suggested that universal benevolence could be used to oppose exclusive or limited attachments, such as a jingoistic patriotism. This political facet of universal benevolence came out clearly as supporters of the Revolution used it to help provide a ground for, justify, and explain their support of France and French ideals—something particularly necessary when the British government opposed France.

This initial reason to appeal to universal benevolence was accompanied by others, as supporters of the Revolution pursued earlier philosophical discussions or developed new avenues. For example, by following up the implications of Hutcheson's formula of "the greatest happiness for the greatest numbers," advocates of reform could gain a perspective from which to judge and propose changes to any British institution. Does any given institution support the good of the whole, and how can it be made to do so? Thus, to George Dyer, "the present sad state of society" means that "every philanthropist should be a reformer."[29] Godwin followed up utilitarian suggestions even more strictly. Despite having become an atheist, Godwin acknowledged the influence of Jonathan Edwards's uncompromising view of universal benevolence. (As the conservative minister Robert Hall noted, many "fashionable infidels" had a definition of virtue that "perfectly coincides with that of . . . that most acute reasoner, JONATHAN EDWARDS."[30]) Coupling these utilitarian implications with the further implication that no one should be valued more than anyone else except insofar as he or she might better serve the general good, Godwin's rational system of political justice profoundly challenged what his novel *Caleb Williams* (1794) called "things as they are."

In contrast to Godwin's antireligious approach, others—especially Dissenters—followed up the links between universal benevolence and Christianity. Previously this link had been made chiefly by showing the (necessarily) universal benevolence of God, which may guarantee our own or become an ideal for us. But to Dissenters in the early 1790s, the Revolution raised hopes of change in Britain, change that could include an improvement in their own position. For them, universal benevolence provided a way of opposing the way they were treated; their exclusion could be thought of as the result of the establishment acting on the basis of limited local attachments. In his *Inquiry into the Nature of Subscription to the Thirty-nine Articles*, George Dyer connects his arguments against subscription to the controversy over the Revolution, and states that his points are those of humanity, not of a single sect: "These reasonings which plead the cause of mankind are not the partial arguments of a dissenter against a churchman," for subscription "will appear abhorrent from the first principles of natural justice and of common benevolence" (60–61).[31] The Dissenters' hopes for reform, visible also in Price's *Discourse*, are founded on a reading of Christianity; Price and Joseph Fawcett, an early and continued friend of Godwin, portray Christ as urging not friendship or patriotism but a universal community.[32] (In attacking the Revolution in 1793, Samuel Horsley, the Bishop of Rochester, said he felt compelled "to remark, that brotherly love embraces only brethren.")[33] And another way in which universal benevolence could be invoked to serve the purposes of reform was Mary Wollstonecraft's feminist cause; Wollstonecraft frequently used the argument that women (or anyone) can be virtuous and perform their duties to society only when their interests are broad and include "the love of mankind."[34]

In practice many of these aspects of universal benevolence are combined. In no case was the combination more threatening to conservatives than in *Political Justice*, though Godwin was a foe of revolutions.[35] In Godwin the notion of the general good not only generates criticism of virtually all institutions, but also, as we have seen, entails the extirpation of all attachments to anything smaller than the whole. (The Godwinian character in an anti-Godwin novel says, "I opposed all political and moral order, and endeavoured to overturn every system that time and experience had sanctioned and approved."[36]) Godwin follows to its logical conclusion the use of universal benevolence to oppose factions, clear in Shaftesbury and Hutcheson; but whereas most British moral philosophers, including Shaftesbury and Hutcheson, had tried to show that universal benevolence and local attachments could support each other, Godwin's position takes the demands of universal benevolence to be thoroughgoing and paramount, just as in the strict definition of virtue made by Jonathan Edwards. For Godwin, ties of kinship, affection, or gratitude simply inhibit us from choosing the proper action. And he renounces the reliance on the affections common in British moral philosophy, invoking abstract justice, rather than fellow-feeling or sympathy, as the basis of his system. Indeed, Godwin could set justice at odds with "philanthropy" (his term for affection for others), calling philanthropy "rather an unreflecting feeling, than a rational principle" (*Political Justice,* 1:261 [4. 4. appendix 1]); this emphasis on justice links him to Price rather than Hutcheson.

Godwin's was an extreme position, even among supporters of the Revolution, and many of them disagreed (or came to disagree) with it. A common topic for debate became, "Is private affection inconsistent with universal benevolence?"—a question debated at a meeting of the Royston book club (a well-known group in which Dissenters were prominent)[37] and asked in the *Monthly Magazine* by the Enquirer (William Enfield).[38] Most supporters of the Revolution appealed to fellowfeeling as well as justice,[39] and few wanted to deny local attachments; thus, they followed the mainstream of British moral philosophy. Even writings that set out to criticize patriotism, such as Price's and Fawcett's addresses on the love of country, resemble this moral philosophy in praising local attachments and affections—including patriotism—as not only natural but also valuable, because they lead us to help those whom we are best able to help (Price *Discourse*, 9; Fawcett *Sermons*, 2:158).[40]

Nevertheless, supporters of the Revolution were a little readier than earlier philosophers to focus on the antisocial dimension of local affections, what Fawcett calls our "disposition to imprison the social principle within a certain circle of society" (*Sermons*, 2:161). And they were particularly ready to criticize patriotism—or, more precisely, unworthy forms of patriotism; as Price says, though patriotism "is certainly a noble passion," it has largely been "a blind and narrow principle, producing in every country a contempt of other countries, and forming men into combinations and factions against their common rights and liberties" (*Discourse*, 2, 4–5). Accordingly, we should not let this (or any other) "narrower interest" stand in the way of a "more extensive interest" such as universal benevolence (*Discourse*, 10), and we should rely on universal benevolence to govern and limit—in Price's words, "correct and purify" (*Discourse*, 6–7)—these lesser attachments. As Fawcett puts it: "Those, with whom we are particularly connected, we innocently may, and necessarily must, prefer to strangers: but we should not suffer them either so to *distort* our hearts, as to make us wish them well, at the expence of a greater sum of welfare to others; or so to *exhaust* our affections, as to leave us no interest in the . . . surrounding society" (*Sermons*, 2:170). And after describing the many ways in which a "Patriot of the Christian school" should love and help his country, Fawcett adds a warning—in what is an application of Hutcheson's suggestion that we should choose and value friends and country in part according to their virtue—that unjust actions by fellow citizens, actions such as opposing the rights of fellow citizens or engaging in "unrighteous war," will lead the true patriot to oppose them in his heart (*Sermons*, 2:166–67).[41]

Thus for both Price and Fawcett, universal benevolence helps lead to a proper patriotism, and both writers seek to show that our many affections, when rightly understood, need not pull us in different directions—in true patriots, for example, love of country and love of humankind will work together. (As Mary Wollstonecraft puts it, "genuine duties support each other"; in the case of the apparently patriotic Cato, who though loving Rome hated Carthage, love of country turns out actually to be vanity, "unjust" and counter to the interests of "humanity" [*Rights of Woman*, 189].) It is common, accordingly, to see supporters of the Revolution asserting that universal benevolence is a high (perhaps one's highest) duty, but that it ought not to destroy other affections. Wollstonecraft writes not just that affections such as the love of women for men should be "only a part of that glowing flame of universal love" encircling humanity and ending in God, but also that "I do not mean to insinuate that either sex should be so lost in abstract reflections or distant views as to forget the affections and duties that lie before them" (*Rights of Woman*, 68, 26). Or, as Hazlitt summed up the issue some years later, "natural affection, patriotism, benevolence" are all "good in their place and degree"; "it is only *exclusive* selfishness, *exclusive* patriotism, *exclusive* philanthropy, that are inconsistent with the order of Providence, and destructive of the nature of man." True patriotism is founded on or consistent with "truth, justice, and humanity"; any other patriotism is "the watchword of faction, the base pander of avarice and pride" ("Illustrations of Vetus"; *Works,* 7:66, 68).

Although almost no supporters of the Revolution treated universal benevolence as exclusive and thus menacing, the opponents of the Revolution repeatedly portrayed it as a devastating principle, one that would virtually destroy civilization. While the harshness of attacks on the Revolution in general was due to many reasons, including the British government's encouragement of anti-Revolutionary hysteria, the extreme position of conservatives in relation specifically to universal benevolence had three chief sources: the power of Burke, whose virulent attacks on the Revolution often singled out for blame the sentiment of universal benevolence; the French version of universal benevolence, especially as filtered through Burke; and the radical denial of the value of affections (and the wide though short-lived popularity) of Godwin, who was taken to indicate the real tendency of universal benevolence.

For Burke, as for Hume, universal benevolence simply did not exist, except perhaps as a faint final extension of closer attachments; our loyalties naturally should and actually do stem from our "subdivision," the "little platoon we belong to in society."[42] Burke profoundly mistrusts any principle that distracts us from our habitual or familiar feelings, and to him universal benevolence is a philosophical abstraction; we cannot have with a universal humanity the same "secret, unseen, but irrefragable bond of habitual intercourse" that we have with smaller groups, nor can we have the "old prejudices and unreasoned habits" that help join together provinces or nations (*Regicide Peace*, first letter, 79; *Reflections,* 315). Yet however factitious or weak he may think universal benevolence to be as an affection, as a principle Burke sees it as posing a great threat because of its great power to destroy. Unlike earlier moral philosophers, Burke emphasizes the practical results of a belief in universal benevolence. These results are in his view catastrophic, for what universal benevolence destroys is what civilization depends on: all our social feelings and attachments, beginning in the family and ending in the nation.

This view helps explain the violence of Burke's and his followers' attacks on universal benevolence. What characterizes this "new philosophy," Burke says, is "Benevolence to the whole species, and want of feeling for every individual for whom the professors come in contact" (*Letter,* 537). Burke's great symbol for this perversion is Rousseau, "a lover of his kind, but a hater of his kindred," who "melts with tenderness for those only who touch him by the remotest relation, and then, without one natural pang, casts away . . . his children. . . . The bear loves, licks, and forms her young: but bears are not philosophers" (*Letter,* 538, 537). France reveals clearly to Burke one of

Rousseauism's chief results—its tendency to bring universal benevolence into conflict with particular affections. Because of the revolutionaries' concern for the public welfare, he says, they view "Tenderness to individuals . . . as treason to the public" (*Reflections,* 161). In the name of the greatest good, they "dispose of all the family relations of parents and children, husbands and wives," and "endeavor to subvert those principles of domestic trust and fidelity which form the discipline of social life" (*Letter,* 539, 541). The end result, in Burke's vision of the Revolution and its belief in universal benevolence, is murder, what he calls "the homicide philanthropy of France" (*Regicide Peace,* third letter, 153): "children are encouraged to cut the throats of their parents; mothers are taught that . . . they ought to make no scruple to rake with their bloody hands in the bowels of those who came from their own" (*Regicide Peace,* first letter, 76).

Because Burke treats universal benevolence as connected to abstract theorizing, a lack of natural feelings, and a failure to value traditional institutions, it can stand for nearly everything wicked and destructive about the Revolution. And he sees signs that universal benevolence will function in Britain as it does in France, particularly in "The factions, now so busy amongst us," that are seeking "to divest men of all love of their country" (*Appeal,* 76). He asserts that the "perverted minds" of British supporters of the Revolution "have no delight, but in contemplating the supposed distress, and predicting the immediate ruin, of their country" (*Regicide Peace,* third letter, 239). (When Hazlitt blames Burke for changing the "tone of politics" in Britain, he has in mind moments like this, when Burke helped to set "The two noblest impulses of our nature, the love of country and the love of kind, . . . in hostile array, . . . armed with inextinguishable fury against each other" [*Life of Napoleon*; *Works,* 13:50].)

Other British opponents of the Revolution followed Burke in seeing universal benevolence as a threat to British patriotism; the *Anti-Jacobin* refers to "Philanthropy,—beneath whose baneful sway / Each patriot passion sinks, and dies away."[43] But these opponents also did more. They took Burke's analysis of the general destruction caused by French principles in France and applied it more broadly than he had to what was taking place at home. At times, they took universal benevolence to be not a belief that people might actually hold but rather a convenient excuse for attacks on British society. In a poem in the *Anti-Jacobin,* a "Friend of Humanity" shows no real concern for the poor; when he learns that a poor Knife Grinder cannot be used for propaganda because he has no grievances against the existing order, the "Friend" reacts by forgetting his compassion, kicking the knife-grinder, and exiting "in a transport of. . . universal philanthropy" (*Poetry of the Anti-Jacobin,* 11 [no. 2; 27 Nov. 1797]). But more often opponents of the Revolution were concerned with universal benevolence as an idea with powerful subversive implications. They feared that by raising questions about society's values and arrangements—an activity epitomized, by the mid-1790s, in Godwin and *Political Justice*—universal benevolence could serve as a universal solvent of tradition, hierarchy, and order in general. They saw this dissolving taking place because for them as for Burke (and Godwin) universal benevolence jeopardized local attachments. The threat of universal benevolence thus could encompass the destruction of things like local charity arrangements: Hannah More's Mr. Fantom, a man of "wide-stretched benevolence," prefers to think of "Poles and South Americans" rather than help a local parish apprentice who has been wronged.[44] But as the 1790s progressed, conservatives who feared that universal benevolence threatened the local focused on what was most local, and what was to them the foundation of everything else valuable. They took universal benevolence to undermine what their conservative ideology placed at the core of society: marriage and the family.

The importance of the idea of the family is everywhere visible in Burke's *Reflections*, where it not only serves as the source of our feelings but repeatedly appears as an image of society itself.[45] As the *Annual Register*, in a discussion of the Revolution, sums up this domestic ideology: "The grand spring and cement of society is, the divine principle of love, branching forth from conjugal into parental, fraternal, and filial affection, an attachment to kindred, neighbours, countrymen."[46] Thus James Mackintosh, who after writing one of the best-received attacks on the *Reflections* had become a convert to Burke, gives the family a crucial role in his famous lectures of 1799 on "The Law of Nature and Nations," criticizing "every system that would sacrifice the particular affections to general benevolence," and stressing that the "duties of private life" arise "almost all from the two great institutions of property and marriage."[47] Almost no opponent of universal benevolence failed to mention that it would weaken family affections and duties.

To opponents of the Revolution, being seduced by the promises of universal benevolence not only destroyed one's family loyalties, it also left one with nothing in their place—with, to use the words of Robert Hall, a "chilling frost of universal indifference" (*Modern Infidelity,* 42). Burke's followers took up the contention—which was also Hume's and others'—that universal benevolence was an illusory abstraction and did not exist (Hannah More's Mr. Trueman tells the philanthropic Mr. Fantom that he is ignoring our "sinful nature," that human beings are incapable of universal benevolence [*Works,* 1:7]). Yet, like Burke, what these followers stressed was not their doubts that universal benevolence could exist but the practical effects on society that would result from believing in that ideal. In a strong attack on Godwin—the attack that finally spurred Godwin to respond to his critics—Samuel Parr contends that pursuing "duties" that are only "imaginary" would lead to "the neglect of all the usual duties by which social life is preserved or adorned."[48] To Edward Sterling, universal benevolence (which he takes to include many correlative notions) is "destructive of the nature of man—. . . it unfixes our moral land-marks—melts into air every practical virtue and definite duty—substitutes words for salutary deeds—and by directing our most natural and useful passions to objects indistinct or unattainable, leaves these powerful agents afloat, and ends by abusing them to the production of crime and misery" (qtd. by Hazlitt, "Illustrations of Vetus"; *Works,* 7:63–64).

This all sounds hyperbolic, but when Sterling speaks of threats to our "nature," or when Parr asks "what would become of society" (*Sermon,* 2:381), underlying their words is a real fear of the irrecoverable loss of what it means to be human—a fear Burke also shared.[49] As Parr explains, "when any dazzling phantoms of universal philanthropy have seized our attention, the objects that formerly engaged it shrink and fade. All considerations of kindred, friends, and countrymen, drop from the mind during the struggles it makes to grasp the collective interests of the species; and when the association that attached us to them has been dissolved, the notions we have formed of their comparative insignificance will prevent them from recovering . . . that strong and lasting hold they once had upon our conviction and our feelings" (*Sermon,* 2:375). This was not a fear that the eighteenth-century moral philosophers had expressed; but it was as true for some of Burke's followers as it was for Burke that, in David Bromwich's summary, "human nature can come to an end in a moment of historical catastrophe" (*Choice of Inheritance,* 48).

Parr had once supported the Revolution (and been a friend of Godwin), but events in the 1790s had changed his allegiances, as they had for Mackintosh and many others who took the course of the Revolution to reveal the true tendencies and threats of Revolutionary ideology. Even for many of those whose allegiances did not change so rapidly, the progress of the Revolution put beliefs under siege, and forced the question of how to salvage at least part of those beliefs.

For Wordsworth, the inclusion of universal benevolence among the beliefs associated with the Revolution was a matter not just of doctrine but of deeply felt experience. In his involvement with the Revolution, the experience of love was central—and not just because of his relationship with Annette Vallon. In *The Prelude* he presents his identification with the Revolution as analogous to participating in a literary romance, and in his romantic view France appears as an occasion for and exemplification of universal benevolence. His account of the Revolution repeatedly alludes to universal benevolence, as in his portrait of the ideal benevolence of Michel Beaupuy, or his sense that in France "benevolence [was] . . . / Spread like a fragrance everywhere" (6: 368–69). It is during and as a result of the Revolution that the culmination of Wordsworth's own feeling of benevolence takes place: "my heart was all / Given to the people, and my love was theirs" (9:125–26).[50]

Although the reverses of the Revolution threatened Wordsworth deeply enough to shake his beliefs and lead him to a personal crisis, in *The Prelude* Wordsworth wants to show that his universal benevolence did not collapse along with hopes for the regeneration of France. Early in the poem, writing in the present tense, Wordsworth echoes a letter from Coleridge, in which Coleridge had suggested that Wordsworth write a poem directed at those men who are "sinking into . . . selfishness" "in consequence of the complete failure of the French Revolution" (*CL*, 1:527; ca. Sept. 10, 1799). In response Wordsworth wrote a passage that appears as early as the two-part *Prelude* of 1799, in which he contrasts himself to men who both sneer at "visionary minds" and turn to "selfishness, disguised in gentle names / Of peace and quiet and domestic love" (2:449–56). This contrast, which criticizes those who would attack universal attachments by opposing those attachments to domestic ones, places Wordsworth in a particular camp: on the side of "visionaries" who continue to believe in the possibility of universal benevolence.

But Wordsworth not only asserts the survival of this belief; he also seeks in the poem to show *how* that belief survived. He consistently implies, for example, that he could retain his ideal because it was based not on the Revolution but on his own personal experience of growing up in nature. (This link between universal benevolence and nature also gives Wordsworth a way to present an image that can bring together, instead of set in opposition, local and universal attachments; while his experience is connected with particular English scenes, scenes in nature may also function as representatives of universal experience.) Still, the importance and depth of the association between universal benevolence and the Revolution require a further strategy to rescue his ideal. I would suggest that this strategy involves a distinctive but unacknowledged role for Godwinian philosophy.

For many supporters of the Revolution, one of the attractions of Godwin was that, in the face of events in France, he "offered a philosophic justification for progress that eliminated recourse to revolutionary action" (Roe *Radical Years*, 11). By founding the philosophy of *Political Justice* on abstract principles, Godwin seemed to lift ideals out of the welter of current events; instead of depending on their embodiment in France, or in anyone, ideals could rest on the ground of pure rationality. Accordingly, Wordsworth could keep his beliefs intact by slipping them off their old base in the Revolution and onto a new base in Godwinian philosophy. So although Wordsworth had identified universal benevolence with the Revolution, Godwin enabled him to detach his benevolence from actual human beings and thus to keep it alive; Wordsworth could still imagine human beings living according to universal benevolence and other ideals. Because he saw "The man to come parted as by a gulph / From him who had been" (11:59–60), he could still "pursu[e] / A higher [human] nature" (10:834–35).

As Wordsworth presents it, then, Godwin's philosophy provided a ready-made lifeboat, so that the Revolution's failures did not drag a belief in universal benevolence down with them. Once detached from the Revolution, universal benevolence was at much less risk of being taken over by the "selfishness" that both Wordsworth and Coleridge saw in the late 1790s. And when Godwin and his philosophy failed Wordsworth, helping to cause Wordsworth's crisis in *The*

Prelude, universal benevolence did not need to form part of that crisis. As we have seen, Godwin represented only one version of that ideal, so forswearing Godwin did not mean forswearing the ideal. In the account constructed for *The Prelude*, Wordsworth could identify his crisis not so much with the ideals themselves as with the Godwinian version of those ideals.

What Godwin finally provides Wordsworth in *The Prelude* is something to blame and to cast out. Wordsworth can jettison Godwin's version of universal benevolence without losing the ideal itself. After he recovers from his crisis he can still find "in man an object of delight / . . . and of love" (12:54–55); as he had already hinted in the passage about visionary minds in Book 2, universal benevolence can survive. In Wordsworth's telling of the story, Godwin gives him crucial help—although not in any way Godwin might have expected. Like Fénelon's chambermaid (or valet), Godwin is in effect the sacrifice that enables Wordsworth's ideals to live.

Whether Godwin actually played some such role for Wordsworth in the 1790s is impossible to know. Certainly *The Prelude* provides an incomplete and carefully constructed version of the poet's history; Roe, who provides a valuable account of Wordsworth's relation to Godwin, notes that "*The Prelude* does not suggest the complex significance of *Political Justice* for Wordsworth and his contemporaries" (*Radical Years,* 161). And in the poem Wordsworth passes over his postcrisis history so quickly that he never shows his universal bene-volence in practice; the persistence of his ideal is something he simply asserts, without corroborating evidence. Indeed, Wordsworth's writings from the mid-1790s on show that—whatever *The Prelude* suggests—repudiating "the philosophy / That promised to abstract the hopes of man / Out of his feelings" did not in itself make his attitudes toward human feelings and benevolence simple or secure. Wordsworth's comments on sympathy and relationship in the "Preface" to *Lyrical Ballads*, for example, seem to me to reveal a particular urgency—an urgency that stems from his experience of the 1790s. Wordsworth and many others could not simply remove themselves from the decade's dizzying arguments and counterarguments about what it was right to feel for: the French queen, as in Burke's *Reflections*? the people, as in many of the replies to Burke? abstract justice, as in Godwin? victimized lovers, as in Helen Maria Williams's *Letters*? And these conflicts had their personal correlative for Wordsworth in his experience of deep conflicts between loyalties: to the French or to the English? to his family in France or to his family in England? to universal ideals or to local attachments? By unsettling old patterns and practices, the 1790s helped lead Wordsworth to believe that, in questions of human passions and sentiments, he could take little for granted, and that it was politically as well as culturally important, as he wrote in a letter, "to rectify men's feelings, to give them new compositions of feeling."[51] Wordsworth's poems, especially the narratives, insistently raise questions about how we respond to others. Through them Wordsworth, like the political controversialists of the 1790s and the moral philosophers who preceded them, carries on the exploration of the ideal of benevolence. Wordsworth's poetic stances do represent some retreat from his earlier radical positions, as he knew; but they also retain important connections to—and build on or renew—both the prorevolutionary arguments of the 1790s and a liberal philosophical tradition.

Acknowledgment

I wish to thank the National Endowment for the Humanities for supporting much of the research for this essay.

NOTES

1. All quotations from *The Prelude* refer to the 1805 text, as given in *The Prelude: 1799, 1805, 1850*, ed. Jonathan Wordsworth, M. H. Abrams, and Stephen Gill (N.Y.: Norton, 1979).

2. *The Complete Works of William Hazlitt*, ed. P. P. Howe, 21 vols. (London: J. M. Dent, 1930–34), 11:20.

3. *An Enquiry Concerning Political Justice*, 2 vols. (1793; rpt. Oxford: Woodstock, 1992). In what follows, I refer to 1:82–83 (bk. 2, ch. 2).

4. The continuing interest of Godwin's illustration is suggested in a recent book by George P. Fletcher, *Loyalty: An Essay on the Morality of Relationships* (Oxford: Oxford University Press, 1993), which uses the Fénelon case as a startingpoint for a defense of the value of particular loyalties against the claims of impartiality (see 12–14). For another example, see Terrance McConnell, *Gratitude* (Philadelphia: Temple University Press, 1993), esp. 130–31.

5. See *St. Leon*, ed. Gina Luria (N.Y.: Garland, 1974), viii–xi. Godwin then quotes from a similar statement he had made in the second edition of his 1798 *Memoirs* of Mary Wollstonecraft.

6. *Thoughts Occasioned by the Perusal of Dr. Parr's Spital Sermon* (London: 1801), 37, 42, rpt. in *Uncollected Writings by William Godwin (1785–1822)*, ed. Jack W. Marken and Burton R. Pollin (Gainesville, Fla.: Scholars' Facsimiles and Reprints, 1968), 326, 331. Coleridge's view, in his marginalia to this text, was that the furor over the Fénelon passage was "a striking Instance of the Danger" philosophers run in choosing "contemporary Examples, as Illustrations" (reproduced in Godwin, *Uncollected Writings,* 332, and also in *The Collected Works of Samuel Taylor Coleridge*, vol. 12: *Marginalia*, pt. 2: *Camden to Hutton*, ed. George Whalley [Princeton: Princeton UP, 1984], 848). The example of Brutus, incidentally, was often invoked in reference to the Revolution.

7. See Hazlitt's *Life of Thomas Holcroft* (1816), in *Works*, 3:135 (bk. 4, ch. 1).

8. For a good discussion of Godwin's thought, especially in relation to previous moral philosophers, see D. H. Monro, *Godwin's Moral Philosophy: An*

Interpretation of William Godwin (Oxford: Oxford University Press, 1953).

9. For some immediate precursors to the arguments of these philosophers, see R. S. Crane's discussion of English divines from about 1660 to about 1725, in "Suggestions Toward a Genealogy of the 'Man of Feeling,'" *ELH* 1 (1934):205–30.

10. In the subsequent sections on the philosophical and political debates, I am adapting and condensing my essay "Revolutionary Writing, Moral Philosophy, and Universal Benevolence in the Eighteenth Century," *Journal of the History of Ideas* 54 (1993):221–40.

11. Although he is usually treated as part of an American (Puritan) tradition, Edwards was a British subject who not only knew well the writings of British moral philosophers, but was highly regarded by British writers of the middle and later eighteenth century. For a valuable discussion of Edwards's relation to his predecessors, see Norman Fiering, *Jonathan Edwards's Moral Thought and Its British Context* (Chapel Hill: University of North Carolina Press, 1981).

12. *The Nature of True Virtue* (1765), ed. William K. Frankena (Ann Arbor: University of Michigan Press, 1960), 78, 24.

13. *A Treatise of Human Nature*, ed. L. A. Selby-Bigge, 2d ed. by P. H. Nidditch (Oxford: Clarendon, 1978), 318 (bk. 2, pt. 1, sec. 11), 481 (bk. 3, pt. 2, sec. 1).

14. See (Bishop) Joseph Butler, "Upon the Love of Our Neighbor," Sermon 12 of *Fifteen Sermons Preached at the Rolls Chapel* (1726), rpt. in *Five Sermons Preached at the Rolls Chapel*, ed. Stuart M. Brown Jr. (Indianapolis: Bobbs-Merrill, 1950), 66–67.

15. Henry Home, Lord Kames, *Essays on the Principles of Morality and Natural Religion* (1751; rpt. NY: Garland, 1983), 121 (pt. 1, essay 2, ch. 8); *Elements of Criticism*, vol. 1, 6th ed. (1785; rpt. N.Y.: Garland, 1972), 71 (ch. 2, pt. 1, sec. 5); and *Essays* 90–91 (ch. 1, pt. 2, sec. 5).

16. See *Collected Works*, vol. 1: *Lectures 1795 on Politics and Religion*, ed. Lewis Patton and Peter Mann (Princeton: Princeton University Press, 1971), 46, 163, and also *Collected Letters of Samuel Taylor Coleridge*, ed. E. L. Griggs, 6 vols. (Oxford: Oxford University Press, 1956–71), 1:86 (13 July 1794, to Southey); abbreviated in the text as *CL*.

17. For a brief and clear explanation of Hutcheson's contribution and wide popularity, see Garry Wills, *Inventing America: Jefferson's Declaration of Independence* (Garden City: Doubleday, 1978), ch. 13. The editions of Hutcheson's works that I am using are as follows: *An Essay on the Nature and Conduct of the Passions and Affections,* 3d ed. (London: 1742); *An Inquiry Concerning Moral Good and Evil*, Treatise 2 *of An Inquiry into the Original of Our Ideas of Beauty and Virtue, in Two Treatises*, 4th ed. (1738; rpt. Glasgow: 1772); *Illustrations on the Moral Sense* (1742), ed. Bernard Peach (Cambridge: Belknap Press of Harvard University Press, 1971); *A System of Moral*

Philosophy, 2 vols. (1755; rpt. in one vol., N.Y.: Augustus M. Kelley, 1968).

18. Richard Price, *A Review of the Principal Questions in Morals* (1758; 3d ed. 1787), ed. D. Daiches Raphael (Oxford: Clarendon, 1948), 152, 76–77, 121.

19. *An Enquiry Concerning the Principles of Morals* (1751), ed. L. A. Selby-Bigge, 3d ed. rev. P. H. Nidditch (Oxford: Clarendon, 1975), 225n (sec. 5, pt. 2, art. 182).

20. *The Theory of Moral Sentiments* (1759; 6th ed. 1790), ed. D. D. Raphael and A. L. Macfie (Oxford: Clarendon, 1976; rpt. Indianapolis, 1982) 235 (pt. 6, sec. 2, ch. 3, par. 6); abbreviated in the text as *TMS*. In some of his revisions for the sixth edition of 1790, Smith may have been reacting to the French Revolution (see the comments by Smith's editors: *TMS* 18–19, 229n, 231n). Most of the sections relevant to my argument are added at that time.

21. See Hume, *Enquiry,* 225n (5. 2. 182), and Smith, *TMS* 237 (6. 2. 3. 6).

22. *An Essay on the Freedom of Wit and Humour* (pt. 3, sec. 2), in *Characteristicks of Men, Manners, Opinions, Times,* 3 vols. (1714; rpt. Farnsborough, England: Gregg International, 1968), 1:113–14. Hutcheson quotes from this section, and follows it with a criticism of factions (*Inquiry,* 192 [4. 4]).

23. In his valuable book *The French Revolution and the Enlightenment in England* (Cambridge: Harvard University Press, 1988), Seamus Deane takes Hutcheson to be stating here "an early version of the Burkean theory of local affections" (15). It seems to me, however, that Hutcheson is not emphasizing local attachments; rather, he is downplaying them, as in his statement that we can acquire "national love" for a country even if we only "observe" that it shares qualities with our own. Moreover, he is noting with approval (as Joseph Fawcett did later) that when our country acts badly, we are able to give up our love of it.

24. See, for example, Shaftesbury, *Essay on Wit and Humour* (3. 2), in *Characteristicks* 1:110; Hutcheson, *Inquiry* 200–1 (5. 5); Hume, *Treatise,* 486 (3. 2. 2); Hartley, *Observations on Man, His Frame, His Duty, and His Expectations,* 2 vols. (1749; rpt. in one vol., Gainesville: Scholars' Facsimiles and Reprints, 1966) 1:481–82 (1. 4. 4. 97), 2:228–29 (2. 3. 2. 53), 2:301–2 (2. 3. 6. 70); Kames, *Elements* 71 (2. 1. 5); Adam Ferguson, *Principles of Moral and Political Science* (1792), rpt. in Louis Schneider, ed., *The Scottish Moralists on Human Nature and Society* (Chicago: University of Chicago Press, 1967), 84.

25. *A Discourse on the Love of Our Country*, 6th ed. (London, 1790).

26. *Remarks on the Speech of M. Dupont* (1793), in *The Complete Works of Hannah More*, 7 vols. (N.Y.: Harper's, 1855), 5:296.

27. For a discussion of how ideas and prejudices about France were central to the debate on the Revolution, see Deane, *French Revolution*.

28. *Thoughts on the Probable Influence of the French Revolution in Great-Britain* (London: 1790), 3, 4, 6.

29. *A Dissertation on the Theory and Practice of Benevolence* (London:

1795), 35–36 (pt. 2, ch. 1).

30. *Modern Infidelity*, in *The Works of Robert Hall*, vol. 2, *Sermons, Charges, and Reviews* (London: Henry G. Bohn, 1846), 44–45n.

31. Qtd. in M. Ray Adams, *Studies in the Literary Backgrounds of English Radicalism* (Lancaster, Pa.: Franklin and Marshall, 1947; rpt. N.Y.: Greenwood, 1968), 240–44. As Adams notes, "the long fight" against the Corporation and Test Acts was given "an extraordinary impetus during the early period of the French Revolution."

32. See Price's *Discourse,* esp. 7–8, and Fawcett's 1791 sermon "Christianity vindicated in not particularly inculcating Friendship and Patriotism," in *Sermons*, 2 vols. (London: 1795), sermon 17, 2:149–173. Godwin acknowledged Fawcett's "great influence" on him (MS., qtd. in Nicholas Roe, *Wordsworth and Coleridge: The Radical Years* [Oxford: Clarendon, 1988], 24). Wordsworth, who read Fawcett's bitter antiwar poem *The Art of War* (1795) and attended his sermons in 1791, said he used Fawcett as the model for the Solitary in *The Excursion.* For other Dissenters' benevolist interpretations of Christ, see Dyer's *Dissertation* 12 (1. 1), and William Frend's self-defense at his Cambridge trial (qtd. in Roe, *Radical Years,* 112).

33. Qtd. in Alfred Cobban, ed., *The Debate on the French Revolution 1789–1800*, 2d ed. (London: Adam and Charles Black, 1960), 427.

34. *A Vindication of the Rights of Woman* (1792), 2d ed., ed. Carol H. Poston, 2d ed. (N.Y.: Norton, 1988), 4. See also 151, 183, 191–92.

35. As he puts it in his 1801 reply to several critics: "I never went so far, in my partiality for the practical principles of the French Revolution, as many of those with whom I was accustomed to converse. I uniformly declared myself an enemy to revolutions." *Thoughts Occasioned by the Perusal of Dr. Parr's Spital Sermon* 5, rpt. in *Uncollected Writings,* 289.

36. See Count Reginald de St. Leon (Edward Dubois), *St. Godwin: A Tale of the Sixteenth, Seventeenth, and Eighteenth Century* (1800), 233, qtd. in Peter H. Marshall, *William Godwin* (New Haven: Yale University Press, 1984), 218.

37. See Anthony Lincoln, *Some Political and Social Ideas of English Dissent 1763–1800* (Cambridge: Cambridge University Press, 1938), 42. The meeting is mentioned by Henry Crabb Robinson, *Diary, Reminiscences, Correspondence*, ed. Thomas Sadler (London: Macmillan, 1872), 1:21.

38. Vol. 1, no. 4 (May 1796), 273–76.

39. As Helen Maria Williams wrote, in reference to having been present at the first anniversary of the fall of the Bastille, to become "in that moment a citizen of the world" "required but the common feelings of humanity" (*Letters Written in France* [London: 1790; rpt. Oxford: Woodstock, 1989], 14).

40. Fawcett does, however, note that "partiality" to persons, unless founded on their "moral pre-eminence," does not constitute "social *virtue*," or "moral rectitude," or "Goodness or Charity" (*Sermons,* 2:153–54). (In this he is following Edwards; he apparently discussed *The Nature of True Virtue* with

Godwin during their time together in Hertfordshire in the late 1770s. See Marshall, *Godwin,* 47.)

41. For a discussion of how, in the wake of their achievement of independence, Americans sought to reconcile "the self-interested nature of patriotism with the Christian ethic of disinterested benevolence," see Jay Fliegelman, *Prodigals and Pilgrims: The American Revolution Against Patriarchal Authority, 1750–1800* (Cambridge: Cambridge University Press, 1982), 227–230.

42. Edmund Burke, *Reflections on the Revolution in France* (1790), ed. Conor Cruise O'Brien (Harmondsworth, 1968), 135. The editions of the other works of Burke that I am using are as follows: *An Appeal from the New to the Old Whigs* (1791), in *The Works of the Right Honourable Edmund Burke,* 8 vols., Bohn's British Classics (London: 1872), vol. 2; *A Letter to a Member of the National Assembly* (1791), in *Works of Burke,* vol. 2; *Four Letters on the Proposals for Peace with the Regicide Directory of France* (1796–97), in E. J. Payne, ed., *Burke: Select Works,* vol. 3 (Oxford: Clarendon, 1878).

43. "New Morality," ll. 95–96, in no. 36 (9 July 1798), rpt. in *Poetry of the Anti-Jacobin,* 2d ed. (London: 1800) 224.

44. *The History of Mr. Fantom, the New-Fashioned Philosopher* (1794), in *Works,* 1:11, 8. The literary descendants of Mr. Fantom include Mrs. Jellyby and her "telescopic philanthropy" in Dickens's *Bleak House.*

45. See *Reflections* 120, 315; and James T. Boulton, *The Language of Politics in the Age of Wilkes and Burke* (London: Routledge, 1963), 112–14.

46. *The Annual Register for 1798,* 2d ed. (London: 1806) 229–30, qtd. in Mitzi Myers, "Reform or Ruin: `A Revolution in Female Manners,'" *Studies in Eighteenth-Century Culture* 11 (1982): 211.

47. *Memoirs of the Right Honourable Sir James Mackintosh,* ed. R. J. Mackintosh, 2d ed., 2 vols. (London: 1836), 1:116, 102. Edward Sterling ("Vetus"), who echoed Mackintosh's lectures (according to Hazlitt) as late as 1813, took "universal love" to undermine marriage, sibling love, parental affection, and "filial piety," in order that "the great republic" could play the role of "sister, husband, wife, son, and mother." Qtd. by Hazlitt, "Illustrations of Vetus"; *Works,* 7:63.

48. *A Spital Sermon, Preached at Christ Church, Upon Easter Tuesday, April 15, 1800* (1801), in *The Works of Samuel Parr,* 8 vols., ed. John Johnstone (London: 1828), 2:376.

49. See David Bromwich's chapter on "Burke, Wordsworth, and the Defense of History," in *A Choice of Inheritance: Self and Community from Edmund Burke to Robert Frost* (Cambridge: Harvard University Press, 1989), esp. 48.

50. I have treated the place of universal benevolence in *The Prelude* in "Saving Ideals: Revolution and Benevolence in *The Prelude,*" forthcoming in *JEGP.*

51. To John Wilson (5–7 June 1802), in *Wordsworth: Selected Prose*, ed. John O. Hayden (Harmondsworth: Penguin, 1988), 312.

"Great Burke," Thomas Carlyle, and the French Revolution

Lowell T. Frye

Born in 1795, not writing about the French Revolution until the mid-1830s, Thomas Carlyle obviously did not participate in the Revolution debate in England during the 1790s—at least not firsthand. But neither the Revolution itself nor the debate about its meaning were safely "historical" during the 1830s. True, in the years following the Bourbon Restoration in 1815, a moderate, emotionally neutral interpretation of the French Revolution seemed distinctly possible. Whig writers for the *Edinburgh Review*, notably Francis Jeffrey, absorbed Edmund Burke's vision of organic social development along with his belief in the inviolability of property; meanwhile, writers for the *Tory Quarterly Review* distanced themselves from Burke's unremitting hostility to the Revolution *in toto*. In 1826 Richard Wellesley, reviewing Prior's *Life of Burke*, judged that "the French Revolution has in the *ultimate* issue of events, proved beneficial to France," and not to France only, for "other nations of the old and of the new world have, on the sequel, if not in consequence of [the Revolution], advanced in freedom and the general improvement of their institutions" (471). Three years later Robert Southey, surveying "The State and Prospects of the Country," refused "to join Mr Burke in the eulogiums he has bestowed on the court and aristocracy of France. . . . They contradict the whole mass of facts which are before the public." Southey treats almost as a commonplace the conclusion that "it was the degeneracy, corruption, and thoughtlessness of the court and government which was the chief source of . . . the revolution" (483).[1]

The fall of the Bourbon monarchy in July 1830, however, even as it reinvigorated the campaign for parliamentary reform in Britain, forced a breach between Whig and Tory interpretations of the Revolution of 1789–1795 as wide as that between the views of Edmund Burke and Charles James Fox forty years earlier. British statesmen and journalists between 1830 and 1832 sought in the French Revolution of 1789, as well as in the English revolutions of the 1640s nd 1688, arguments for and against reform. As a result, the protracted and acrimonious debate leading to the passage of the Reform Bill of 1832 clearly echoed the Revolution debate of the 1790s in substance and tone. Proponents of parliamentary reform like Macaulay traded rhetorical jabs with opponents of reform like John Wilson Croker.[2] In an atmosphere so charged, any sort of evenhanded historical understanding of the French Revolution was subordinated to the partisan use of revolutionary *exempla*. The beginnings of a moderate, dispassionate view of the Revolution gave way to rhetorical extremism of the sort that characterized the exchanges between Edmund Burke and his opponents—notably Fox, Paine, and Wollstonecraft—in the 1790s.

From his distant vantage point at Craigenputtoch in rural Scotland, Thomas Carlyle paid close attention to this fiercely partisan exchange and was impatient with it, persuaded that England itself stood on the brink of revolution and needed something more constructive than the mutual execrations hurled at each other by advocates and opponents of parliamentary reform. Before 1830 Carlyle, although certainly aware of the French Revolution as a crucial event in modern history, expressed no special interest in writing about it; in September 1833, however, he confidently asserted that the French Revolution was "the grand work of our era" and the repository of "all possible knowledge important to us," if only he and his contemporaries could understand it.[3] During these pivotal years Carlyle came to believe that an *historical* understanding of the French Revolution—the achievement of a language and an interpretive method not subordinated to Whig, Tory, or Radical political concerns—could help Britain to transform itself without suffering the horrors of revolutionary violence.[4]

Throughout the 1830s Carlyle's analysis of contemporary social ills was rooted in his study of the French Revolution, as he makes clear in "Chartism" (1839):

Since the year 1789, there is now half a century complete; and a French Revolution not yet complete! Whosoever will look at that enormous Phenomenon may find many meanings in it, but this meaning as the ground of all: That it was a revolt of the oppressed lower classes against the oppressing or neglecting upper classes: not a French revolt only; no, a European one; full of stern monition to all countries of Europe. These Chartisms, Radicalisms, Reform Bill, Tithe Bill, and infinite other discrepancy, and acrid argument and jargon that there is yet to be, are *our* French Revolution: God grant that we, with our better methods, may be able to transact it by argument alone![5]

But at the beginning of the decade, Carlyle held little hope that the revolution would be one of words only, as his letters and journals reveal. In December 1830, commenting on the shift in government from Tory to Whig, he writes: "The Whigs in office, and Baron Brougham Lord Chancellor! Hay-stacks and corn-stacks burning all over the South and Middle of England! Where will it end? Revolution on the back of Revolution for a century yet?"[6] The following September found him in a mood still more apocalyptic: "There will be rickburning I imagine as last winter. We live in the 'end of the days'" (*Letters,* 5:402). "Poor country!" he lamented in October 1831. "Millions in it nigh starving; and for help of them, Talk, talk, and nothing but Talk" (*Letters,* 6:18). Carlyle never believed that the Reform Bill would solve Britain's problems, but he greatly feared what might occur if the House of Lords succeeded in defeating the bill: "By the mysterious arrangement of this world, it has been ordered that 200 bipeds, few of them with sense or stuff enough to make a moderate taylor, should be called *Peers,* and have the power to keep all Britain in a ferment for months, perhaps to drive it into desperation, and anarchy" (*Letters,* 6:21). "Nothing on all hands but broken heads, broken hearts, woe, want, wickedness, and madness over the whole world," he writes in November 1831. "Truly the political aspects of England give even me alarms: a second edition of the French Revolution is distinctly within the range of chances: for there is nowhere any tie remaining among men" (*Letters,* 6:37, 52).

One might expect that final passage of the Reform Bill in June 1832 would have weakened Carlyle's interest in the French Revolution; for many of his countrymen, interest in the revolution peaked during the debate over reform.[7] But Carlyle's interest did not wane—rather, it intensified—with the passage of the Bill, a fact reflecting his bitter dissatisfaction with those who viewed the Revolution as merely a political event rather than a social force. He found Tories and Whigs and even Radicals similarly tiresome: writing in January 1833, Carlyle notes that "in politics . . . I take no pleasure at all: the Tories, now happily driven into holes and corners, are quite out of date; all the rest is Whiggery and Reform-Bill-for-ever, a most sandblind feeble sort of concern" (*Letters,* 6:307). Addressing Mill in April 1833, Carlyle was far from hopeful in the wake of Reform, asserting that a day of reckoning was fast approaching in Britain: "unless some extensive far-reaching system of Emigration be organized, the result in a few years must be a rebellion fearful to contemplate; the fierce implacable rebellion of Hunger and Ignorance against Wealth and Idleness, whose very imbecility has become tyrannous, deadening and killing" (*Letters,* 6:373). In this mood Carlyle turned to study the French Revolution, admitting that he was "following anew the developments of that frightful world-drama with a new interest" and looking for "any tolerable History of the Revolution. . . . I am curious about France" (*Letters,* 6:302, 242). Increasingly, Carlyle felt that if the British misinterpreted or ignored the meaning of the French Revolution—and they seemed only too likely to do so—they would have to learn it through revolutionary upheaval at home. With a profound sense of mission, then, Carlyle paradoxically set out to influence action and policy in England in the 1830s by wresting the French Revolution away from the politicians, by asserting his own right to define the Revolution and interpret for his age the significance of its "flaming reality"—a task he brought to completion with the publication of *The French Revolution: A History* in three volumes in 1837.[8]

Given the nature of Carlyle's ambition, it is not surprising that the ghost of Edmund Burke haunts Carlyle's history of the French Revolution. Anyone writing about the Revolution for a British audience between 1790 and 1837 had to grapple with Burke, for it was Burke's *Reflections*, and his four strident *Letters on a Regicide Peace*, that established the terms and tenor of the Revolution debate in England. More surprising is the fact that, given the vast amount written in this century about Carlyle, relatively little has been written about Burke in conjunction with Carlyle: it has long been the fashion to seek chiefly in Germany or France for the writers and ideas that influenced Carlyle's thinking.[9] Carlyle himself contributed to this tendency by speaking and writing of Burke infrequently: he mentions Burke by name only a handful of times in the roughly nine hundred pages of his history; references to Burke are nearly as rare in Carlyle's letters of this period. Nonetheless, there is a profound Burkean presence in Carlyle's history of the Revolution, especially in the first volume, which closes with the narration of the October Days of 1789, the central symbolic event of Burke's *Reflections*.[10] There is not a clear Burkean *influence*, if by that word we mean close interpretive agreement: ultimately Carlyle disagreed sharply with Burke's judgment of the events in France. Still, a reading of Burke's *Reflections* followed by a reading of Carlyle's *The French Revolution* is very suggestive: the number of thematic and rhetorical reverberations between the two books suggests that Carlyle labored consciously to *displace* Burke's view of the Revolution first by appropriating that which he wished to retain from the earlier book and second by dispelling the rhetorical power of that which he wished to reject. Carlyle harbored no special grudge against Burke—nowhere against Burke does Carlyle unleash the sort of criticism he levels at Rousseau or Voltaire, for example, or even against eighteenth-century British historians. But to interpret the French Revolution for the 1830s, to move the Revolution out of the arena of partisan debate, Carlyle had to topple the prevailing view of the Revolution which, if not precisely that of Burke, was certainly one whose terms had been established by Burke.

Carlyle himself offers theoretical justification for the argument I am making. In the third volume of his history, just as he begins to narrate the events of the Terror of 1793, Carlyle calls our attention to the task of the historian in the 1830s:

History . . . in dealing with this Reign of Terror, has had her own difficulties. While the Phenomenon continued in its primary state, as mere 'Horrors of the French Revolution,' there was abundance to be said and shrieked. With and also without profit. Heaven knows, there were terrors and horrors enough: yet that was not all the Phenomenon; nay, more properly, that was not the Phenomenon at all, but rather was the *shadow* of it, the negative part of it. And now, in a new stage of the business, when History, ceasing to shriek, would try rather to include under her old Forms of speech or speculation this new amazing Thing; that so some accredited scientific Law of Nature might suffice for the unexpected Product of Nature, and History might get to speak of it articulately, and draw inferences and profit from it; in this new stage, History, we must say, babbles and flounders perhaps in a still painfuler manner. (*Works,* 4:203)

Carlyle proceeds to ridicule Roux and Buchez's *Histoire Parliamentaire*

(1833–1836) for its babbling and floundering, for its thesis that "the French Revolution was a dead-lift effort, after eighteen hundred years of preparation, to realise—the Christian Religion!" Undoubtedly Roux was trying to do what all history must do, "what Father Adam began life by doing: strive to *name* the new Things it sees of Nature's producing" (4:204). Roux's failing was not that he attempted to interpret the Revolution but that he spruced up an old theory to explain a new event:[11]

What if History were to admit, for once, that all the Names and Theorems yet known to her fall short? That this grand Product of Nature was even grand, and new, in that it came not to range itself under old recorded Laws of Nature at all, but to disclose new ones? In that case, History, renouncing the pretension to *name* it at present, will *look* honestly at it, and name what she can of it? Any approximation to the right Name has value: were the right Name itself once here, the Thing is known henceforth; the Thing is then ours, and can be dealt with. (4: 204)

In these passages Carlyle outlines a series of stages in the human response to an historical event and at the same time implies that earlier attempts to explain the French Revolution are inadequate. In the wake of an event as horrible as the Terror, Carlyle says, it is natural for us first to shriek: our response is immediate, passionate, intemperate. Writing about the September Massacres of 1792, Carlyle approves of strong moral response: "That a shriek of inarticulate horror rose over this thing, not only from French Aristocrats and Moderates, but from all Europe, and has prolonged itself to the present day, was most natural and right. . . . Well may mankind shriek, inarticulately anathematising as they can. There are actions of such emphasis that no shrieking can be too emphatic for them" (4:42–43). But note the words *inarticulate* and *inarticulately*: shrieking allows us to express our moral revulsion at the barbarity of revolutionary violence, but it does not help us to understand it. To understand an event we must *articulate* it, find the right words to narrate it.[12]

In the second stage of our response to an historical event, then, we attempt to describe, to "name." Too often, however, the only language and perspective we have at our disposal are outmoded by the event itself: Carlyle concludes that we cannot adequately describe the French Revolution by means of a perspective and style exploded along with the ancien regime. The Revolution is a "new amazing thing"—Carlyle is clearly echoing Burke's judgment that "all things taken together, the French Revolution is the most astonishing that has hitherto happened in the world" *(Reflections, 92)*. We therefore cannot understand its meaning and significance if we attempt to do so with "old Forms of speech or speculation," if we employ the assumptions and language of the Enlightenment to explain an event that demonstrates the fallibility of those assumptions about human behavior. Carlyle had thought deeply about the writing of history between 1830 and 1833; he is constantly aware as he writes his history of the Revolution that narration cannot be separated from interpretation. Rather, to narrate *is* to interpret, to make sense of a series of occurrences. Instead of explaining a new event with an old language and set of assumptions, we ought to renounce "the pretension to *name* it at present" and instead "*look* honestly at it." In the third stage of our response to historical events, then, we must admit the inadequacy of existing narrative forms and explanatory methods and develop new names, a new language, if we are to have any chance of understanding "the new Things . . . of Nature's producing."

Carlyle here calls unmistakably for a revolution in historiography to mirror the social revolution the historian attempts to describe. Just as clearly, though less explicitly, Carlyle presents himself as the historian able to invent the perspective and language needed to explain the French Revolution to the British in the 1830s. As he wrote to John Sterling in January 1837 while awaiting proofs from the printer, he judged his history of the Revolution "a wild savage book, itself a kind of French Revolution" *(Letters,* 9:116). This well-known statement no doubt refers to the book's jarring, idiosyncratic narrative style that seeks to recreate for the reader something of the energy of revolutionary events. But the metaphor also suggests that the book, like the Revolution itself, works to overthrow an ancien regime, in this case one of historical interpretation and narration. According to Hannah Arendt, "theoretically, the most far-reaching consequence of the French Revolution was the birth of the modern concept of history."[13] She attributes to Hegel the development of a philosophy of history designed to explain change. Carlyle too understood history as a record of change and rupture; he was one of the first British thinkers to act on this new understanding. John Rosenberg has noted, "History as Gibbon wrote it is unimaginable after the French Revolution; history as Carlyle conceived it would have been unthinkable before the Revolution."[14] To a remarkable degree, Carlyle succeeded simultaneously in transforming British understanding of the nature of history and of the French Revolution. Lord Acton at the end of the nineteenth century claimed dramatically that Carlyle's history of the French Revolution "delivered our fathers from thraldom to Burke."[15]

It is important to note that Carlyle did not deliver his contemporaries from Burke by engaging in a polemic that openly contests Burke's interpretation of the French Revolution. To have explicitly rejected Burke's argument—as to have explicitly accepted it—would have ceded control of the debate to Burke and additionally would have aligned Carlyle with one or another of the political parties—a fate he very much wished to avoid, given his disenchantment with Tories, Whigs, and Radicals alike. Carlyle did not wish simply to agree or disagree with Burke on specific events of the Revolution, but rather to gain control of the debate altogether. He achieved his goal by *renaming* particular events on which Burke had lavished his attention, rhetorically refusing them the meaning Burke had assigned them. By so doing Carlyle shaped a narrative that leads to conclusions other than the conclusions Burke reached, without ever attacking Burke's interpretation outright and without rejecting a significant body of Burke's insights into society and human nature.

The rhetorical strategy Carlyle employs vis-à-vis Burke becomes understandable against the backdrop of his complicated relation to Burkean ideas. Whether influenced directly by his reading of Burke or indirectly by his reading of Coleridge, the *Edinburgh Review*, and Herder (among other German thinkers), Carlyle clearly shares many of the assumptions that constitute Burke's understanding of human beings in society.[16] Both men conceive of society organically and historically, as a living thing deeply, even mysteriously, rooted in the past: where Burke writes of society as a "partnership not only between those who are living, but between those who are living, those who are dead, and those who are to be born" (194–95), Carlyle speaks of an oak that "grows silently, in the forest, a thousand years" (2:27). Both men distrust those who attempt to explain or improve society by means of rational analysis and theory. Burke opposes the healthful "choice of inheritance" to the "fallible and feeble contrivances of our reason" (120–21); Carlyle grudgingly recognizes the surgical use of analysis to detect and destroy incoherencies in society but asks skeptically, "What thing was victorious Analysis ever known to make?" From theory and theorizing, we can expect only "'endless vortices of froth-logic'; whereon first words, and then things, are whirled and swallowed" (2:53). Ultimately, says Carlyle, theories of human nature and society, precisely because they are abstracted from the real thing "by the very conditions of them must be incomplete, questionable, and even false" (2:54). Both Burke and Carlyle, in studying the French, use the image of paper to capture the disjunction between theory and reality. The *assignat*, substituting printed paper for honest gold, fictitious value for real value, becomes for Burke a chief symbol of the falsity of revolutionary social engineering (142, 308). Carlyle extends Burke's symbol, dubbing the late eighteenth century in France the Age of Paper, "which in many ways is the succedaneum of Gold. Bank-paper, wherewith you can still buy when there is no gold left; Book-paper, splendant with Theories, Philosophies, Sensibilities. . . . Paper is made from the *rags* of things that did once exist; there are endless excellences in Paper" (2:29).

Real value for Burke and Carlyle resides not in theory but in things, not in our "own private stock of reason" but in customary practices deeply ingrained in a people. Burke therefore celebrates a nation's prejudices, cherishing them the more the longer they have lasted, for prejudice does what "naked reason" cannot: "it renders a man's virtue his habit; and not a series of unconnected acts. Through just prejudice, his duty becomes a part of his nature" (183). We do what is right, we perform our obligations, not through moral analysis and conscious decision but by reflex, provided that we have been reared properly. Indeed, our very nature—what it means to be human—is constituted by and in layerings of habit and prejudice. What are mores, manners, customs but habit extended through the nation at large? Without such ligatures to bind us together, society and human nature dissolve in "madness, discord, vice, confusion, and unavailing sorrow" (195). Like Burke, Carlyle identifies habit as that which makes our world and ourselves cohere. He too is aware of the fragility of that coherence: "our whole being is an infinite abyss, *overarched* by Habit, as by a thin Earth-rind, laboriously built together." Without a "System of Habits, in a word, *fixed* ways of acting and of believing,—Society would not exist at all. . . . Herein too, in this its System of Habits lies the true Law-Code and Constitution of a Society. . . . The thing we call written Code, Constitution, Form of Government, and the like, what is it but some miniature image, and solemnly expressed summary of this unwritten Code?" (2:38). Without *habit*, we are *naked*—throughout *The French Revolution*, as in *Sartor Resartus*, Carlyle puns on the word *habit* and notes the link between *custom* and *costume*. We clothe ourselves—we become human and civilized—in habits and mores: "man lives not except with formulas; with customs, *ways* of doing and living" (4:68). When we shed our habits, we are naked, s*ansculottes*. And an entire nation without clothes, composed of men "suddenly stript bare" of their manners and mores, is terrible indeed, something no longer human.

Carlyle's reflections on human beings in society, then, are in some measure Burkean, if not derived directly from Burke. But working from shared assumptions, Burke and Carlyle arrive at radically opposed judgments of the French Revolution, the nature and process of social change at the center of their disagreement. Burke believed in the necessity of gradual, incremental reform. "A state without the means of some change is without the means of its conservation" (106). But except in rare instances when a people is impelled by necessity, change ought never to be radical or abrupt. Rather, like nature itself, the healthy state, in a condition of unchangeable constancy, moves on through the varied tenour of perpetual decay, fall, renovation, and progression. By aligning themselves with nature in this way, the English have prospered: "in what we improve we are never wholly new; in what we retain we are never wholly obsolete" (120). Burke distinguishes more clearly between change and reform in his *Letter to a Noble Lord* (1796): "[Change] alters the substance of the objects themselves; and gets rid of all their essential good, as well as of all the accidental evil annexed to them. Change is novelty. . . . Reform is not a change in the substance, or in the primary modification of the object, but a direct application of a remedy to the grievance complained of. So far as that is removed, all is sure. It stops there."[17] But those who seek to change rather than to reform an institution or government are usually not willing to stop there. They do not show reverence for that which has stood the test of time; instead, they bare their moral shortcomings and parade their lack of wisdom: "A spirit of innovation is generally the result of a selfish temper and confined views" *(Reflections,* 119). Burke asserts resoundingly in the *Letter to a Noble Lord*, "To innovate is not to reform" (9:155–56). In the face of energetic innovators, a state finds security in the inertia of its people. Resistance to change is a virtue.

Burke believed in a state's ability to reform itself without cutting loose from traditional moorings. Carlyle, however, was not so sanguine about the possibility of smooth, continuous reform, though he admits that "stillest perseverence were our blessedness; not dislocation and alteration,—could they be avoided" (2:27). But dislocation and alteration—abrupt change—cannot be avoided. History itself is not a chronicle of smooth continuity but a record of sharp breaks. "Consider it well, the Event, the thing which can be spoken of and recorded, is it not, in all cases, some disruption, some solution of continuity? Were it even a glad Event, it involves change, involves loss (of active Force); and so far, either in the past or in the present, is an irregularity, a disease" (2:27). Human history, like geologic transformation, is catastrophic and uneven rather than uniform and continuous, not least because it is the nature of peoples and societies to refuse all change until forced by circumstance to accept it. Unlike Burke, Carlyle does not reject innovation in favor of conservative reform but instead sees innovation as a force necessary to counter the conservative impulse:

So . . . in this world of ours, which has both an indestructible hope in the Future, and an indestructible tendency to persevere as in the Past, must Innovation and Conservation wage their perpetual conflict, as they may and can. Wherein the "daemonic element," that lurks in all human things, *may* doubtless, some once in the thousand years, get vent! But indeed may we not regret that such conflict . . . should usually be so spasmodic? For Conservation, strengthened by that mightiest quality in us, our indolence, sits for long ages, not victorious only, which she should be; but tyrannical, incommunicative. She holds her adversary as if annihilated; such adversary lying, all the while, like some buried Enceladus; who, to gain the smallest freedom, has to stir a whole Tinacria with its AEtnas. (2:39)

Carlyle concedes significant value to the desire to conserve—it ought to be victorious, for it preserves the system of habits by which we live our lives—but Burkean inertia becomes Carlylean indolence, a moral failing not a social virtue. Suppressed by the weight of self-satisfied indolence long past the time when innovation was needed, change erupts volcanically, cataclysmically: "The fountains of the great deep boil forth; fire-fountains, enveloping, engulfing. Your 'Earth-rind' [of custom and habit] is shattered, swallowed up; instead of a green flowery world, there is a waste wild-weltering chaos;—which has again, with tumult and struggle, to *make* itself into a world" (2:38).

In other words, habits and customs, like costumes, wear out and must be replaced with new clothes: old garments do not reweave themselves. Old social forms and traditions and structures cannot—or at least do not—evolve or reform themselves as quickly as is necessary, especially in an aristocratic society in which the privileged classes feel no pressure for change until it is too late. For Carlyle, turbulent revolution comes from below, though the opportunity for its welling up often arises from weakness at the top. The real revolution is in the streets among the sansculottes, not in the national assembly where, for the most part, Burke locates it. Burke looks at France and sees a political revolution with dire social consequences. Carlyle, on the other hand, sees an upheaval of dark social forces which a series of politicians seek unsuccessfully to control. Far from a political choice, revolution is "the Madness that dwells in the hearts of men. In this man it is, and in that man; as a rage or as a terror, it is in all men" (4:28). It is "the open violent Rebellion, and Victory, of disimprisoned Anarchy against corrupt worn-out Authority: how Anarchy breaks prison; bursts-up from the infinite Deep, and rages uncontrollable, immeasurable, enveloping a world; in phasis after phasis of fever-frenzy" (2:211). Burke judges the French Revolution to be horrible, destructive, and unnatural, a catastrophe willfully ignited by a cabal of philosophers, journalists, and lawyers—landless adventurers all. "Were all these dreadful things necessary?" he asks. "No! nothing like it" (126). Carlyle disagrees. The Revolution was horrible and destructive, yes, but also natural and even necessary, though not inevitable, and in the end productive. It was the forcible transformation of a society that either could not or would not transform itself peaceably. It was an event driven by the discontent of the mob, not a conspiracy of intellectuals, though the philosophes certainly helped create the climate of opinion in which revolution became imaginable. Burke's and Carlyle's divergent judgments of revolution are partially grounded in sharply opposed ideas about social hierarchy, particularly about the nature of poverty and the place of the poor in society. In his *Reflections*, if not in his writings about India and Ireland,[18] Burke asserts that the poor, who will always be with us, must accept their lot. He does not argue that the poor should not be helped, but his emphasis is on spiritual rather than material consolation:

The body of the people must not find the principles of natural subordination by art rooted out of their minds. They must respect that property of which they cannot partake. They must labour to obtain what by labour can be obtained; and when they find, as they commonly do, the success disproportioned to the endeavour, they must be taught their consolation in the final proportions of eternal justice. Of this consolation, whoever deprives them, deadens their industry, and strikes at the root of all acquisition as of all conservation. He that does this is the cruel oppressor, the merciless enemy of the poor and wretched. (372)

Whether a society is good in which the poor are "tractable and obedient" *(Reflections,* 372) is for Carlyle moot, for as he looks about him in the 1830s, he sees not "tractable and obedient" multitudes but powder kegs on the verge of explosion. Even in the 1790s, Carlyle writes, the French sansculotte "was but the *second*-miserablest of men," the Irish "sans-potato" more miserable still. In 1837 Carlyle looked to the continuing poverty of the Irish and wondered how long before such wretchedness vented itself in rebellion—a topic he would explore more fully in *Past and Present* (1843). For him the lesson of the French Revolution is clear:

'if the gods of this lower world will sit on their glittering thrones, indolent as Epicurus' gods, with the living Chaos of Ignorance and Hunger weltering uncared-for at their feet, and smooth Parasites preaching, Peace, peace, when there is no peace,' then the dark Chaos, it would seem, will rise;—has risen, and, O Heavens, has it not tanned their skins into breeches for itself? That there be no second Sansculottism in our Earth for a thousand years, let us understand well what the first was; and let Rich and Poor of us go and do *otherwise*. (4:313)

Both Burke and Carlyle hoped that their books would safeguard the British from violent, bloody revolution at home, but they looked in different directions for salvation. Burke in the 1790s lobbied hard for war against the regicides abroad and repression of the "Jacobins" at home; Carlyle in the 1830s believed that rejecting the French Revolution, and thereby refusing to understand its lessons, would not eliminate but rather increase the likelihood of violent revolution in Britain. As Chris Vanden Bossche has aptly noted, "Whereas Burke . . . sought a return from revolution to authority, Carlyle sought a return to authority through revolution." Burke looked to the past, Carlyle to the future.[19]

Given his complex relation to Burkean ideas, as well as the prevailing political climate in the early 1830s, in which attitudes toward Burke and the French Revolution helped define one's own political position, Carlyle faced a delicate task in writing his history of the Revolution. He needed to displace the Burkean interpretation without at the same time demeaning Burke himself or rejecting the whole body of Burke's thinking. He achieves his goal with the help of several rhetorical strategies. First, on the rare occasions that he mentions Burke, Carlyle does so favorably, a tactic not dishonest given the Burkean flavor of Carlyle's social thought. Second, when he differs from Burke, Carlyle does so forcefully but indirectly. For example, in the passage on outmoded interpretive strategies discussed earlier, Carlyle criticizes Roux's *Histoire Parliamentaire*, though his strictures might just as easily have been directed at Burke's *Reflections*. Elsewhere Carlyle attacks the moral hypocrisy of the ancien regime, noting scornfully "how 'sweet' are the manners; vice 'losing all its deformity'; becoming *decent* (as established things, making regulations for themselves, do); becoming almost a kind of 'sweet' virtue!" (2:30). Rather than attribute the sentiment openly to Burke ("that sensibility of principle, that chastity of honour . . . under which vice itself lost half its evil, by losing all its grossness" [*Reflections*, 170]), Carlyle inserts it as if it were an immoral *French* idea and uses it to damn the French court and nobility. His audience would have recognized immediately that the idea was Burke's, slightly reworded, but the lack of overt mention of Burke mutes the critique. Combined, these two strategies permit Carlyle to use Burkean ideas as he wished without aligning himself for or against Burke, for or against Tories or Whigs.

But Carlyle's awareness of the power of rhetoric in historical writing extends beyond such local, instrumental techniques. His belief that the historian must find new names for new things rests on an acute understanding of the historian as *writer*. As he wrote in "Count Cagliostro" (1833), history must soar on the double pinions of fact and imagination, for readers of history as of other forms of argument are persuaded not merely by reason but by emotion as well. The persuasive power of a written history resides jointly in the reliability of its facts and in the way the historian chooses to narrate those facts. It was possible, therefore, for Carlyle to write a history of the French Revolution that drew on sources and records inaccessible to Burke, that altered Burke's judgments—and that still did not accomplish the chief goal, to "rename" the Revolution and thereby explain to his contemporaries in the 1830s the meaning of "the grand work of our era." Burke was a master rhetorician, and—not to take away from his care with the sources at his disposal—the power of the *Reflections* does not rest solely or even primarily in the reliability of its facts. To displace the Burkean interpretation would require a *rhetorical* as well as a factual triumph. Nowhere is the rhetorical overthrow of his predecessor more evident than in Carlyle's treatment of the revolutionary journée of October 5–6, 1789, which culminated in the march of the Parisian women on Versailles and the forced return of the royal family to Paris.

The October Days constitute the emotional and thematic heart of Burke's *Reflections*; the most famous passage in the book is Burke's vision of Marie Antoinette. "It is now sixteen or seventeen years since I saw the queen of France, then the dauphiness, at Versailles; and surely never lighted on this orb, which she hardly seemed to touch, a more delightful vision" (169). From the start of this highly elaborated passage, Burke is looking to the past, remembering the vision of glory that was Marie Antoinette. He deifies the queen ("I saw her just above the horizon, decorating and cheering the elevated sphere she just began to move in,—glittering like the morning-star") and interprets the assault on her in the palace at Versailles as the collapse of a culture: "Little did I dream that I should have lived to see such disasters fallen upon her in a nation of gallant men, in a nation of men of honour and of cavaliers. I thought ten thousand swords must have leaped from their scabbards to avenge even a look that threatened her with insult.—But the age of chivalry is gone.—That of sophisters, economists, and calculators, has succeeded." Burke then describes movingly the loss he feels: "Never, never more, shall we behold that generous loyalty to rank and sex, that proud submission, that dignified obedience, that subordination of the heart, which kept alive, even in servitude itself, the spirit of an exalted freedom. The unbought grace of life, the cheap defence of nations, the nurse of manly sentiment and heroic enterprize is gone!" (170). The elegiac power of this passage connects the assault on the queen and the assault on civilization, both of which Burke images as rape. "A band of cruel ruffians and assassins . . . rushed into the chamber of the queen, and pierced with an hundred strokes of bayonets and poniards the bed, from whence this persecuted woman had but just time to fly almost naked" (164). What happens to the queen is happening to French culture and civilization. "All the decent drapery of life is to be rudely torn off. All the super-added ideas, furnished from the wardrobe of a moral imagination, which the heart owns, and the understanding ratifies, as necessary to cover the defects of our naked shivering nature, and to raise it to dignity in our own estimation, are to be exploded as a ridiculous, absurd, and antiquated fashion" (171).

The passage on Marie Antoinette and the October Days immediately proved a locus of controversy. Even before publication of the *Reflections* in November 1790, Burke's friend Philip Francis, in a well-known letter of February 1790, responded candidly to an early manuscript of the book and dismissed scathingly the picture of the queen as "pure foppery": "If she be a perfect female character you ought to take your ground upon her virtues. If she be the reverse it is ridiculous in any but a lover, to place her personal charms in opposition to her crimes." Francis especially deplored the perceived emphasis on the queen's beauty: "Are you such a determined Champion of Beauty as to draw your Sword in defense of any jade upon Earth provided she be handsome?" Despite their bluntness and clumsy jocularity, Francis's strenuous objections seem to rest on a sincere concern for Burke and Burke's reputation. "Look back, I beseech you and deliberate a little. . . . The mischief you are going to do yourself is, to my apprehension, palpable. It is visible. It will be audible. I snuff it in the wind. I taste it already. I feel it in every sense and so will you hereafter" (*Correspondence of Edmund Burke*, 6:86–87).

An injured Burke vehemently rejected Francis's counsel, defending his description of the queen and the feelings that evoked it, but Francis was right that the passage would rouse an uproar. Mary Wollstonecraft attacked it in *A Vindication of the Rights of Men* (1790), claiming that Burke reserves his tears for "the declamation of the theatre, or for the downfall of queens, whose rank alters the nature of folly, and throws a graceful veil over vices that degrade humanity; whilst the distress of many industrious mothers" elicits no response.[20] She continues:

Man preys on man; and you mourn for the idle tapestry that decorated a gothic pile. You mourn for the empty pageant of a name, when slavery flaps her wing. . . . Did the pangs you felt for insulted nobility, the anguish that rent your heart when the gorgeous robes were torn off the idol human weakness had set up, deserve to be compared with the long-drawn sigh of melancholy reflection, when misery and vice are thus seen to haunt our steps, and swim on the top of every cheering prospect? *(Works, 5:58)*

In *The Rights of Man* (1790) Thomas Paine also cudgels Burke's rendering of the October Days, noting famously that Burke "pities the plumage, but forgets the dying bird"—pities the queen but ignores the suffering of the people at large.[21] Paine spends several pages attacking Burke's handling of October 5–6, 1789, exposing the factual errors he believes Burke has committed. But the brunt of his critique is on the rhetorical "tragic paintings by which Mr. Burke has outraged his own imagination, and seeks to work upon that of his readers": such dramatic set-pieces as the lament on chivalry are "very well calculated for theatrical representation, whose facts are manufactured for the sake of show, and accommodated to produce, through the weakness of sympathy, a weeping effect. But Mr. Burke should recollect that he is writing history, and not *plays*; and that his readers will expect truth, and not the spouting rant of high-toned declamations."[22]

Though purporting to show the weakness and inaccuracy of Burke's treatment of the October Days, the attacks by Francis, Wollstonecraft, and Paine paradoxically demonstrate the immense power of Burke's rhetoric to rouse an emotional response in the reader and thereby to set the terms of debate if not to persuade all who disagree with his views. All the attempts to refute *directly* Burke's paean to Marie Antoinette and the lament for the collapse of civilization fail, and indeed must fail, because they end up reflecting badly on the moral imagination of the critics who write them. Burke himself points out the limits of Francis's moral sensibility, rejecting the view that he must "prove juridically the Virtues of all those I shall see suffering every kind of wrong, and contumely, and risk of Life, before I endeavour to interest others in their sufferings" *(Correspondence,* 6:90). Similarly, objections to Burke's sympathy for the queen when the people are suffering reduces moral response to a sort of arithmetic: we must compare the sufferings of one queen with the sufferings of the multitude before we allocate our concern. Put that way, the objections of Paine and Wollstonecraft seem like moral quibbling that substitutes the suffering of one for that of another without in the least undermining the legitimacy of Burke's vision and feeling. Besides, by contesting Burke in this way, Paine and Wollstonecraft find themselves bound to follow Burke's lead: to refute his position, they must treat it at length, making of their own work a commentary on his.

In the 1830s the passage on Marie Antoinette and the October Days was still the most famous in the *Reflections*, as indeed it is today. I argue that any British writer who wished to supersede Burke's interpretation of the French Revolution necessarily would have to deal rhetorically with this passage, somehow strip it of its power to inflame the moral imagination of its readers. Carlyle took up the challenge, but not directly as did Wollstonecraft and Paine. His disagreement with Burke's overall judgment of the queen and the collapse of chivalry did not mean he agreed with other of Burke's critics. Carlyle respected the queen as a courageous human being more admirable than her husband; he pitied her fall even though he saw symbolized in her much of the frivolity of the ancien regime. The coarseness of Philip Francis's attack, referring to the queen as a jade, would have disgusted Carlyle. Nonetheless, in his own narrative Carlyle needed to treat the October Days in such a way as to dissipate the power of Burke's portrayal without at the same time belittling the queen or Burke. His solution is masterly, one based on Burke's own understanding of the connection between rhetoric and emotion, between aesthetic response and moral response.

In the midst of his paean to Marie Antoinette, Burke apostrophizes on the springs of his own capacity to feel: "Oh! What a revolution! and what an heart must I have, to contemplate without emotion that elevation and that fall!" (169).

It is not primarily the queen's suffering but rather the contrast between her exalted past and her diminished present that generates powerful emotion. In his letter to Philip Francis, Burke defends these lines in the tone of a master schooling a recalcitrant pupil:

I tell you again that the recollection of the manner in which I saw the Queen of France in the year 1774 and the contrast between that brilliancy, Splendour, and beauty, with the prostrate Homage of a Nation to her, compared with the abominable Scene of 1789 which I was describing did draw Tears from me and wetted my Paper. (*Correspondence*, 6:91)

In other words, the mental *composition* of the scene, reproducing as it does the structure of tragedy, evokes the classic response of pity and terror. Furthermore, Burke's narration of the tragic scene evokes the same response in the well-schooled reader—in this case Burke himself—as does the initial recollection and imaginative construction: "These Tears came again into my Eyes almost as often as I lookd at the description" (*Correspondence*, 6:91). In both instances, an initial aesthetic reaction to the imaginatively composed or artfully described scene generates a powerful moral sentiment. Both Paine and Wollstonecraft deride Burke's "tragic paintings," his dramatic rhetoric, as if the emotions roused by drama and language were somehow counterfeit. But Burke sees a natural connection between the aesthetic response to tragic drama and the moral response to events in the world outside the theater.[23]   Indeed, the theater is a school of moral sentiment, for appropriate response to tragedy in the theater teaches us appropriate response to events in the world. By the fall of kings or queens—on stage or in real life—"we are alarmed into reflexion; our minds . . . are purified by terror and pity; our weak unthinking pride is humbled, under the dispensation of a mysterious wisdom" (*Reflections*, 175–76).   It would be perverse, Burke concludes, for us to weep in the theater but remain dry-eyed in the face of real-life tragedy, but he does not really fear this possibility. As he writes to Francis in defense of the tears he has shed for Marie Antoinette, "You do not believe this fact, or that these are my real feelings, but that the whole is affected, or as you express it, 'downright Foppery'. My friend, I tell you it is truth—and that it is true, and will be true, when you and I are no more, and will exist as long as men—with their Natural feelings exist" (*Correspondence*, 6:91). So long as natural human feeling is not debased, we will weep when we read of the fall of Marie Antoinette.

Carlyle apparently did not always agree with this sentiment. In 1818, as a young man of twenty-two, he quoted Burke in a letter to a friend, using Burke's grand prose to deflate the pretensions of a local dandy:

I saw that admirable creature, Mr Esbie, some weeks ago at Kirk[c]aldy. . . . To-day I saw him enter the college-yard [in Edinburgh]—'and surely there never lighted upon this earth, which he scarcely seemed to touch, a more beauteous vision. I then thought (to continue, in the words of Burke) that ten thousand swords (fists rather) would have leapt from their scabbards to avenge even a look that threatened him with insult—But alas' poor Esbie must be content, he thinks, '*with some devil of a curacy*' as he calls it; tho' his acquaintance with 'the first houses in England' is of the most intimate nature. (*Letters*, 1:149)

This impromptu burlesque tells us something about Carlyle beyond his own early pretensions. By 1818 Carlyle had read Burke's *Reflections*—at least this famous excerpt from it. He seemed to recognize the riskiness of Burke's prose which, as Bromwich notes, "has seemed to many readers not just quaintly provocative but overheated, self-indulgent, absurd" (141), perhaps just a step removed from the foppery that Francis perceived. But Carlyle also registered the power of the passage and expected his friend to know it, too; otherwise, he would not have memorized and used the lines. The humor of the letter depends on his friend's recognizing the passage—Carlyle names Burke, just in case— and knowing too the incongruous use to which Carlyle puts it.

In the mid-1830s, writing his history of the Revolution, Carlyle chooses to remember the power of Burke's paean to the queen instead of its proximity to melodrama. Furthermore, the way Carlyle handles Burke's passage suggests a clear recognition that its power resides less in the events themselves than in Burke's rhetorical ability to make us feel the tragedy of Marie Antoinette—in his composition and narration of the events. In other words, as long as we read the scene *as* Burke has dramatized it, we will weep for the queen and for France. Scornful rebuttal of the passage will not dispel its power; to do that, one must reimagine the scene, emplot it, and narrate it a different way. And that is precisely what Carlyle does. Rather than attempt to refute Burke's narrative by attacking its moral sentiments, Carlyle dismembers the scene: he dismantles the aesthetic structure of the passage so as to remove the efficient cause of our tears and therefore undermines the specific moral response Burke evokes. By dismembering Burke's famous passage and scattering the pieces elsewhere in his own history of the Revolution, Carlyle does a kind of homage to Burke but overthrows him at the same time.

To begin with, Carlyle, echoing Burke, presents Marie Antoinette as a goddess, but he moves the scene back in time, dissociating it from the October Days of 1789. Carlyle's laudatory description comes at the beginning of his history, immediately following the death of Louis XV: "Meanwhile the fair young Queen, in her halls of state, walks like a goddess of Beauty, the cynosure of all eyes. . . . Weber and Campan have pictured her, there within the royal tapestries, in bright boudoirs, baths, peignoirs, and the Grand and Little Toilette; with a whole brilliant world waiting obsequious on her glance" (2:32). Burke describes the assault on the queen in 1789 and then shocks us with a contrasting glance back to the glorious vision he saw in 1773; Carlyle describes the queen as a goddess in a passage narratively situated in 1774, then looks ahead to 1789 and beyond: "fair young daughter of Time, what things has Time in store for thee! Like Earth's brightest Appearance, she moves gracefully, environed with the grandeur of Earth: a reality, and yet a magic vision; for, behold, shall not

utter Darkness swallow it!" (2:32). This rhetorical strategy erases the tragic
pathos, the sublime nostalgia, of Burke's paean and offers in its place a sense of
inexorability, of the fatality of time. Second, Carlyle rewrites the narrative of
the assault on the queen's chambers:

The terror-struck bodyguards fly, bolting and barricading; [rabid Insurrection] follows.
Whitherward? Through hall on hall: wo, now! towards the Queen's Suite of Rooms, in
the farthest room of which the Queen is now asleep. Five sentinels rush through that
long Suite; they are in the Anteroom knocking loud: 'Save the Queen!' Trembling
women fall at their feet with tears: are answered: 'Yes, we will die; save ye the Queen!'
Tremble not, women, but haste: for, lo, another voice shouts far through the outermost
door, 'Save the Queen!' and the door is shut. It is brave Miomandre's voice that shouts
this second warning. . . . Trembling Maids-of-Honour, one of whom from afar caught
glimpse of Miomandre as well as heard him, hastily wrap the Queen; not in robes of
state. She flies for her life, across the Œil-de-Boeuf; against the main door of which too
Insurrection batters. She is in the King's Apartment, in the King's arms; she clasps her
children amid a faithful few. The Imperial-hearted bursts into mother's tears: 'O my
friends, save me and my children.' The battering of Insurrectionary axes clangs audible
across the Œil-de-Boeuf. What an hour! (2:278–79)

Note how quickly the action takes place in Carlyle's version: we are given a
sense of people sweeping by. Burke, in contrast, lingers on the details of the
entrance into the chamber: "From this sleep the queen was first startled by the
voice of the centinel at her door, who cried out to her, to save herself by flight—
that this was the last proof of fidelity he could give—that they were upon him,
and he was dead. Instantly he was cut down. A band of cruel ruffians and
assassins, reeking with his blood, rushed into the chamber of the queen"
(Reflections, 170). Note too that in Carlyle's version, the queen is dressed,
though "not in robes of state"; Carlyle does not tell us, as Burke does, that the
queen is "almost naked." Carlyle pictures the queen, even under attack, as
attended by her maids-of-honor; Burke emphasizes the queen's isolation and
vulnerability. Carlyle describes Marie Antoinette as concerned mother ("'O my
friends, save me and my children'"), whereas Burke focuses our attention on the
body of the queen. By these means Carlyle eliminates the nebulous eroticism of
Burke's description and weakens the association with rape, thereby further
diminishing the sense of tragedy. For Carlyle, the scene is painful but not
tragic, a pathetic episode "wherein Governed and Governor ignominiously
testify that their relation is at an end" (2:279). Ignominy, but no tragedy.
Carlyle refuses to plot the scene as a tragedy, refuses to let us feel too strongly
the queen's distress.

    Carlyle reserves tragic pathos for other events in his history, perhaps most
surprising among them the death of Robespierre. Through most of the narrative,
Robespierre is treated slightingly; he is "the sea-green Incorruptible," not near
so grand a figure as Mirabeau or even Danton. Yet as his death approaches,
Robespierre acquires tragic grandeur and dignity. Carlyle paints the death scene

so as to evoke pity and terror, with Robespierre cast typologically as Christ sacrificed for us all.[24] Most shockingly, Carlyle echoes Burke ("what an heart must I have to contemplate without emotion that elevation and that fall") in asking our sympathy not for the queen but for Robespierre: "'He had on the sky-blue coat he had got made for the Feast of the Être Supreme'—O Reader, can thy hard heart hold out against that?" Carlyle knows his audience will question the call for sympathy, and he justifies his plea:

following the execution of Robespierre, there bursts forth shout on shout of applause. Shout, which prolongs itself not only over Paris, but over France, but over Europe, and down to this generation. Deservedly, and also undeservedly. O unhappiest Advocate of Arras, wert thou worse than other Advocates? Stricter man, according to his Formula, to his Credo and his Cant, of probities, benevolences, pleasures-of-virtue, and suchlike, lived not in that age. A man fitted, in some luckier settled age, to have become one of those incorruptible barren Pattern-Figures and have had marble-tablets and funeral-sermons. His poor landlord, the Cabinet-maker in the Rue Saint-Honore, loved him; his Brother died for him. May God be merciful to him and to us! (4:284–86)

We are not asked to judge or to condemn Robespierre, rather to weep for the man and his suffering. This is a far cry from Burke's cold refusal, in the *Fourth Letter on a Regicide Peace*, to permit any softening toward the revolutionists: "I trust that our countrymen will not be softened to that kind of crimes and criminals; for if we should, our hearts will be hardened to everything which has a claim on our benevolence. . . . They who bear cruelty are accomplices in it. The pretended gentleness which excludes that charitable rancor produces an indifference which is half an approbation. They never will love where they ought to love, who do not hate where they ought to hate" (*Writings & Speeches,* 9:101). The transfer of feeling from Marie Antoinette to Robespierre—the rejection of "charitable rancor" towards those who took part in the revolution— signals clearly Carlyle's sense that historical judgment and moral judgment are not the same.

Carlyle completes his dismemberment of Burke's famous scene by relocating the great lament—"But the age of chivalry is gone"—two hundred pages away, toward the end of the second of his three volumes:

Great Burke has raised his great voice long ago; eloquently demonstrating that the end of an Epoch is come, to all appearance the end of Civilised Time. Him many answer: Camille Desmoulins, Clootz Speaker of Mankind, Paine the rebellious Needleman, and honourable Gaelic Vindicators in that country and in this: but the great Burke remains unanswerable; 'the Age of Chivalry *is* gone,' and could not but go, having now produced the still more indomitable Age of Hunger. (3:228)

The great Burke remains unanswerable: nowhere does Carlyle praise his predecessor more highly, setting Burke clearly above the many who have sought to repudiate him. Nonetheless, the passage deflates even as it praises: Burke sounded the death knell of an era, yet, Carlyle implies, he proved unable to accept its passing.[25] If Burke could say that "the age of chivalry is gone," that "never, never more, shall we behold that generous loyalty," why did he struggle rhetorically from 1790 to his death in 1797 to reinstate a government and a way of life that he himself had pronounced dead?

Though Carlyle nowhere says so in his history of the French Revolution, it is clear elsewhere that he faults the far-sighted Burke for a failure of nerve, not for an inability to see the truth but for an unwillingness, when confronted with the great event of the age, to accept emotionally what he saw clearly enough. Carlyle never accuses Burke of venality, as Burke's contemporaries often did. Instead, as Carlyle reads his character, Burke the Whig looked into the abyss of the present and future and turned his back on what he saw—a charge made openly in the essay "Boswell's Life of Johnson" (1832), which Carlyle wrote just as he was beginning to think seriously about the French Revolution. In this essay Carlyle praises Samuel Johnson as "the last genuine Tory; the last of Englishmen who, with strong voice and wholly-believing heart, preached the doctrine of Standing-still" *(Works,* 28:121). Though Carlyle could not himself believe in the virtue of standing still during an era of change, he nonetheless admires Johnson's courage and the depth of his belief. Because of these virtues, Carlyle credits Johnson, not Burke or Pitt, with so far saving England from bloody revolution. In contrast to Johnson, "Burke was essentially a Whig, and only, on reaching the verge of the chasm towards which Whiggism from the first was inevitably leading, recoiled; and, like a man vehement rather than earnest, a resplendent far-sighted Rhetorician rather than a deep sure Thinker, recoiled with no measure, convulsively, and damaging what he drove back with him" (28: 121).

Carlyle here echoes Hazlitt's acerbic judgment that "a modern Whig is but the fag-end of a Tory."[26] To Hazlitt and Carlyle, a Whig is something of a hypocrite. He foments a revolution to gain his own ends, only to outlaw future attempts to change the structure of government. He is interested in conserving those customs that safeguard his own property and status; all that threatens them is decried as dangerous innovation. When those attentive to Whig example actually lobby for additional change—Richard Price and the Revolution Society, for example—the Whig disowns them and recoils "with no measure," horrified at the affront to tradition. In calling Burke "essentially a Whig," Carlyle is therefore passing sentence on Burke's character rather than merely noting his political affiliation. And in doing so in 1832, he jabs at the modern Whigs who saw in the Reform Bill—a cautious extension of the franchise and a reform of boroughs likely to benefit Whigs above all—the answer to all England's problems. To Carlyle, Whiggism was synonymous with timidity and smug self-interest.

"Boswell's Life of Johnson" presents a harsh judgment of Burke, at least in part because Carlyle chooses to exalt Johnson at Burke's expense. As I have argued, Carlyle's treatment of Burke in *The French Revolution: A History* is at once less explicit and, within limits, more generous and respectful, for both philosophical and rhetorical reasons. Yet one can argue that Carlyle was right about Burke's unwillingness to gaze into the abyss.[27] Several letters Burke wrote late in life support such a view. Clearly the enormity of the Revolution filled Burke with despair, a fact he was willing to admit privately if not publicly. As he wrote to Fitzwilliam in October 1793, "I cannot proceed, as if things went on in the beaten circle of Events, such as I have known them for towards half a Century. The moral State of Mankind fills me with dismay and horrour. The Abyss of Hell itself seems to yawn before me" (*Correspondence*, 7:494–97). In March 1795 Burke exclaims that "My heart is sick; my stomach turns; my head grows dizzy; The world seems to me to reel and stagger. The Crimes of Democracy, and the madness and folly of Aristocracy alike frighten and confound me. The only refuge is in God who sees thro' all these mazes" (*Correspondence*, 8:215–16). A year later he wrote in a black mood to the émigré Abbe de la Bintinaye. "It seems as if it were God's will, that the present order of things is to be destroyed; and that it is in vain to struggle against that disposition" (*Correspondence*, 8:412)—a sentiment he had approached in print in the concluding lines of his "Thoughts on French Affairs" (1791): "If a great change is to be made in human affairs, the minds of men will be fitted to it; the general opinions and feelings will draw that way. Every fear, every hope, will forward it; and then they who persist in opposing this mighty current in human affairs, will appear rather to resist the decrees of Providence itself, than the mere designs of men. They will not be resolute and firm, but perverse and obstinate" (254–55).

To which Carlyle would have said, yes, yes—though of course he had the benefit of nearly forty years' hindsight on which to base his assent. For Carlyle it was truly in vain to struggle longer against the French Revolution; those who railed against it were indeed perverse and obstinate. In the mid-1830s the Revolution was no longer something to revile or to defend, to lament or to celebrate, but rather something to understand as an historical reality. Carlyle tells his contemporaries that they need to stop shrieking. They must not recoil from the chasm as Burke did, as many in the 1830s did in the face of Reform and Chartism and Irish poverty. Neither should they "enter exploratively its dim embroiled deeps"—they should not succumb to the nihilistic attraction of violence and anarchy. Instead, sensible, courageous people must approach the edge and "stand with unwavering eyes, looking how it welters; what notable phases and occurrences it will successively throw up" (4:71). It is the role of history and the historian to make that possible. Only by such intellectual brinkmanship would his countrymen be able, if they were blessed and lucky both, to avoid a repetition of the French catastrophe. And, Carlyle implies, only then could they move beyond the Revolution debate that dominated the era.

NOTES

1. Robert Southey, "The State and Prospects of the Country," *Quarterly Review* 39 (April 1829): 475–520. The cited quotation is from 483. Hedva Ben-Israel and J. J. Sack insightfully discuss Whig and Tory attitudes toward the French Revolution during the 1820s; their research calls into question F. P. Lock's assertion that between 1793 and the 1830s, attitudes toward Burke, and therefore toward the French Revolution, were largely determined by party loyalties. Lock's assertion is more true of the 1830s than it is of the 1820s. See Ben-Israel's *English Historians on the French Revolution* (Cambridge: Cambridge University Press, 1968), esp. chapters 1–4; Sack, "The Memory of Burke and the Memory of Pitt: English Conservatism Confronts its Past, 1806–1829," *The Historical Journal* 30 (1987): 623–40, esp. 623–28; and Lock, *Burke's Reflections on the Revolution in France* (London: Allen and Unwin, 1985), 167.

2. Ben-Israel describes in detail the rhetorical battle between Croker and Macauley in the House of Commons and in the major reviews during 1831 and 1832. During these years both men supported their antagonistic positions on reform by appeal to examples and lessons drawn from the French Revolution. Macauley, for example, blames the destruction of the French nobility on its stubborn opposition to reforms, whereas Croker blames it on the nobility's "deplorable pusillanimity" in granting them. See Ben-Israel, 103.

3. *The Collected Letters of Thomas and Jane Welsh Carlyle*, ed. Charles Richard Sanders, K. J. Fielding, and Clyde de L. Ryals, 18 vols. to date (Durham, N.C.: Duke University Press, 1970–). The quotation is from 6:446.

4. Carlyle struggled to articulate his theory of history and history-writing in two essays of this period, "On History" (1830) and "On History Again" (1833).

5. *The Works of Thomas Carlyle*, ed. H. D. Traill, 30 vols. (London: Chapman and Hall, 1899). For the quotation, see 29:149–50.

6. *Two Notebooks: From 23rd March 1822 to 16th May 1832*, ed. Charles Eliot Norton (N.Y.: The Grolier Club, 1893). See 178–79.

7. See Ben-Israel, 102–7, 291–92.

8. Ben-Israel notes that, with regard to the French Revolution, "more than anything else it was the separation of history from politics which was beginning to win" in the wake of the passage of the Reform Bill and that Carlyle had much to do with that separation (108).

9. Studies of Carlyle as historian typically mention Burke and the *Reflections* far less frequently and in far less detail than they mention, for example, almost any of the German writers and thinkers Carlyle read in the 1820s. There are, however, several noteworthy exceptions to this generalization. Louise M. Young, in *Thomas Carlyle and the Art of History* (Philadelphia: University of Pennsylvania Press, 1939), examines Carlyle as an inheritor of Burke through Coleridge, though she reads Carlyle as more orthodoxly conservative than he was (43–46, 69–88). Ben-Israel (1968) recognizes significant affinities between Burke and Carlyle,

perceiving that "Carlyle did not derive entirely from Germany. It seems, curiously, that both the emancipation from Burke and the Burkian influence grew in him in the course of his apprenticeship with Whiggism [roughly between 1815 and 1821], when 'Burkianism' itself was being tranformed" (38; see also 144–46). Philip Rosenberg, in *The Seventh Hero: Thomas Carlyle and the Theory of Radical Activism* (Cambridge: Harvard University Press, 1974), identifies differences between Burke's and Carlyle's views of revolution (123–27), as does Chris R. Vanden Bossche, in *Carlyle and the Search for Authority* (Columbus: Ohio State University Press, 1991), 8–13. Finally, Mark Cumming, in *A Disimprisoned Epic: Form and Vision in Carlyle's* The French Revolution (Philadelphia: University of Pennsylvania Press, 1988), and Elizabeth Wheeler, in "Great Burke and Poor Boswell: Carlyle and the Historian's Task," *Victorian Newsletter* 70 (1986): 28–31 discuss Carlyle's and Burke's treatments of Marie Antoinette. See Cumming, 76 and Wheeler, *passim*.

10. James Chandler, in *Wordsworth's Second Nature: A Study of the Poetry and Politics* (Chicago: University of Chicago Press, 1984), has noted of Wordsworth that "Burkean assumptions tend to sink down into the France books [of *The Prelude*], not to float near the surface. . . . Burkean conceptions seem to underlie the very scheme according to which both social and mental events are narrated. . . . Though verbal echoes can help to show that Wordsworth's story is such a retelling of Burke's, the real debt runs deeper" (49). The Burkean presence is similarly widespread and similarly understated in Carlyle's history of the Revolution, though often Carlyle contests rather than approves Burke's conclusions.

11. In his review of Roux and Buchez's *Histoire Parliamentaire*, published in the *London and Westminster Review* in 1837, Carlyle is more respectful, lauding the invaluable collection of documents though repeating his strictures on Roux's historical interpretation. See *Works,* 29:1–21.

12. In 1839, Carlyle analyzes contemporary responses to Chartism in the same way, though with less patience for shrieking: "What will horror do for it? What will execration; nay, at the bottom, what will condemnation and banishment to Botany Bay do for it? Glasgow Thuggery, Chartist torch-meetings, Birmingham riots, Swing conflagrations, are so many symptoms on the surface; you abolish the symptom to no purpose, if the disease is left untouched" (*Works,* 29:119–20).

13. See Hannah Arendt, *On Revolution* (N.Y.: Penguin, 1977), 51.

14. John Rosenberg, *Carlyle and the Burden of History* (Cambridge, Mass.: Harvard University Press, 1985), 31.

15. The quotation is from Lord John Actons's *Lectures on the French Revolution* (1910), quoted in Ben-Israel. Ben-Israel disputes the sweeping claim while still allowing Carlyle a significant role in redefining British views of the Revolution; see 34.

16. Seamus Deane, in *The French Revolution and the Enlightenment in England, 1789–1832* (Cambridge, Mass.: Harvard University Press, 1988), goes so

far as to include Carlyle in a "Burkean group" that includes Mackintosh, Croker, Southey, and Wordsworth (43). F. P. Lock discusses the difficulty of attributing Burkean echoes in nineteenth-century writers to direct influence, given the wide currency of central Burkean concepts (187–88).

17. See *The Writings & Speeches of Edmund Burke*, ed. Paul Langford, vol. 9, *The Revolutionary War, 1794–1797; Ireland*, ed. R. B. McDowell (Oxford: Clarendon, 1991), 9:155.

18. Conor Cruise O'Brien, in *The Great Melody: A Thematic Biography and Commented Anthology of Edmund Burke* (Chicago: University of Chicago Press, 1992), makes a compelling case for Burke's lifelong concern for the poverty and legal disabilities of the Irish Catholics, as well as for the condition of the Indian people under British colonial rule.

19. Vanden Bossche, 8. In a letter to John Sterling, written in October 1831 during the struggle for parliamentary reform, John Stuart Mill wrote of Carlyle that "he differs from most men who see as much as he does of the age, by a circumstance greatly to his advantage in my estimation, that he looks for a safe landing *before* and not *behind*: he sees that if we replace things as they once were, we should only retard the final issue, as we should in all human probability go on just as we then did, and arrive again at the very place where we now stand" (cited in Carlyle's *Letters,* 6:31).

20. *A Vindication of the Rights of Men, The Works of Mary Wollstonecraft*, ed. Marilyn Butler and Janet Todd, 7 vols. (N.Y.: New York University Press, 1989), 5:3–60. The quotation is found in 5:14.

21. Conor Cruise O'Brien defends Burke against Paine's jibe, noting that Paine dehumanizes such victims of the revolution as the queen by reducing them to mere plumage. See *The Great Melody,* 413.

22. Thomas Paine, *The Rights of Man*, published jointly with Burke's *Reflections* (Garden City: Doubleday/Anchor Press, 1973), 286.

23. I am indebted to David Bromwich's lucid analysis of the way in which Burke links dramatic judgment and moral judgment. See his *Politics by Other Means: Higher Education and Group Thinking* (New Haven: Yale University Press, 1992), esp. 141–43.

24. See Rosenberg, 104–9.

25. Elizabeth Wheeler also notes Carlyle's mingled praise and blame for Burke in this passage. See 29.

26. *The Complete Works of William Hazlitt*, ed. P. P. Howe (London: Frank Cass , 1967), 7:19.

27. Writing about Burke in 1879, in a book shot through with Carlylean influence, the liberal John Morley argues that Burke, with regard to the French Revolution, "did not look the state of things steadily in the face. It was no easy thing to do. But Burke was a man who ought to have done it. He set down all to the ignorance, folly, and wickedness of the French leaders. This was as shallow as the way in which his enemies, the philosophers, used to set down the superstition

of eighteen centuries to the craft of priests, and all defects in the government of Europe to the cruelty of tyrants." See John Morley, *Edmund Burke* (N.Y.: Harper, 1879), 162.

Politics of the Episteme: The Collapse of the Discourse of General Nature and the Reaction to the French Revolution

Paul Trolander

From Alfred Cobban's *Edmund Burke and the Revolt Against the Eighteenth Century* (1929) to Foucault's *The Order of Things* (1966), the political outcome of the French Revolution has rarely figured as a contributory factor in changes in discursive practice after 1790, but rather as a symptom of epistemological or ideological shifts that were already under way.[1] From this perspective, the reaction to the French Revolution can be seen as a reaction to the discursive practices or philosophies of the Enlightenment, and the political outcomes of the Revolution, both in France and England, must be represented as latent in those contemporary texts that championed shifts in epistemic and discursive practice, for instance Burke's *Reflections on the Revolution in France* (1790) or Malthus' *Principles of Population* (1798). Indeed, Foucault's study of epistemic change does not factor in the Revolution at all—in *The Order of Things*, discursive practices develop and mutate according to their own inherent principles. The lesson is apparent by mere exclusion—grand political events such as the Revolution may be defined by epistemic change, but they cannot be a cause of it. Even J.G.A. Pocock's historical account of English political discourse at the end of the eighteenth century discounts the force that the political events of the Revolution may have had on discursive practices. In his article "The Varieties of Whiggism" in *Virtue, Commerce, and History*, he takes the view that entrenched institutional and political structures limited the effects that the Revolution could have in England and by themselves allowed for the inherent conservatism of English political ideology to further develop and flourish against the backdrop of a relatively weak native radical tradition.[2] Ideology and discursive tradition defined and limited the nature of political change.

The argument of this brief essay is at odds with these more traditional views of this intellectual history. The direction that discursive/epistemic change took from the late eighteenth century to the early nineteenth, often represented as a move away from the empiricism and rationalism of the Enlightenment to the idealism and organicism of the Romantic period, hinged upon the outcome of political events centering around the French Revolution. The assumptions of intellectual historians that "idea complexes" or "discursive practices" develop, mutate, or react upon each other according to inherent laws or principles have limited value when they are used to explain shifts in writing practices at the beginning of the nineteenth century in England.

It is generally accepted that Burke's *Reflections on the Revolution in France* (1790) is a significant document in the history of the revolt against the eighteenth century. Burke's *Reflections* is typically treated as a reaction to the intellectual trends that are alleged to have inspired the Revolution—French rationalism and English empirical psychology. But the simple treatment of Burke's philosophical positions, often with a comment on their soundness as justification for a conservative political doctrine, cannot explain why Burke's text helped to shape a viable and lasting reaction to the Enlightenment. For one thing, the ideas that Burke reacted to had been around for over half a century. As this essay will show, the discourse of general nature—which Burke systematically critiqued—had already constituted the terms and arguments Burke would employ to negate it.[3] The inherent problems of empiricism and rationalism were no obstacle to their mutual advance, despite their long-standing critique of each others' assumptions and analyses. Moreover, there was little likelihood in 1785 that their advance would come to an end soon. How, then, could Edmund Burke succeed in dampening the claims of rationalism where David Hume, fifty years before and surely a more forcible critic of rationalism than Burke, had failed?[4] Why was Thomas Reid, a more cogent analyst of the shortcomings of empiricism than Burke, unable to quell the advance of empirical psychology thirty years before *The Reflections*?[5] Indeed, Joseph Priestley had helped bring about a resurgent interest in empirical psychology—regardless of Reid's criticism of it—by the publication in 1775 of an abridged edition of David Hartley's *Observations*.[6]

The answer to these questions is that the reaction Burke initiated *was political, not philosophical*. His intention was not to found a philosophy of "organicism" or "idealism" through a critique of "empiricism" and "rationalism." His intention was to deconstruct the social prestige of the discourse that he, as well as supporters of the French Revolution, believed had made that political event possible. Therefore, the success of the reaction depended upon the political outcome of the Revolution. If the Revolution had developed more in accordance with the predictions of its English supporters, Burke's negation of eighteenth-century philosophical reform (empirical or rational) could not have succeeded.

THE DISCOURSE OF GENERAL NATURE

To appreciate the force of Burke's critique, it is necessary to understand that many modes of writing practiced during the eighteenth century were assumed by readers and writers alike to contribute to a general understanding of the laws or principles of human thought, society, and action.   This encompassing sense that much of what was published participated in the construction of a discursive representation of a general model of mind, government, and morals represented the basis for what we have come to call the Enlightenment. This discourse of general nature served to organize, hierarchize, censure, and marginalize all modes of writing, and, by the 1760s and 1770s, it had eclipsed potential competitors as a master discourse.   Poetry, rhetoric, philosophy, aesthetics, the nascent social and natural sciences, the fine arts, and mathematics were all inscribed into the discourse of general nature and given values within it as discourses that represented particular modes or operations of a general model of mind.

Locke's influential *Essay* already contained several of the features of the discourse that created the desire to participate in its project and to disseminate its features.   Locke presented his general model of the understanding as the result of a personal inquiry into the processes and qualities of his own mind; he desired that this general model of the understanding stand as a necessary precursor to all scientific/philosophical investigation, that it inaugurate new fields of knowledge and writing and reform older ones;[7] he assumed that because the perception of qualities of ideas was not mediated by the senses that such qualities were capable of being perfectly known and accurately represented in writing;[8] he concluded that a science of signs was likely to be more accurate than a science of things, and that this science made possible a precise model of mind as well as a science of morals.[9]

These features had the effect of validating personal introspection as an investigation of the general causes and processes of mind, even as they negated the personal sources of analysis.   The writer of texts on mental philosophy entered an authoritative public sphere which shaped a set of moral and mental procedures meant to substitute for the particular minds and moral systems of individuals.   To constitute laws of mind was to constitute the very (corrected) means and methods of signification, to shape the boundaries of discourse, to hierarchize, order, and marginalize other modes of writing beyond the philosophical text.   To participate in the making of a general model of mind was to present one's text as central to the making and shaping of culture production and social relations.   The discursive productions of individual writers gained importance because while they could not be the origin of processes and qualities of general nature—the result of independent laws of nature—yet, individual writers were the only source for their construction and dissemination.   Writers were given a strong incentive to participate in the discourse of general nature because they gained a truth value for their texts that was difficult to refute.

Locke's *Essay* acquired importance throughout the eighteenth century because it created an incentive to participate in the making of text about the mind and in the making of one's text into a reflection of general processes of mind. It authorized the opening up of fields of inquiry and writing about society, aesthetics, and criticism that predominated during the second half of the century. While all writers of mental philosophy did not replicate Locke's empirical method of analysis (there is a general reaction to his assumptions about the tabula rasa even before midcentury), still most texts of mental philosophy continued to assume that a general model of mind was possible through discursive representation and that this discursive representation was or ought to be more authoritative than individual minds in regulating mental activity and textual production. The suggestive power of Locke's project was so great that it overcame the general empirical bounds of his own undertaking. If writing were to accommodate to a model of mind, then a greater diversity of mental powers and faculties allowed for a greater diversity of text to be inscribed in the larger general model. Consequently, later analyses of mental powers overlooked or countered Locke's critique of faculty psychology even as they reiterated his desire for a model of mind that would correct and guide the discovery of "truth."

The intellectual prestige of the discourse was great, and the incentive to participate in it and disseminate its features powerful. We can see from a just a few titles the diversity of modes of writing that had come to be inscribed within its larger features: Burke's *Philosophical Enquiry into the Origin of our Ideas of the Sublime and Beautiful* (1757; aesthetics), Gerard's *Essay on Genius* (1774; cultural/social theory), Darwin's *The Lives of the Plants* (1789; poetry), Godwin's *Caleb Williams* (1794; novel), Sheridan's *Lectures on the Art of Reading* (1775; elocution and public speaking), Gibbon's *Memoirs* (1796; autobiography), Kames's *Elements of Criticism* (1761; critical theory), Smith's *The Theory of Moral Sentiments* (1759; ethics and moral theory), Stewart's *Elements of the Human Mind* (1792; philosophy), Warton's *The History of English Poetry* (1774–81; literary history), Wollstonecraft's *A Vindication of the Rights of Woman* (1792; feminism, educational theory). The idea that all modes of writing contributed to a general progress of mind impelled writers to continue to duplicate the features of this discourse.

GENERAL NATURE AND ITS INTERNAL CONTRADICTIONS

The growth in specialized discourses after midcentury placed a great strain on the basic assumption of the discourse of general nature that all modes of writing contributed to a uniform model of mind. The discourse accommodated to this growth by extending its model of mind to historical development, in which each age constituted a period of intellectual growth and change analogous to individual development. Within this model, academic theorists and critical practitioners often claimed that the general nature of man was intact only during the first ages of society. As society progressed, distinct sciences, arts, and professions developed separate methods and aims, which, being more or less specialized, deviated from the original general norm. The age of general man gave way to that of reason, criticism, science, and art. Of course, this progress from ignorant original to educated modern—albeit specialized—man was good. No matter what humanity had given up by leaving the natural state, it gained social, moral, and civil progress. This view was expressed with varying degrees of nostalgia in the works of Hugh Blair, Richard Hurd, James Beattie, Adam Ferguson, Thomas Warton, Robert Lowth, Mary Wollstonecraft, Dugald Stewart, and many other writers in England and Scotland after midcentury.[10]

Certainly this tendency toward specialized discourses and the growing emphasis on the individual put pressure upon the basic assumptions of general nature, but the apparent singularity of a particular discourse continued to be validated by reference to the greater general model of mind. Each specialized discourse represented a particular specialized mental faculty or power or combination of these. The progress of humanity was still seen in terms of the general progress of the mind, where individual bents or proclivities participated in a greater effort of progress and reform, albeit, a reform that no single mind could be said to embrace, and, indeed, for which no single individual could be claimed as serving as an ideal model. Even the concept of genius, which before midcentury in England was often proposed as a kind of super Lockean mind embracing the extent of human learning and experience, in the second half of century had been split up into types and modes, each mode reigning over a single aspect of a larger mental economy that no one genius could subsume. Alexander Gerard, whose *Essay on Genius* was considered in the 1770s as the most important work on this subject, saw the division of types of genius as nearly infinite, a division that depended upon social and natural forces that further subdivided the various powers of particular modes of genius.[11] There was no incentive to abandon the assumption that a single model of human mind and nature was sufficient to validate all human activity and writing, especially since this assumption gave great social prestige and power to writing and personal introspection.

Another strain on the perceived unity of the discourse of general nature was that the discourse validated any writer's attempt to restructure and reorder the relations regulating writing activity around a single mode of investigation. Before midcentury and as late as the 1760s, moral and mental philosophy provided most of the terms and concepts by which to order all modes of writing on the arts and sciences. But after 1760, there was a growing tendency on the part of writers to proclaim other modes of writing as vehicles for disseminating, organizing, or representing the total progress of mind and humanity. In a sense, this had always been the danger of a discourse that recommended individual utterances as substitutions for general processes. Locke's pronouncement that his text amounted to a prolegomena to all future writing on the sciences provided the language and example that would be used by writers throughout the century. The result was that while much writing was perceived to be organized and subordinated within a larger framework, other texts competed for the right to act as a guiding light of this effort to order culture production. As each text vied for an equal place within the model of mind, it necessarily posited a center distinct from other competing discourses and recommended a different system of order based upon similar principles. Moreover, different vehicles of textual production within a single discursive field vied among themselves for the right to act as repositories for the general progress of mind.

Champions of particular arts or sciences writing from 1760 to the end of the century claimed preeminence for their charges and consequently fractured the sense that all discourses participated in a well-organized and concerted effort to expand a single general progress of mind. Thomas Sheridan claimed that the arts of eloquence and public speaking ought to serve as models of mental and social reform rather than philosophy.[12] Alexander Gerard and William Duff, both writers on genius, suggested that the concept of genius best served to organize the mental powers of society.[13] Adam Smith arrogated the role of social production to political economics,[14] while Edmund Burke claimed that jurisprudence was the proper discourse of social control, if not reform.[15] Wordsworth, later yet, laid the charge of social and mental reform to poetry and attempted to subordinate all other discourses to its lead, or at least to place poetry on par with them.[16] Dugald Stewart, a late-eighteenth/early-nineteenth century Scottish philosopher, made the best case for philosophy's role as a master discourse of reform and education.[17] Yet their very insistence on the right to call their particular discourses legitimate models for reforming human affairs and learning put pressure on the idea of an homogeneous progression of mind, suggesting that each self-proclaimed master discourse was itself specialized and tending to present the views and opinions not of a general reader, but of readers persuaded to take on the views of particular systems of thought.

The lack of agreement about the role of general processes in ordering the investigation of a particular specialized branch of writing also points out the impulse toward fracturing and instability contained within the discourse. The explication of the concept of taste may be taken as an example. While the term "taste" provided writers a center around which to constitute a particular mode of investigation and writing, investigations were anything but ordered or subordinated to concepts within this mode and hardly contributed to a single or coherent view of the master concept. Hume had argued at midcentury that the faculty of taste could never be found in perfection in a single human mind, suggesting that the perfection of taste depended upon the exertions of a committed group of connoisseurs, their decisions and corrections of each others' peculiar faults coming to represent a general progress of the power or faculty of taste.[18] Kames, on the other hand, maintained that a general standard of taste was innate and yet was accessible only by a cadre of specially trained critics whose role was to develop and represent this standard to the public.[19] Alexander Gerard, too, like Kames and Hume, viewed general processes central to the constitution and dissemination of a corrected standard of taste, but for Gerard, such abstract principles were first derived from general approbation of past literary and artistic works and then corrected.[20]   Archibald Alison derived general processes of taste, not from innate standards, general approbation, or a specialized group of experts, but from the principle of the association of ideas.[21] The explication of taste and its general nature thus created over time not the appearance of a unified model of Taste but a sense of the proliferation and cacophony of systems and specialists.

General nature could serve not to order but to rend apart, disorder, create competition among writers. Francis Jeffrey, in his review essay of Alison's "Essay on Taste" in the *Edinburgh Review*, was quick to point out the eighteenth-century's failure to derive a legitimate standard of taste. He derided the possibility of legislating a general standard through rationalistic laws or systems of mind. Even so, his belief in a public formulation of principles of taste which if not universal could at least be derived from historical conditions of reception, reiterated the eighteenth-century's preoccupation with regulating human activity by recourse to general processes. Jeffrey was unwilling to undo or circumvent the discourse of general nature; its rewards for the individual writer were still too great, even in 1811.[22]

Contentions over the very shape and regulation of the public sphere of knowledge that this discourse sought to organize and hierarchize were emerging as well. Literary reviews and magazines of the second half of the eighteenth century, including reviews as diverse in political orientation as the *Critical* (1756–1817), *Monthly* (1749–1832), *English* (1783–1796), and *Analytical* (1788–1799) and magazines as diverse as *The Gentleman's Magazine* (1754–1907), *The Universal Magazine* (1747–1815), and *Monthly Magazine* (1796–1843), were waging a polite war for the right to proclaim themselves vehicles for an evolving model of human nature. Their concepts of the general reader and of the homogeneous development of human society and mind indicate that even late in the century, the human mind was conceived as an ordered whole which the magazine's boundaries sought to contain. But their competition to act in its behalf and to present their methods of ordering and hierarchizing knowledge as more legitimate than those of their competitors indicates how much the concept of general nature, far from homogenizing culture production and ordering it around a single center, proliferated the number of centers around which knowledge and writing could be disseminated. The perception that various individual peculiar centers had opened up was aided by editorial comments claiming that their competitors' publications were organized not by a general concept of mind and humanity but by biased and peculiar systems—political, national, religious, or economic. Nor did editors go out of their way at this time to suggest that the sum of so many peculiar systems could constitute a single ordered whole.[23]

Another factor that was constantly subverting the desire to subsume all human phenomena into a general model of mind was the discourse's preoccupation with origin and development, a preoccupation that was constantly impelling it toward concepts of natural growth and an account of the individual. The dialectic that assumed the presence of the peculiar in direct contact with the formative general urged the constant invention and detailing of more and more complicated circumstances within which general principles could appear. Thus, the individual, whether a nation, system of thought, mental faculty, person, or profession, was always in contact with the peculiar, but was also developing within circumstances that were special to the general laws of that individual. By knowing these laws, the individual could be reformed and the principles directing this reformation would take on the character not of an homogenizing set of rules or laws that subsumed the individual into a general model but of an already existing set of internal principles that regulated the individual's development. The natural growth or playing out of these general principles eradicated peculiarities that interrupted or waylaid the individual's development.

This dialectic, together with the assumption that general principles of mind were constituted through (or with the aid of) sensory experience, fostered concepts of mental development and education that increasingly focused upon specialized modes of experience and reasoning, including (1) various faculties of mind (senses, understanding, memory, imagination, moral judgment, taste, sympathy, passions, and affections); (2) various disciplines of study and work (philosophy, the arts, the professions, the trades); (3) various modes, kinds, or examples of genius (biography, autobiography, educational tracts, philosophies of genius); and (4) different nations, social systems and historical periods (literary and national histories, criticism, aesthetics). Models of historical, national, genial, professional, artistic, and social difference were modeled on the assumption that each form of individual difference could be constituted from general principles or laws of mind and that deviations from the laws of individual development could be circumvented or reformed.

After having examined how contradictions within the discourse actually aided its formulation and further dissemination, it is difficult to see how the breakdown of general nature could have been brought about by features already contained in it, for instance, by an increasing emphasis on the particular,[24] the advent of a new complex of concepts centering around organicism,[25] or the rise of different conceptualizations of Nature.[26] There seems no internal necessity for purely discursive forces to circumvent a discourse that was already on its way to conceptualizing organic structure.[27] Indeed, the conceptual and discursive inertia was on the side of the discourse of general nature that had maintained increasingly diverse writing/representing practices within familiar moral, philosophical, political, and literary bounds. Put another way, the intentions of the trend away from general nature (e.g., toward the particular or organic, toward special modes of writing and investigation, toward theories/discourses of historical/natural development) were already contained within the aims of general nature. The desire to constitute a scientific project for moral and mental reform, the elevation of reason and/or sympathy over prejudice, the identification of the interests of society with those of the individual, the construction of abstract discursive models of complicated mental and social processes, the historical understanding of social, political, and intellectual development, the progress and differentiation of the sciences and arts, the general advance of all professions, trades, and social ranks—these aims were formulated through the anxiety contained within the discourse that the difference between the particular and general was always in danger of collapsing and that therefore discursive/epistemic closure may be imminent. But by the 1780s, this battle against closure seemed all but won. The literature of the late eighteenth century—scientific, philosophical, critical, literary—points to an increasing confidence in an emerging progressive society based upon the separate powers of distinct discourses and classes of man, rather than to some moment of aporia when the discourse of general nature suddenly failed or gave way to a new episteme or idea complex.

POLITICS OF EPISTEMIC CHANGE: THE REACTION TO THE FRENCH REVOLUTION AND THE SUBVERSION OF THE DISCOURSE OF GENERAL NATURE

If some of the very epistemological features (science of mind and morals, laws or principles of development, constitution of the individual or particular) of nineteenth-century discourse were already present in those of general nature, what was the nature of the grand shifts of thought that supposedly took place between the eighteenth and nineteenth centuries? A more-than-partial answer to these questions is, I think, a political one. Shifts in argument and discursive forms were mediated through the language of political reaction to the perceived philosophical origins of the French Revolution. The progressive tone of the discourse of general nature and its assumptions about the improvability of mind and society marked it as the central cause of the violent social and political changes associated with the French Revolution. For the most part, this reaction was ideological and propagandistic. Its central characteristic was its effort to misappropriate and deform the features of general nature in order to force a reordering or reshuffling of the hierarchy of social and political aims, modes of writing, methods of investigation, analysis and representation that were perceived as central to that discourse.

The rallying point in England of the reaction to the revolution was Edmund Burke's *Reflections on the Revolution in France* (1790), a work whose influence on discussions of the revolution can be seen throughout the decade of the 1790s and much beyond.[28] Burke's work is important to the discursive and epistemic changes under discussion here because it was successful in linking the aims and methods of the discourse of general nature to the violent and chaotic events of the French Revolution, insisting that the Revolution was reason enough to dismantle the values and aims of general nature.

At the heart of Burke's critique of the Revolution was his negation of (philosophic) writing as an adequate means of modeling complex human activity. From Burke's perspective, a British or a French constitution could not be adequately represented by a single set of rational principles, because the very nature of the political and social arrangements of a nation defeated discursive representation. A nation was a great amalgam of written and unwritten laws, local and national prejudices, commercial as well as scientific and intellectual enterprises, political and religious institutions—all of which developed over centuries and combined in unique ways to create a complex and irregular whole.[29] No one system or point of view could explain this whole. By necessity, a government could regulate and balance society's various political, social, and economic interests, but it could not derive a workable science of government from a single set of general laws.[30]

Burke also recharacterized several of the key terms of the discourse of general nature. He referred to general principles of philosophy, which had once validated most modes of writing and investigation, as the peculiar principles of a small group of political subversives, and their efforts to develop and deploy an empire of reason as the efforts of a smallish "clan of the enlightened" intent upon making all human activity and knowledge adhere to their "narrow" rationalism.[31] He reversed, too, the relationship that the discourse of general nature had envisaged between reason and prejudice. Where once prejudice and superstition fled at the slightest light of reason, dangerous reason was now constantly and needfully kept in check by prejudice and superstition. Reason could never match the extensive influence of prejudice, a fact that Burke urged as proof of the unnaturalness of the first and the naturalness of the second.[32]

Burke's travesty of the discourse of general nature was meant to undercut its social prestige and eliminate those incentives that aided its dissemination. Writing was no longer to be interpreted as an entry into a public sphere but into a conspiracy and cabal. Representations of mind and society were no longer to be interpreted as straightforward models of general laws but as ruses that hid the real motives of small interest groups. Readers might find in a text the actual principle that motivated its writer, but they would never find abstract principles that could safely and effectively reshape society. From this new perspective, texts could be valued only as private systems, personal reflections, histories of particular institutions and nations. Readers were no longer encouraged to view text as a potential mirroring of the general laws of their own being—a model of self. They were now spectators of the writer, who was reconstrued as a potentially hostile "other"—an emanation of special laws of nature that were perhaps quite different from those that actuated the English-reading public. In time, this view would become as true for the conservative writer as much as for the liberal.[33]

The message of Burke's *Reflections* was, therefore, not just that philosophers and political extremists had ruined France's chances for a gradual reform of its political institutions, but that all modes of writing must be suspected of political and personal motives. The only cure for taking any text or mode of writing as a model for political and social change was to discredit the discursive practices that made such change possible. Burke, therefore, attempted to revalue the entire field of human activity, within which writing and discursive representation must take a particular role, as a set of "balancing" and "anomalous" political and social interests that could never be homogenized but could nonetheless coexist.[34]

It is this revaluing of writing as necessarily the product of a particular interest that constitutes the nature of the shift we see in the early part of the nineteenth century. But while the shift itself affects discursive practices, it had to be effected by more than discursive or conceptual means. This must be plain when we realize that much of what Burke argued was not new to philosophical discourse. Burke's embracing individual nature as good, historical process and development as counters to speculative reason, political and religious institutions as necessarily founded on prejudice and error, local tradition and experience uncorrected by philosophical principles as natural—all of this had had its echoes in earlier eighteenth-century texts. The simple fact that Burke was audacious enough to reverse the common topoi and aims of the discourse of general nature could not in itself have recommended these ideas to his readers. These concepts had already been deployed by general nature in order to validate its methods and terminology.

The shift relied on the outcome of political events in France that neither Burke nor the supporters of the discourse of general nature had a direct hand in bringing about. Burke's criticism of general nature so much relied upon events in France turning out the way he predicted that his "revolt" against the eighteenth century could hardly have been successful if political moderates in France (monarchicals) had been able to effect by peaceful means liberal reforms of government—elimination of feudal dues, creation of a constitutional monarchy based on the British system, reform of the judicial branch, limited suffrage. Indeed, Burke's critics relied on the relatively bloodless nature of the Revolution prior to 1792 as proof that the universal principles of reason that had motivated the Glorious Revolution in 1688 were manifesting themselves once again in France. They insisted that the threat of violence came from the right, not the left, from counterrevolutionaries intent upon regaining lost political and social power and from foreign governments which feared that ideas of revolution would catch hold in their own countries.[35] From 1790 to 1792, these ideas were not expressed simply by dissenting radicals such as Wollstonecraft, Price, and Priestley but by liberals in the Parliament and House of Lords, such as Charles Fox and Lord Landsdowne. Fox, no friend at the time to dissenters or radicals in London, continued to represent the aims of the Revolution as those of the discourse of general nature right up to his fall from power in 1794.[36] Other vehicles of philosophical reform and champions of universal benevolence, such as the *Analytical Review* (1789–1799) and *The Monthly Magazine* (1799–1823), continued to find sympathetic readers even during the height of the political reaction against Jacobinism.

Quite simply, the wholesale epistemic/discursive shifts seen at the end of the eighteenth century could not have been effected through discursive or conceptual processes alone. They depended upon the mediation of historical precedent or example either through the positive valuation of the discourse of general nature (the strategy of the progressives), or through its negation (the strategy of the conservatives). There were expectations about the predictability of the discourse based upon its known aims, intentions, procedures, and assumed social/moral effects that had to be accounted for. If the Revolution had been moderate and liberal in its effects and if its features could have been coded as such or given positive discursive values within the discourse of general nature, then Burke's negation of them would have fallen on deaf ears. But Burke's critique of the French Revolution seemed borne out because the Revolution did not retain its moderate character. It did not fulfill the aims of the progressives who had insisted that it was an example of the progressive improvement of humanity and society, that is, an agent of class harmony, limited democracy, better living conditions, international peace. Instead, historical events seemed to fulfill Burke's predictions that a revolution based upon abstract philosophical principles could only end in violence, anarchy, and tyranny. Because both sides agreed on what was at stake politically and philosophically in the outcome of the Revolution, once the Revolution could no longer serve as an example of peaceful moderate reform, the rhetorical power in the debate had to shift away from the progressives.

From this perspective, Burke's apparent success in characterizing the nature of the Revolution lent credence to his claim that the entire discursive/epistemic apparatus (which both sides in the debate—not just Burke—had insisted caused the Revolution) must be systematically discredited and subverted. Historical precedent seemed to bear out the conclusion that you could not have a General Man without violent deracination. You could not create General Man without erasing history, destroying institutions and nations, killing individuals.

Acknowledgments

Some of the research for this essay was completed during an NEH Summer Seminar, "The Revolution Debate and English Literature in the 1700s," directed by David Bromwich at Yale University in 1991. Its subsequent conception, writing, and revision were done in collaboration with Zeynep Tenger.

NOTES

1. Alfred Cobban, *Edmund Burke and the Revolt Against the Eighteenth-Century* (N.Y.: Macmillan, 1929), and Michel Foucault, *The Order of Things: An*

Archeology of the Human Sciences (1966; N.Y.: Random House, 1970). Other works influential in establishing these assumptions include Basil Wiley's *The Eighteenth-Century Background: Studies in the Idea of Nature in the Thought of the Period* (1940; Boston: Beacon, 1961); W. J. Bate's *From Classic to Romantic: Premises of Taste in Eighteenth-Century England* (Cambridge, Mass.: Harvard University Press, 1946); M. H. Abrams's *The Mirror and Lamp: Romantic Theory and the Critical Tradition* (London: Oxford University Press, 1953).

2. J.G.A. Pocock, "The Varieties of Whiggism from Exclusion to Reform: A History of Ideology and Discourse," in *Virtue, Commerce, and History: Essays on Political Thought and History, Chiefly in the Eighteenth Century* (Cambridge: Cambridge University Press, 1985), 274–95.

3. The purely rhetorical value of Burke's negation of Enlightenment ideology has been recently noted by Albert O. Hirschman in *The Rhetoric of Reaction: Perversity, Futility, and Jeopardy* (Cambridge, Mass.: Harvard University Press, 1991). Hirschman maintains that Burke's "formulation of a perverse effect theory," where the social policy of the revolutionaries in France brought about an outcome contrary to their intended goal of public good, was a reversal of Mandeville's familiar argument that "individual actions motivated by greed, desire for luxury, [and] self-interest—can have a positive social outcome." Hirschman reasons that "in this manner, the intellectual terrain was well prepared for arguing that on occasion the opposite might happen" (14), which Burke then utilized to his advantage.

4. The failure of Hume's attempt to reach a wide audience with his *Treatise on Human Nature* (1739) is legendary. While he considered this work revolutionary in its attempt to draw out principles of ethics from Locke's empiricist assumptions, his own contribution to moral philosophy was overshadowed in his time by the works of such "ratior ``ts" as Francis Hutcheson.

5. Thomas Reid, *An Inqui, .nto the Human Mind, on the Principles of Common Sense* (1764).

6. Joseph Priestley, *Hartley's Theory of the Human Mind, on the Principle of the Association of Ideas* (1775).

7. John Locke, "The Epistle to the Reader," *An Essay Concerning Humane Understanding*, 4th ed. (London, 1700).

8. Locke, 301–11.

9. Locke, 306–7 and 437–38.

10. Hugh Blair, "Critical Dissertation on the Poems of Ossian," *Eighteenth-Century Critical Essays*, 2 vols., ed. Scott Elledge (Ithaca: Cornell University Press, 1961), 2:848–59, and *Lectures on Rhetoric and Belles Lettres*, 2 vols. (London, 1783; Carbondale: Southern Illinois University Press, 1965), 2:311–24; Richard Hurd, *Letters on Chivalry and Romance*, 2d ed. (London, 1762), 114–20; James Beattie, *Essays*, 3d ed. (London, 1779), 2:62–69. Adam Ferguson, *An Essay on the History of Civil Society* (London, 1773), 286–94; Thomas Warton, *The History of English Poetry*, 3 vols. (London, 1774–81), 3:490–501; Robert Lowth,

Lectures on the Sacred Poetry of the Hebrew People, 2 vols. (1787; Hildesheim: Georg Olms Verlags., 1969), 1:80–88; Mary Wollstonecraft, *A Vindication of the Rights of Men*, *The Works of Mary Wollstonecraft*, eds. Janet Todd and Marilyn Butler (N.Y.: New York University Press, 1989), 5:28–29, and "On Poetry," *Posthumous Works of the Author of a Vindication of the Rights of Woman*, 4 vols., ed. William Godwin (London, 1798), 4:166–75; Dugald Stewart, "Of Imagination," *Elements of the Philosophy of the Human Mind*, 2 vols. (Cambridge, 1829), 1:355–94; William Duff, *An Essay on Original Genius* (London, 1767; Gainsville, Fla.: Scholars' Facsimiles and Reprints, 1964), 260–96.

11. Alexander Gerard, *An Essay on Genius* (London, 1774).

12. Thomas Sheridan, "Discourse I," *Lectures on the Art of Reading* (London, 1775), 286–315.

13. Gerard, *Essay on Genius,* 125–47 and 215–31; and Duff, 3–5.

14. Adam Smith, *An Enquiry into the Nature and Causes of the Wealth of Nations*, ed. Edwin Cannan (N.Y.: The Modern Library, 1937), 3–16.

15. Edmund Burke, *Reflections on the Revolution in France*, 3d ed. (London, 1790), 141–42.

16. William Wordsworth, "Wordsworth's Prefaces of 1800 and 1802," *Lyrical Ballads*, eds. R. L. Brett and A. R. Jones (1963; N.Y.: Methuen, 1984), 254–61n.

17. Stewart, "Introduction," *Elements of the Human Mind,* 1:15–40.

18. David Hume, "Of the Standard of Taste," *Essays Moral, Political and Literary*, ed. Eugene Miller (Indianapolis: Liberty Classics, 1985), 243.

19. Henry Home, Lord Kames, "Standard of Taste," *Elements of Criticism*, 8th ed., 2 vols. (1761; Edinburgh, 1807), 2:487–504.

20. Alexander Gerard, *An Essay on Taste*, 3d ed. (Edinburgh, 1780; Gainesville, Fla.: Scholars' Facsimiles and Reprints, 1963), 232–68.

21. Archibald Alison, "Analysis of this Exercise of Imagination," *Essays on the Nature and Principles of Taste*, 5th ed. (1790; Edinburgh, 1817), 69–80.

22. [Francis Jeffrey,] "Art. I. *Essays on the Nature and Principles of Taste*," *Edinburgh Review* 35 (May, 1811): 43–46.

23. This competition is plainly visible in prospectuses to new reviews and magazines and in yearly prefatory addresses to readers. See especially "Preface," *The Critical Review* 34 (Dec. 1772); "To the Literary World," *The Monthly Review; or, Literary Journal, Enlarged* ns 1 (1790): i–iv; "Preface," *The English Review* 1 (1783): 3–4, and "Prospectus" 23 (1794): 1–15; "To the Public," *The Analytical Review, or History of Literature, Domestic and Foreign, on an Enlarged Plan* 1 (1788): i–vi; "Preface," *The British Critic* 1 (1794): i–iii; "Preface," *Gentleman's Magazine* 60 (1790): iii, and "Preface" 66 (1796): iii; "Preface," *The Universal Magazine of Knowledge and Pleasure* 82 (1788): 3–4; "Preface," *The Monthly Magazine and British Register* 5 (1798).

24. Bate, 93–94.

25. See M. H. Abrams's account of Coleridge's importation of German

concepts of organicism in *The Mirror and the Lamp*, 218–25.

26. Wiley, 205–11.

27. Foucault, 220–32.

28. The influence of Burke's *Reflections* can be felt in several arenas. At first, his work sparked many liberal/radical responses, and for the moment Burke appeared among political and intellectual circles to have lost the debate about the nature of the Revolution. Among the many liberal and radical responses to Burke were several works important to the debate about the philosophical foundations of the Revolution, including Mary Wollstonecraft's *A Vindication of the Rights of Men* (1790), Paine's *The Rights of Man* (pt. 1, 1791; pt. 2 1792), James Mackintosh's *Vindiciae Gallicae* (1791). For a thorough treatment of the fortunes of liberal/radical ideology and related political movements during the 1790s, see Albert Goodwin's *The Friends of Liberty: The English Democratic Movement in the Age of the French Revolution* (Cambridge, Mass.: Harvard University Press, 1979). Also useful are J. E. Cookson's treatments of the liberal press and the loyalist reaction in his *The Friends of Peace: Anti-War Liberalism in England, 1793–1815* (Cambridge: Cambridge University Press, 1982), 84–141. Burke's efforts were perhaps most felt in the British House of Commons, where he was successful in marginalizing the liberal arm of the Whig party, notably Charles Fox and his supporters. Fox and the cause of political reform would not make a political comeback until after the turn of the century. For the political effects of Burke's split with Fox, see L. T. Mitchell's *Charles James Fox and the Disintegration of the Whig Party, 1782–1794* (Oxford: Oxford University Press, 1971), 153–238, as well as Mitchell's recent biography of Fox, *Charles James Fox* (Oxford: Oxford University Press, 1992), 108–35 and 194–219. Burke's successful campaign against liberal/radical politics in the House helped foster the general social reaction against Jacobinism. In the late 1790s, conservative publications began their assault on the liberal press, their rhetoric often taken directly from Burke or inspired by him. Among the more influential include *The Anti-Jacobin* (1797–98) and *The Anti-Jacobin Review* (1798–1821), both of which were successful in slurring liberals and radicals as instruments of French republican propaganda. Even after the height of the reaction to the Revolution, Burke's arguments and tone continued to influence conservative rhetoric of such periodicals as *The Satirist* (1807–14), *The Quarterly Review*, *Blackwood's Magazine* (1817–90), and *Fraser's Magazine* (1830–82). Outside of England, Burke's *Reflections* was influential in shaping the international reaction to the French Revolution; see Jacques Godeschot's *The Counter-Revolution: Doctrine and Action, 1789–1804*, trans. Salvator Attanasio (1971; Princeton: Princeton University Press, 1981), 50–66.

29. Burke, 45–54 and 255.

30. Burke, 90–91, 232–35 and 249–51.

31. Burke, 130–33 and 165–67.

32. Burke, 129–30, 143, and 235–36.

33. This process can be seen especially in conservative popular literary magazines of the 1820s and 1830s, such as *Fraser's Magazine* and *Blackwood's Magazine*.   Peter Murphy's recent essay, "Impersonation and Authorship in Romantic Britain," *ELH* 59 (1992): 625–49, demonstrates the consequences of this new ideology of reception for both writers and readers.

34. Burke, 251.

35. Goodwin, 86–91, 110–29, and 239–53; and Cookson, 30–83.

36. Mitchell, 195–238.

Representations of Revolutionary Women in Political Caricature

Jane Kromm

The critical role played by visual culture in shaping the arguments of the Revolution debate is most evident in the political caricatures of the 1790s. Engravings of revolutionary events and of British responses to them provided a visual apparatus through which basic information about key players and occurrences could be communicated. Because representations are not transparent reflections of actualities, a significant attribute of these political prints is the way they constructed incidents and personalities through the canny manipulation of verism and distortion. These tactical adjustments positioned the engravings to function as formative influences on public opinion, and this influence was pivotal to the debate's exchanges over the nature of human nature and social change. In an effort to clarify the terms of these exchanges, representations of French revolutionary women in British political caricature cast them in an unflattering and particularly unnatural light.[1] This essay analyzes the cultural, political, and visual elements that supported the formation of this representational practice. Indeed, the interdependence of these elements enabled the practice to assume, even in the face of obvious satirical exaggeration, a position of documentary accuracy, eventually extending to include not just the revolutionary women themselves, but the figures of any woman with political or public sphere associations.

The market for political caricatures was well-established by the 1780s, when London boasted a number of printshops, like those of S. W. Fores in Piccadilly and of William Holland in Oxford Street, both of which had opened in January 1784.[2] At these and other locations around the city, engravings on topical subjects including images of the most recent revolutionary events in France were published, exhibited, and sold. From 1789 through 1794, Holland and Fores advertised permanent exhibitions of caricatures on French revolutionary subjects in the hopes of attracting and maintaining an interested clientele.[3] William Humphrey, with a shop in the Strand, and Mrs. Hannah Humphrey, who offered Gillray's prints exclusively after 1791 at her Bond Street establishment, were similarly keen competitors for the market in political caricature.[4]

The first prints on revolutionary subjects were largely favorable reactions, which appeared not long after the events themselves. Most were shaped by preoccupations with domestic advantage, such as the decline of French military potential or the victory of reform over privilege.[5] These favorable constructions of French events were eventually replaced by more negative responses, which feared a contagion of revolutionary causes among reformers, especially dissenters, at home.[6] According to Dorothy George, the very first negative prints on French revolutionary events targeted such high profile dissenters as Richard Price and Joseph Priestley.[7] A more anxious, negative position was enhanced by events just before and during the Terror, and subsequent prints after 1792 and through as late as 1799 construed revolutionary activities as mindless, anarchic, destructive acts of Jacobinism. This outright hostile position was reinforced by the outbreak of war between France and England in 1793.[8]

Those revolutionary events that first attracted the most attention in British political caricature were the storming of the Bastille and the October Days march to Versailles.[9] Both incidents were treated as variations on a generic mob or riot scene derived principally from the Gordon riots of recent British experience in which the crowd-defining characteristics of destructive and libertine behavior had been most lately reinforced.[10] Yet each of the two revolutionary incidents received a significantly different emphasis and valuation. Whereas the Bastille scenes received a clearly positive treatment in their emphasis on the vagaries of French carceral practices and on liberation as a suitable response to them, the march on Versailles was treated as a more potentially negative processional scene of marginal women. The earliest caricatures in which French women figure prominently are those which make reference to the October Days events.

Representative of this second group of crowd scenes is Isaac Cruikshank's (1756–1811) *Le roi esclave ou les sujets rois, Female Patriotism*. It shows the return of the women from Versailles and was published on October 31, 1789, by Fores and sold at his shop in Piccadilly. Born in Edinburgh, Cruikshank was established as an artist in London by 1784. His work in caricature was fairly modest throughout the decade, but he hit his stride by 1789, and thereafter, his work was confident and profuse.[11] He established a specialty in French subjects early on, and so was well-positioned to interpret revolutionary subjects from the outset.[12] His personal political bearings are difficult to detect: some of his caricatures are pro-French, but he attacked Paine and Priestley in others. Burke, Pitt, and Fox also were targets of his satire. He was in direct competition with Gillray, which had the effect of making both artists influences on each other, although Gillray's bite was usually the more caustic and his orientation the more consistently conservative, antirevolutionary one.[13]

In *Le roi esclave*, a range of women from several classes prods and threatens the slightly caricatured royal family and much exaggerated General Lafayette on the return march from Versailles to Paris. Sharp implements, including pikes, muskets, and swords, a hoisted decapitated head, and bodies hanging from a gibbet in the distance attest to the women's violent inclinations. The threatening snippets of French dialogue above their heads similarly underscore their belligerent capabilities. Soldiers of the National Guard are visible behind, but the most specifically delineated individuals in the phalanx of marchers are the women who, significantly, seem at first glance to be *less* caricatured than are the royal family and Lafayette. The practice of mixing degrees of caricatural exaggeration with more realistic, seemingly documentary aspects within a single political satire has been occasionally noted, but the significance of the mixture and the interpretative weight such mixing bears have received less scholarly attention.[14] In *Le roi esclave*, precisely because the women are in close proximity to more obvious objects of satirical license, their own delineation achieves, by virtue of this contrast, a less ambiguous position of documentary validity.[15]

The varied range of depicted women likewise encourages the viewer to regard this part of the image as a convincing rendition of the October Days events. There are well-dressed, elaborately coiffed, upper-class women, lower-class women in mobcaps, and wagon-hauling political activists, possibly including the militant feminist revolutionary Theroigne de Mericourt.[16] This latter group's association with the Cordeliers is proclaimed by a banner. Interspersed among all classes of participants are women whose decolletage under the circumstances marks them as possible prostitutes. There is thus a distinct and persistent emphasis on the attractive and seductive demeanor of these women which is combined with the threat of their violent potential, here visually directed pointedly towards men (Louis XVI, the decapitated head, Lafayette, bodies suspended from the gibbet). While it might seem that the two elements of violence and seduction ought to carry a more symbolic than realistic inflection, the relative absence of visual distortion serves rather to indicate that French women actually looked and behaved this way, whereas the royal family and Lafayette were unlikely to have been as hapless and ineffectual as they are here rendered. Thus, the less-caricatured elements could be used to show the greater distortion of reality.

In a subsequent engraving published in December 1792, Cruikshank adapted this gendered combination of violent potential and seductive demeanor from the level of actual revolutionary participants in delimited events to that of allegory in *The Genius of France Extirpating Despotism, Tyranny and Oppression from the Face of the Earth or the Royal Warriors Defeated*. The print is a reaction to several defeats that had been recently suffered by various allied forces.[17] Amidst numerous heads of state, including the two female rulers Catherine of Russia and Maria I of Portugal, the Republic is portrayed as a revolutionary partisan conceived in an unusually positive light for a British image as both allegory *and* contemporary description.[18] The Republic is young, attractive in her phrygian bonnet, the popular red cap of liberty, and is shown as a staunch defender of human rights against various forms of tyranny. Her captioned exertions suggest that France will set the example for democracy among the debased and deficient European powers. Notable among these are the two women: Catherine is a helmeted militant warrior who goads into the fray the rulers she physically overwhelms, and the already "dismounted" Maria of Portugal is shown dishevelled and tearing her disordered hair. These sexualized effects of madness, along with her staring, unfocused expression, are recognizable indexes of the insanity from which Maria is known to have suffered. Although the print in its entirety offers a positive assessment of the French cause, these three figures, the allegorical yet descriptive Republic and the two royal female bodies, continue to circulate the phenomena of violence and allure as contiguous, gendered elements among women active in the political sphere. While falling far short of the more typical British renderings of the Republic or Liberty as a monstrous summation of those contiguous elements, nevertheless their plausible distribution across three female historical figures in Cruikshank's image actually adds to, rather than detracts from, their veristic potential.

Yet even this minimally positive stage in representing French revolutionary events in relation to the idea of women connected with them was shortlived. By 1793, the monstrous collation of negative attributes for the female Republic or Liberty had become the norm.[19] This development is immediately apparent in two caricatures of December 1793 and February 1794 respectively, William Dent's *The French Feast of Reason, or the Cloven-Foot Triumphant* and Cruikshank's *A Peace Offering to the Genius of Liberty and Equality*.[20] Dent's engraving is a satire on the recent (November 10) festival of reason (held in the de-Christianized interior of Notre Dame) in which an opera singer had enacted the role of Liberty.[21] She is shown as a hefty Medusa, seated atop Pandora's box, a staff surmounted with a phrygian cap decorated with a guillotine inelegantly placed between her legs. Dent here makes use of an increasingly common satirical device in which the female horrors of Greek legend who showcased sexualized violence, especially Medusa, Medea, and the furies, are invoked as representations of the Republic.[22] They are deployed as inversions of the more positive, Athena-derived allegorical figures favored increasingly among the French. This British satirical practice is an indication that Burke's description of the October Days women had not only flourished but had multiplied. Burke envisioned them "amidst the horrid yells, and shrilling screams, and frantic dances, and infamous contumelies, and all the unutterable abominations of the furies of hell, in the abused shape of the vilest of women."[23] One man kisses Liberty's extended cloven hoof, while a group behind him sings a revised ode that advocates killing and plunder. To the left, two aristocrats kneel praying at Liberty's feet; they are encroached upon by a mob of the people, the most prominent of whom are destroying cross and crozier. As before, the French mob is depicted through the template of the Gordon riots as an uncontrollable, insatiable, destructive force.

The plate is accompanied by an elaborate array of verbal accessories as well as a lengthy explanatory key along the print's lower portion in which Dent assures us that "tho' a satyrical [it is] a just representation." There are references to specific, recently assassinated revolutionaries, like "Tyger" Marat and "Monkey" Lepelletier. The banners held aloft by the crowd show Truth, Reason, Nature, Liberty, and Equality, but these are represented by inversions of the standard iconography for such abstractions. For example, Reason is a reason-less, raving maniac in chains, and Nature is an unnatural, Medea-like woman depicted in the act of killing a child. References to actual revolutionary women have been omitted in this print, but the emphasis on violence and sexuality associated with their earlier presence in similar satires continues to be present in the images of Liberty and Nature. This allusory mechanism, along with the awareness of the French practice of using contemporary women to act out allegorical personae, keeps the connection between the behavioral tendencies of actual women participants in revolutionary events and gendered representations of abstractions on a recognizable continuum.

In Cruikshank's print, this representational practice has an even more grotesque outcome. Here various British politicians of the Opposition are satirized as sansculottes approaching a monstrous Republic and proffering gifts to secure the peace.[24] She is a Medusa-as-sansculotte slattern: the snakes entwined in her hair proclaim rapine, murder, famine, and atheism, while snakes also appear from between her pendulous, phallic-like breasts as she sits, armed with a knife, swilling gin. Before her throne of gin barrels lies a decapitated Liberty, her classicizing raiment in sexualized disarray. Cruikshank's anti-Terror configuration for this caricature, in which it is implied that the state of France is a chaos of all kinds of human disorders, was in reaction both to Stanhope's attempt to move that the Republic be offically acknowledged and to fears that Jacobin attacks at home were accelerating.[25] Consequently, the emphasis on the actions of British politicians receives the most elaboration, insulting these men as supplicants of a debased principle. Still, the delineation of the Republic in the form of a masculinized, hard-drinking, knife-wielding woman of the people, as well as her immediate victim, the decapitated, breast-baring Liberty, continues to be focalized around a debased, public sphere iconography for the rendering of female figures.

These images of female figures can be seen to occupy points in a significant representational trajectory. This trajectory begins with depictions of actual participants whose violent, seductive tendencies could be construed as documentary features when shown in contrast to the more caricatural elements which accompanied them. It then moves to an exaggerated insistence on these qualities in what would appear to be the more abstract, less realistic format of the allegorical figure, but which despite some distancing effects, keeps these qualities in visual circulation. The trajectory comes full circle after 1793 when British caricatures of the situation in France, motivated by an injunction to show scenes of a persisting state of Terror and inspired by Burke's prophetic "horrid paintings" of that eventuality, return to the subject of actual women participants.[26] Among numerous examples, another print by Cruikshank demonstrates this return to what can be described as the October days iconography of a mob comprised primarily of unruly women.

Cruikshank's *Lord Mum Overwhelmed with Parisian Embraces*, published in November 1796 and sold out of Fores' shop, shows the entourage of Lord Malmesbury being overrun by a crowd in which Parisian women figure prominently. The event to which the print refers actually took place outside Paris in Evreux, but many in addition to Cruikshank repositioned the unseemly reception to the city.[27] A tattered, impoverished assemblage, seemingly capable of varied destructive and/or licentious acts, surrounds Malmesbury's coach. There are many mentally crazed, eye-bulging visages, much cap-waving and cap-throwing among the men in the background, while the foreground consists principally of the female, radical, lower-class *poissardes*. Some seem to be pulling the coach along, a function similar to that performed by the revolutionary participants of the march from Versailles; others queue up to kiss the British lord, bringing the essentially frivolous, sexualized nature of their participation to the fore. In other words, this is yet another British construction of crowd behavior in France that sustains an inaccurate picture of events and participants. The scene is still indebted to the Gordon riots' behavioral paradigm, but with the difference that here, the masculine majority provides a mere chorus for the women who are the more visible, active elements in the mob. Their enthusiastic participation, ugliness, as well as the repeated motif of exposed pendent breasts, show the libertine unnaturalness of their condition. These qualities indicate that such a degree of enthusiasm is still very much in evidence among French women, and that it is dangerous, unreliable, and inseparable from an aggressive, and hence undesirable, sexuality. The significance of this amalgamation of qualities threaded throughout all the representations of politically effective women discussed here lies in their resemblance to those associated with the rising gender stereotype for madness in women.[28]

As is well-known, imputations of madness were regularly directed against key players and events throughout the Revolutionary decade. Numerous attempts were made to relate different constructions of mental imbalance to French revolutionary acts, processes, discourses, and personalities, as well as to the dominant participants in the Revolution debate in England. There were initially some who advocated an optimistic position about madness and revolution, thinking that as the latter brought an end to hierarchies of oppression, so would it bring an end to the incidence of the former.[29] However, especially after the Terror, the opinion that revolutionary upheavals aggravated or even produced dangerously disordered behavior became increasingly common.[30] Some further claimed that an inevitable side effect of the social "leveling" advocated by revolutionaries was an exacerbation of mental instability.[31]

One common device by which the absence of reason had been gauged, in part in response to the experience of the Gordon riots, was the spectre of mob behavior understood as the unruly conduct of the common people when social constraints were no longer respected, opening a "Pandora's box" of destructive and sexual impulses. Much of Burke's rhetoric conforms to this distinction between reason, social order, and tradition versus madness as unreason, discord, and confusion. It is evident when, for example, he contrasts "this world of reason, and order, and peace, and virtue, and fruitful penitence" with "the antagonist world of madness, discord, vice, confusion, and unavailing sorrow."[32] But Burke's unambiguous stance in advocating such a clear-cut binary distinction ironically did not protect him from attracting charges of insanity himself which were leveled by friend and foe alike.[33] A similar situation afflicted Paine: while his writings urged the necessity of distinguishing mad acts from revolutionary ones, he was regularly satirized as "Mad Tom," a reference to the traditional wandering insane beggar, Tom O' Bedlam.[34]

Many draftsmen and engravers were likewise drawn to take up this satirical discourse of madness in their topical political prints. When the subject of this satire is male political players, the discourse is focalized around the issues of rationality, agency, and obsessional pride.[35] Thomas Rowlandson's *A Peep into Bethlehem* (c. 1792–93) is representative of the use to which imputations of madness could be put in the print culture of the revolutionary decade.[36] Burke, a rosary visible against his naked chest, strikes the traditional pose of the deluded rhetorician, a common device in eighteenth-century British constructions of madness deployed to signify eloquence without judgment. Wolcot (Peter Pindar) is the spellbound audience of one, his rapt attention to Burke's verbal excesses demonstrating that madness among men is located in the world of ideas and debate.[37] They fail to acknowledge the presence of a raving woman behind them, despite her attention-attracting features of decolletage, disordered hair, upraised fists clenched with straw, and fierce expression. She is Margaret Nicholson, who had been admitted to Bethlehem in 1786 following an assassination attempt upon George III with a dessert knife.[38]

The gendered constructions of madness that Rowlandson relied upon here were in the one case totally familiar, even old-fashioned, and in the other, a novel invention first appearing in the 1780s and 90s.[39] While wild, dishevelled hair, dress, and behavior as indices of madness in women had a venerable ancestry going back at least as far as Ophelia, visual representations of this cluster of attributes did not appear until the 1780s. These attributes stress those features of madness in women that associate it with the excessively natural and nonrational, usually also with a sexual, sometimes even bestial and violent, cast.[40] By concentrating on female madness as a nonrational phenomena and masculine madness as a condition of *too much* rationality, this satirical device keeps the issue of masculine rational ability separate and pre-eminent, ensuring that it appear to be a higher order of dysfunction to the extent that it remains defined by reason than that suffered by the de-natured women. As in Dent's festival banners, reason may be visualized in inverted form as a raving maniac in chains as it often was throughout the eighteenth century, but nature inverted is a woman abusing her child in what is clearly gauged to be the more startling, antisocial act of madness. It is woman as a flawed creature of nature who fails to conform to her familial role that qualifies her for a madness of sexualized monstrosity like the furies, Medusa, or Medea.

During the Revolutionary decade, the features associated with the new gender stereotype for madness in women were combined with the particularly British iconography of the French mob scene to produce the figure of the unruly female participant in revolutionary events. The representational and political significance of this development for women can be further demonstrated by two other prints produced just before and just after the 1790s. Both prints make reference to a specific person engaged in political activities, the Duchess of Gordon.

The earlier print of February 1789 by Rowlandson relates to a group of satires he produced around the political intrigues catalyzed by George III's mentally disabling attacks. At least five of these question the mental stability of the various court factions, some favoring the king's recovery and others not, and three specifically refer to Dr. Francis Willis who had been called in on December 5, 1788, to serve as special consultant to the ailing king.[41] In *The Hospital for Lunatics*, two men and a woman occupy individual cells as a doctor and keeper approach.[42] The doctor observes, "I see no signs of convalesence," and the keeper responds, "They must all be in a state of coercion." He brings the straitjackets that will effect this coercion. Among the inmates, William Pitt wears a straw crown; the caption explains that he went mad from picturing himself as the royal heir. The Duke of Richmond sports a chamberpot as headgear; he has gone mad from the study of fortifications, toy versions of which lie at his feet. The seated female figure is chained by the neck to her cell. Her hair is attractively loosened, her dress is in disarray, baring much of the breast that she is scratching. The caption above explains that she has been "Driven mad by a Political itching." The sexual nature of her political interest and engagement is thus unambiguously expressed. Dorothy George has suggested that this woman is the Duchess of Gordon, well known for her quarrelsome interventions throughout the Regency crisis. In the anonymous *Female Politicians* of 1801, she is depicted tearing the hair of a young female opponent after first having torn off her bodice.[43] These portrayals just before and after the Revolutionary decade set and maintain the construction of women's participation in political processes as symptomatic of madness, calling attention to its sexualized, regressive unnaturalness.[44] Hence the significance of the features—decolletage and/or exposed breasts, hair and clothes in sexualized disarray—given to French women revolutionaries and female allegorical figures in British political satires of the revolution is that they are visual indices for a narrowly conceived and recently established gender stereotype of madness which considerably underscores the unnatural quality already associated with women's public sphere engagement.[45]

Before the Revolution, French women were typically viewed as exemplifying too much of the wrong kind of influence in public life. During the

Revolutionary era, when the ideology of separate spheres widened the gender divide between private and public spaces, many conservatives in Britain were convinced that women's interference in politics constituted what was wrong with French republicanism.[46] Decrying the political participation of women as a specifically French practice increased after the outbreak of war in 1793.[47] A preoccupation with the need to reinstate familial authority by insisting that women's place be in the home became major elements in anti-Jacobin, counterrevolutionary propaganda.[48] And one of the most effective representations deployed to prove that the conditions of Terror persisted in France and threatened to cross the channel were those in which the streets of Paris were shown to be overrun with madwomen.[49]

Presenting women's political activity as an especially undesirable aspect of revolutionary upheaval was achieved in part by situating that activity within the satirical discourse of madness just at the moment when truth claims being made for the rising gender stereotype of madness in women were gaining credibility. Depictions of revolutionary women in political caricature are thus exemplary of the ways in which the visual reconstruction of French revolutionary events was subjected to persistent misrepresentation in the service of the Revolution debate's principal contested issues. The porous relations between allegory and realism, and between realism and distortion that are peculiar to the genre of political caricature, rendered it particularly useful in the campaign to redefine the Revolutionary decade so as to ensure the representational order of the future.

NOTES

1. On French women revolutionaries and their representation, see Lynn Hunt, *Politics, Culture and Class in the French Revolution* (Berkeley: University of California Press, 1984); Joan Landes, *Women and the Public Sphere in the Age of the French Revolution* (Ithaca, N.Y.: Cornell University Press, 1988); Paule-Marie Duhet, *Les femmes et la révolution 1789–1794* (Paris: Julliard, 1971); Darline Levy, Harriet Applewhite, and Mary Johnson, *Women in Revolutionary Paris 1789–1795* (Urbana: University of Illinois Press, 1979); Maurice Agulhon, *Marianne into Battle*, tr. Janet Lloyd (Cambridge: Cambridge University Press, 1981); Madelyn Gutwirth, "The Representation of Women in the Revolutionary Period: The Goddess of Reason and the Queen of the Night," *Consortium on Revolutionary Europe, Proceedings 1983* (Athens: University of Georgia Press, 1985), and *Twilight of the Goddesses* (New Brunswick: Rutgers University Press, 1992); Vivian Cameron, "Political Exposures: Sexuality and Caricature in the French Revolution," *Eroticism and the Body Politic*, ed. L. Hunt (Baltimore: Johns Hopkins University Press, 1991), 90–107. On British representations of revolutionary subjects, see David Bindman, *The Shadow of the Guillotine: Britain and the French Revolution* (London: British Museum, 1989); Ronald Paulson,

Representations of Revolution 1789–1820 (New Haven: Yale University Press, 1983); Linda Colley, *Britons Forging the Nation 1707–1837* (New Haven: Yale University Press, 1992). Of the many recent publications on caricature and printmaking during the Revolution, see Musée Carnavalet, *L'art de l'estampe et la Révolution française* (Paris: Musée Carnavalet, 1977); *Representing Revolution* (Amherst, Mass.: Amherst College, Mead Art Museum, 1989); *French Caricature and the French Revolution 1789–1799* (Los Angelos: Grunwald Center. for Graphic Arts, 1988); Robert Darnton and Daniel Roche, eds., *The Revolution in Print* (Berkeley: University of California Press, 1989); *Face to Face, French and English Caricatures of the French Revolution and its Aftermath* (Toronto: Art Gallery of Ontario, 1989); Michel Jouve, "L'Image du sans-culotte dans la caricature politique anglaise," *Gazette des Beaux-Arts* ser. 6 no. 92 (1978): 187–96. Jouve argues that the sansculotte replaces the aristocratic fop as the most insulting image of a French man.

2. M. D. George, *English Political Caricature*, 2 vols. (Oxford: Clarendon, 1959–1960), 1:173.

3. George, 1:205.

4. George, 1:175; John Wardroper, *The Caricatures of George Cruikshank* (Boston: Godine, 1978), 8. See also E. B. Krumbhaar, *Isaac Cruikshank, a Catalogue Raisonné* (Philadelphia: University of Pennsylvania Press, 1966); William Bates, *George Cruikshank* (N.Y.: Schramm, 1972). Before 1791, Gillray's prints were published by William Humphrey and Fores. See George, 1:175 and Richard Godfrey, *Printmaking in Britain* (N.Y.: New York University Press, 1978), 74, 77.

5. Sura Levine, "Print Culture in the Age of the French Revolution," *Representing Revolution,* 10; George, 1:206; Bindman, 28; John Brewer, "'This Monstrous Tragi-Comic Scene': British Reactions to the French Revolution" in Bindman,13.

6. Brewer 13, 17, and 19; Mark Philp, "The Fragmented Ideology of Reform," *The French Revolution and British Popular Politics*, ed. Philp (Cambridge: Cambridge University Press, 1991), 60.

7. George, 1:206.

8. George, 2:1.

9. George, 1:205.

10. Bindman, 45. Some caricatures of the Gordon riots include marginal women, seemingly prostitutes, among the crowd. See British Museum, *Catalogue of Political and Personal Satires*, 11 vols. (London: British Musuem, c. 1870–1954), cat. nos. 5684, 5844.

11. George, 1:172. Krumbhaar states that the British Museum catalogue lists 278 of Cruikshank's caricatures produced between 1793 and 1797 (20). He exhibited in the Royal Academy in 1789, 1790, and 1792. The titles of these now lost works suggest that they were sentimental narratives (Bates, 9; Wardroper, 8).

12. George, 1:205.

13. Krumbhaar, 21. Bindman notes that Gillray found Burke's position persuasive as early as 1790 (28).

14. Paulson has commented that such mixing is especially typical of Gillray (203). Levine claims that such mixtures are typical of all revolutionary caricatures (7).

15. This is also true of the figure of Marie Antoinette: she is less exaggerated than her son or husband, and Louis XVI's remark also isolates her as the cause of the family's difficulty.

16. George proposed the identification of one of these women as Theroigne (British Museum cat. no. 7560). Theroigne's involvement in the march to Versailles is now known to be a legend, but it was widely held at the time. See Duhet, 47; Marcellin Pellet, *Étude historique et biographique sur Theroigne de Mericourt* (Paris: Maison Quantin, n.d.), 25, 28.

17. Krumbhaar, 73; George, 1:218. George adds that it also acknowledges the Convention decree which promised to aid all those seeking liberty.

18. George comments that "In English prints the genius of Republican France is commonly a monstrosity. Here—uniquely—she is a comely young woman, wearing a Phrygian cap" (1:218).

19. As Lynn Hunt and others have shown, this is also the period during which French prototypes for the Republic became less radical, less related to the appearance of contemporary women, and more timeless and classized. See Hunt, *Politics* 61–62; chapters 2 and 3 *passim*.

20. Dent was an amateur caricaturist whose work was sold in various shops from 1783 to 1793. This, his last caricature, was sold at Aitken's in Leicester Square. See George, 1:205; 2:8. Cruikshank's engraving was published by Fores.

21. Such festivals often included, when held in the provinces, local beauties as Liberty, but also women from the various performing arts, all of whom were regarded as marginal to polite society. On the festivals, see Agulhon, *Marianne*, and Mona Ozouf, *Festivals and the French Revolution* (Cambridge, Mass.: Harvard University Press, 1988).

22. Brewer, 22; Kromm, "Representing Revolutionary Feminism and Madness: the 'Case' of Theroigne de Mericourt," unpublished manuscript.

23. *Reflections on the Revolution in France* (1790; N.Y.: Penguin, 1986), 165.

24. George, 2:9; Krumbhaar, 118, n. 882; British Museum cat. no. 8426.

25. George, 2:9. However, Cruikshank does not seem to have produced any explicitly propagandistic works for British anti-Jacobin, anti-Dissenter associations as Rowlandson did for the Anchor and Crown society. See Brewer, 18; George, 2:1.

26. The reference to Burke's description of the events in France as "horrid paintings" is Paine's. See *The Rights of Man* (1791; N.Y.: Penguin, 1984), 50. For the imperative of configuring the French situation, a one of abiding Terror, see Bindman 58–61; Brewer 27–28.

27. George, 2:26.

28. For a more detailed account of this development, see Kromm, "The Feminization of Madness in Visual Representation," *Feminist Studies*, 20.3 (1994): 507–35. For a general overview of women and madness during this period, see Elaine Showalter, *The Female Malady* (N.Y.: Pantheon, 1985); Roy Porter, *A Social History of Madness* (N.Y.: Weidenfeld and Nicolson, 1987), esp. ch. 6; Philip W. Martin, *Madwomen in Romantic Writing* (NY: St. Martin's, 1987); Yannick Ripa, *Women and Madness* (Cambridge: Polity, 1990).

29. See Elisabeth Roudinesco, *Theroigne de Mericourt, a Melancholic Woman during the Revolution*, tr. Martin Thom (London: Verso, 1991), 158 for the optimistic Montagnard orientation toward the relation between revolution and madness.

30. Several treatises and reports emphasizing the importance of revolutionary upheavals as causes of madness are cited in Françoise Jacob, "Faire la Révolution, est-ce devenir fou?: les aliénistes français du XIXP siècle jugent 1789," *L'Image de la Révolution française*, ed. Michel Vovelle, 4 vols. (Oxford: Pergamon, 1990), 3:2055–60. Her examples include a report from l'an III of the Hôpital général of LaGrave, Toulouse; Jean-Pierre Falret's *Observations et propositions médico-chirurgicales* (Paris, 1819); and J-B Bonfils, *De la folie or l'aliénation mentale* (Paris, 1819).

31. On the relationship between the revolutionary emphasis on "leveling" as an aspect of social instability conducive to madness, see Jan Goldstein, *Console and Classify* (Cambridge: Cambridge University Press, 1987), 159–60; Bindman, 26.

32. Brewer, 16; Burke, 195.   For other references to the insanity of revolutionary actions, see Burke, 90, 121, 127, 181–82, 195, 232, 279, 332.

33. Among various sources, see Roy Porter, *Mind-forg'd Manacles* (Cambridge, Mass.: Harvard University Press, 1987), 15, 233, 234.

34. Paine 50–51; 58–59.   Political caricatures in the British Museum collection showing Paine as Mad Tom include cat. nos. 7900, 8087, 8132, 8143. The author is working on a separate study of Mary Wollstonecraft's constructions of madness in her political writings and her novels.   Wollstonecraft was particularly critical of those aspects of women's education and socialization that made them vulnerable to mental conditions such as neurasthenia.   Her own unconventional behavior and suicide attempts, however, qualified her in the eyes of many as an example of the psychological trauma associated with women who engaged in public-sphere activities.

35. British Museum cat. nos. 7624, 7626, 7656, 7691, 7867.

36. British Museum cat. no. 8367. Other satires of Burke insane include nos. 7529, 7685, 7689.

37. This construction of madness is more like Locke's position that madness consists in the "putting together [of] wrong ideas" than Burke's own insistence that madness is an *absence* of reason.   See Michael Deporte, *Nightmares and Hobbyhorses* (San Marino, Calif.: Huntington Library, 1974).

38. Porter, 115. Engravings of the men who attempted to assassinate George III, such as James Hadfield, are not caricatured visually as madmen. See British Museum cat. nos. 9539, 9540.

39. See Kromm, "The Feminization of Madness."

40. For an interesting discussion of the persistent association of women with the natural as opposed to the cultural, see Sylvana Tomaselli, "The Enlightenment Debate on Women," *History Workshop Journal* 20 (1985): 101–124.

41. On the nature of George III's illness, see Richard Hunter and Ida Macalpine, *George III and the Madbusiness* (N.Y.: Pantheon, 1970). Satires of the king that broach issues of madness or incarceration include British Museum cat. nos. 5979, 7378, 7394, 7495, 7504, 7514, 7519, 7527, 7529, and 7546. None shows the king insane. This contrasts with the case of Maria I of Portugal, another royal client of Dr. Willis, who was represented in a state of insanity (British Museum cat. no. 8143).

42. British Museum cat. no. 7504. Joseph Grego suggested that Henry Wigstead had worked with Rowlandson on this print. See his *Rowlandson the Caricaturist*, 2 vols. (London: Chatto & Windus, 1880), 1:247. There is another version which, instead of the woman, has a man who "went mad and fancied himself a Taylor's Goose" (Grego, 1:247).

43. British Museum cat. no. 9775.

44. See Kromm, "Gender and the Scopic Economies."

45. The Duchess of Devonshire received a similar treatment in satires of the mid to late 1780s (Colley, 245).

46. Colley, 404, n. 23; 250–52. For a more complete discussion of separate spheres ideology, see Mary Poovey, *The Proper Lady and the Woman Writer* (Chicago: University of Chicago Press, 1984); and Landes, *Women and the Public Sphere*.

47. Colley, 253. Ironically, women's participation in French politics was systematically discouraged at this time through different measures: Marie Antoinette was executed on October 16, 1793; women's political clubs were ordered closed on October 30, 1793; Olympe de Gouges was executed on November 1, 1793. The *Moniteur universel* of November 19, 1793 hoped that these events would be effective in "teaching women a lesson."

48. Brewer, 25; Philp, 60.

49. Isaac's son, the more successful caricaturist George Cruikshank, continued to use the unruly, sexually pointed features for depicting politically active women, as in *The Belle Alliance, or the Female Reformers of Blackburn* and *The Radical's Arms*, both of 1819.

Postscript: The French Revolution and Romanticism

David Bromwich

English departments have long offered courses on the Romantic poets which featured Blake, Wordsworth, Coleridge, Byron, Shelley, and Keats: the great originals of the time, only one of them a fashionable writer. A cultural approach may now add Hemans, Southey, and a number of others felt to be interesting as they reveal the conditions of contemporary success: one reads them to understand the taste of the age at its best, its worst, and its most typical. For the past several years, I have taught a lecture course on "The Literature of Romanticism" with a more confused design than either of these. I ask students to read the poets from Blake to Keats; but we begin with Burke's *Reflections* and Paine's *Rights of Man*; we end with Scott's *Heart of Mid-Lothian*; in the middle we read, for counterpoint, and for a possible harmony with each other *Pride and Prejudice* and the *Vindication of the Rights of Woman*. The idea is to place the writers who seem, in a broad sense, conservative—Burke, Austen, Scott—in dialogue with exemplars of the radical spirit of the age and to suggest that certain anxieties and certain interests were shared by all. To complicate the picture, we turn, in the middle of Shelley, to read Mary Shelley's *Frankenstein* as an anti-Promethean tract, a criticism of *Alastor* that seems to have prompted the extraordinary self-revision that is *Prometheus Unbound*. The aim is to show that "the personal is political," in a way not intended by the coiners of that slogan. An observation by a well-situated friend, critic, and novelist, regarding the influence of a moral imagination, might dispose a great poet to change his faith from an ethic of solitude and revenge to an ethic of solidarity and reform, accompanied by a more than Christian appeal to forgiveness. The power of Romantic writing and the permanence of the questions it returns to us are such that a change like this can always seem a vivid possibility. Or so the anecdote of Mary Shelley's effects on Percy Bysshe Shelley is meant to suggest.

To characterize the period 1789–1832 as Romantic is merely to accept a convention. It is a useful convention, I think, for scholarship as well as teaching, but in accepting it one must recall that no author we now read under this heading would have recognized the description. To the extent that the authors associated themselves with a movement—Byron, at moments, did, and Coleridge and Shelley knew what he meant—they would have been surprised to see the other names and the works with which we link them. Romanticism is a term convenient for us, not them; but it can still help us to think about some motives for reflection and action that had their start two centuries ago; and given sufficient irony, one need not be embarrassed by the word: the trouble with the alternative—with a detached systematic vocabulary about anything—is that its equipment for thinking is apt to come from even simpler anachronisms about "class," "discourse," "conjuncture," or "status quo." Romanticism, from Burke and Wordsworth on, had to do with thoughts of a new liberality and frankness about oneself, about the larger communities in which one was a participant, and about everything that persists beyond the reach of those communities. We may call the last thing "nature," but nature in a sense that includes mankind, since it incorporates an idea of human nature. When in Romantic writing one encounters the word *nature*, it almost never seems to draw a circle around rivers, mountains, forests, and the other constituents of the living world. These belong to the idea but are far from the whole of it. To acknowledge such elemental forces as outside the human frame of things could only mean to adopt them as symbols of the integrity of things-as-they-are. Yet a leading premise of Romanticism is that one can hardly think even of natural objects without insensibly connecting them with an idea of things as they ought to be.

The writers of the period offer fresh thoughts "about oneself"—what can that mean? The beliefs we share today about the distinctness of personal identity seem so plainly a *given* that we are apt to assume they were always so; that this kind of self-consciousness was known, quite generally, in earlier times and that it was known to carry a peculiar importance. But neither supposition is true. Nietzsche said the idea of the self was so improbable a fruit of progress that it had remained unplucked on the tree of thought for millennia. This need not mean that in classical Greece and Rome and under the feudal system there were no individuals, not one person who harbored the thought, "I am a unique and inseparable being; there are truths I know respecting myself and the world that nobody else knows in the same way." Doubtless there were such people. It is an important fact about them and their cultures that in every earlier time of the world they were people who had nowhere to go. There was no broader life—no life of experience and reflection—in which their intuitions of a self could be confirmed. Intellectual historians like J. H. Van Den Berg and Charles Taylor have variously located the beginnings of the modern idea of the self. The germ of it, we are sometimes told, was already in Luther and Montaigne; it does seem traceable to the general spirit of reformation in religion, and of secularization in letters. However, the kind of individual consciousness that we find in Romantic poets and prose writers has a more immediate source a generation before, in the writings of Rousseau.

For French politics and moral theory, Rousseau's most influential works are the *Social Contract* and the *Discourse on Inequality*. For the English writers we are now considering, the great book is his *Confessions*, which opens with a remarkable sentence: "I have resolved on an enterprise which has no precedent, and which, once complete, will have no imitator. My purpose is to display to my kind a portrait in every way true to nature, and the man I shall portray will be myself." I do not think Rousseau can have meant that no one after him would write an autobiography—though his egotism certainly made him capable of such a conceit. What, then, when he spoke of an enterprise without precedent and without an imitator, did he imagine his readers would take him to be saying? Rousseau implies that he has seen and felt certain things, that there are experiences that are uniquely his; he believes that the record of those experiences will have value as an exemplary human testimony. Could the same be true of the story of any of us? The inference from the *Confessions* is: yes, potentially yes, for any of us. We cannot be sure in advance how somebody else's story may affect our imagining of our own: that is the only excuse for reading such a book and the only excuse for writing it. This may seem a simple truth about literature generally; but even with the innovative fictions of the eighteenth century, with Diderot and Laclos as much as Richardson, we read in some degree forearmed by an existing impression of character—whether the character represents a particular social role or the predicament of a whole society. On the other hand, to come to terms with Rousseau means for a self to regard another self. The effects of the discovery will not be the same in any two such encounters. This suggestion, from the opening pages of the *Confessions*, will have broad consequences for criticism and interpretation in the nineteenth century. Emphatically, for Rousseau there is a truth of reading; there are wrong readings and empty readings; but it is not possible to suppose that criticism is a progress toward one right reading.

The Rousseauian thought about the individuality of any life and its unique testimony points to a psychological change in the understanding of books and writers. The fact was observed at the time—suspicion of the effects was part of the burden of the anti-Rousseau invective of Burke's *Letter to a Member of the National Assembly*—and the change was supposed to have direct political implications of a leveling sort. Any writer of whatever class, rank, or status, could now be judged individually by any reader. This is another way of saying that the interest of autobiography comes with a shift from a culture based on patronage to a culture based on public opinion. I am giving a strong version of an analysis which was itself common in the years between the French Revolution and the first Reform Bill—an analysis which took for granted that an interest in reading about the self might foreshadow the enfranchisement of many as yet unacknowledged persons. But the radical perception for those who first ventured it was stronger than any conceivable summary. Here is William Hazlitt in 1829, remembering what it felt like to read Rousseau in the 1790s:

Before we can take an author entirely to our bosoms, he must be another self; and he cannot be this, if he is "not one but all mankind's epitome." It was this which gave such an effect to Rousseau's writings, that he stamped his own character and the image of his self-love on the public mind—*there* it is, and there it will remain in spite of everything. Had he possessed more comprehension of thought or feeling, it would only have diverted him from his object. But it was the excess of his egotism and his utter blindness to everything else, that found a corresponding sympathy in the conscious feelings of every human breast, and shattered to pieces the pride of rank and circumstance by the pride of internal worth or upstart pretension. Till then, birth and wealth and power were all in all, though but the frame-work or crust that envelopes the man; and what there was in the man himself was never asked, or was scorned and forgot. And while all was dark and grovelling within, while knowledge either did not exist or was confined to a few, while material power and advantages were everything, this was naturally to be expected. But with the increase and diffusion of knowledge, this state of things must sooner or later cease; and Rousseau was the first who held the torch lighted at the never-dying fire in his own bosom) to the hidden chambers of the mind of man—like another Prometheus, breathed into his nostrils the breath of a new and intellectual life, enraging the Gods of the earth, and made him feel what is due to himself and his fellows. Shall we think only rank and pedigree divine, when we have music, poetry, and painting within us? Tut! we have read *Old Mortality*; and shall it be asked whether we have done so in a garret or a palace, foot? Or knowing them, shall we not revere the mighty heirs of fame, and respect ourselves for knowing thee?

It is a striking commentary and itself a sort of confession.

When Hazlitt speaks of Rousseau as another Prometheus, the allusion may seem a personal extravagance. But the same comparison of Rousseau with Prometheus occurs with surprising insistence elsewhere—for example, in an early notice of his writings by Mary Wollstonecraft. And in one way or another this becomes a powerful element in the Romantic idea of any original imagination. Why Prometheus? He stole the gift of fire from the gods, conveyed it to man, and by doing so made man able to rival the gods themselves. The fire, in the story Hazlitt is telling, corresponds to the new and radical standard of internal worth, the belief that a thought has some value by virtue simply of being mine. Once the gift is given, the hierarchies of the earth, the whole established order in politics and morality and religion, will be shaken to the foundations. So it appears that self-knowledge, of this unprecedented kind, is a knowledge from which there can be no turning back, any more than for paganism there could be a turning back from the humanized god of Christianity. The discovery of one self inseparable from the discovery of "another self" is part of a long history of progress, or as Hazlitt gladly consents to call it, the March of Intellect. It is the latest step and its effects he says ought now to command our attention. His *Life of Napoleon*, written about the same time, gives a literal and historical translation of the same fable: "The French revolution might be described as a remote but inevitable result of the invention of the art of printing." In the act of reading and judging alone are contained the seeds of a self-respect which will be broadcast as a belief in democratic equality and representation.

In the Romantic view, the discovery of the self is not a selfish discovery. By reading, by abstraction, it connects me with a community beyond the parochial demands I associate with my parents or the beliefs and prejudices I inherit from my placement in a given culture at a given time. That larger and impalpable community, which I was not given but chose, relates me conceivably to anyone, and therefore it seems to everyone. The belief in the self is thus the only faith still available that makes the sort of universalist claims we usually identify with religious commitments or with moral duties. And the advocates of the French Revolution were the first to capture that intuition when they made liberty, the liberty of the individual in questions of conscience and property, the concomitant of fraternity and equality: the fraternity of persons who owe something to each other as fellow citizens even before they know each other's identity; and the equality of persons who do not rule out any kind of person as a possible sharer in the project of liberty. That the belief in the self had a potency to take the place of religion has been conceded by those least apt to sympathize with the belief itself. I have in mind a passage of Matthew Arnold's "Function of Criticism at the Present Time" which admits the "force, truth, and universality" of the ideas of the French Revolution and commends the ideas for their "unique and still living power." The challenge that remained for writers after Burke and Wordsworth was how far such hopes could govern the moral conduct of a community apart from the thrall of religious authority. Today the self and its liberties continue to pose the same challenge, though the institutions against the self now commonly shun the name of religion and call themselves by names drawn from the quasi-religious authority of politics or culture.

The idea that the freedom of an experimenting self might belong to *everyone* gives the literature that followed that revolution its character of novelty and universality. This is so because, to repeat, only the self connects me with humanity at large. The point appears in the past decade or two to have become counterintuitive, and will bear some elaboration. It feels more natural, more logical, to many people now, to suppose that the self links up with local interests, and that only an actual community of persons sharing certain practices could lead us by association to the universal community of mankind. Lurking somewhere in this mental picture is a scheme of impenetrable boundaries:

self—local interests

---

community—universal interests

On the modern communitarian hypothesis, the self is composed of stray particulars, captivating perhaps, but with no meaning on their own; these constitutive interests pick up reality as they are shared, and the sharing happens of course in a community. The community, then, of which one is a conscious member—this entity connects one with the fate of an otherwise unfathomable humanity, itself dimly distinguishable from its contributing lesser communities.

Part of the appeal of Romantic idealism is that it reverses these now intuitive and conventional expectations. It does so by means of the imaginative identification of a self with the community of humankind. There are Enlightenment echoes in my phrasing, from Hume above all, for this power of general sympathy from an abstraction of personal experience is the single greatest inheritance Romanticism owes to the Enlightenment. In the early Wordsworth, in Shelley, and even in Keats for all his hatred of didacticism, a very different scheme is presumed:

self—universal interests

community—local interests

When the Dissenting preacher and metaphysician Dr. Richard Price affirmed, in his sermon of November 4, 1789, that he rejoiced in the triumph of the French people over tyranny and oppression, and that he rejoiced as a "citizen of the world," he signalled the hold of this latter idea of moral association upon the minds of a generation. To celebrate "the love of our country," as Price did in the title of his sermon, implied no "conviction of the superior value of it to other countries, or any particular preference of its laws and constitution of government." One's country is the contingent home for oneself among a world of others. For me alone, in thinking about my duties toward them alone, will the bonds of principle be absolute. Price, more than other writer of the time, shows the long reach of Protestant liberty of conscience to a Romantic freedom of thought and action.

Price was a thinking man and a genuine moralist and deserves better than to be known chiefly for Burke's attack in the *Reflections*. But Burke at any rate was consistent. He distrusted the claims of all Protestant exceptionalism, and his irony hardened into scorn when he thought he could see an argument favoring "the dust and powder of individuality." It was a central and not an incidental purpose of the *Reflections* to meet head-on the pretension of generosity in Price's cosmopolitanism. You believe, says Burke, that your liberty relates you immediately to all mankind, but a sympathy like yours is morally impossible. Before you can be a citizen of the world, you must be a member of a family, then a neighbor of others in a small community, then and only then a citizen of a nation. "To be attached to the subdivision, to love the little platoon we belong to in society, is the first principle (the germ as it were) of public affections. It is the first link in the series by which we proceed towards a love to our country and to mankind." After the abstraction of a nation, long after, comes mankind. The self on this theory can have no authority for asserting an intimate relation to humanity at large, except through the mediating layers of attachment that give a reliable texture to its experience.

We come to a puzzle here. It would seem that Romanticism in literature, so plainly associated with the dignity of the individual mind, altogether warrants the rebuke from the antirevolutionist Burke, who writes to deplore the dust and powder of individuality. And yet Burke is viewed by many historians as a predecessor of Romanticism precisely for his naturalism, the "organicism" or "localism" of his thinking about the necessary bonds of a community. Wordsworth, for one, credited him as a formative influence for just such thoughts as those. The fairest conclusion may be that Romanticism cannot mean the taking of a single side in the debate about the self. It may imply rather an engagement in the debate at a certain intensity, and a dramatic feeling for what is at stake in the choice of any side at all. Not every writer of the period recognized that something new had come into the world with the French Revolution, something on which the fate of individuals and communities might depend for a long time after. Those who wrote without some such awareness, on amusing subjects and with amusing results, we now think of as talented writers who happened to work in the years 1789–1832. But for the ones we read with the interest I have been sketching, the debate about the political and moral world could evoke so strong a personal response as to force their language into code, or elicit a response at two removes in the form of an allegory. In the Preface to the *Lyrical Ballads*, Wordsworth calls the poet "the rock of defense for human nature; an upholder and preserver, carrying everywhere with him relationship and love." Why is human nature in need of defense? Why now? And why this character, the poet, in this particular cause? Wordsworth's argument is really circular, as Rousseau's idea of sympathy also was, but its power is none the less sustaining for that. We look to the poet for a defense of human nature because it is from the poet that we learn the adequacies of the imagination and the inadequacies of things as they are. The person who can make us start to see this, so that we continue to see it for ourselves, is the person whom we call the poet.

Select Bibliography

Abrams, M. H. *Natural Supernaturalism*. New York: Norton, 1973.

Ben-Israel, Hedva. *English Historians on the French Revolution*. Cambridge: Cambridge University Press, 1968.

Bindman, David. *The Shadow of the Guillotine: Britain and the French Revolution*. London: British Museum, 1989.

Blakemore, Steven. *Burke and the Fall of Language: The French Revolution as Linguistic Event*. Hanover, N.H: University Press of New England, 1988.

Boulton, James T. *The Language of Politics in the Age of Wilkes and Burke*. London: Routledge, 1963.

Bradley, James E. *Religion, Revolution, and English Radicalism*. Cambridge: Cambridge University Press, 1990.

Butler, Marilyn, ed. *Burke, Paine, Godwin, and the Revolution Controversy*. Cambridge: Cambridge University Press, 1984.

——. *Romantics, Rebels, and Reactionaries: English Literature and its Background, 1790–1830*. Oxford: Oxford University Press, 1981.

Chandler, James. *Wordsworth's Second Nature: A Study of the Poetry and Politics*. Chicago: University of Chicago Press, 1984.

Cobban, Alfred, ed. *The Debate on the French Revolution 1789–1800*. 2d ed. London: Adam and Charles Black, 1960.

——. *Edmund Burke and the Revolt Against the Eighteenth Century*. New York: Macmillan, 1929.

Cookson, J. E. *The Friends of Peace: Anti-War Liberalism in England, 1793–1815*. Cambridge: Cambridge University Press, 1982.

Deane, Seamus. *The French Revolution and the Enlightenment in England 1789–1832*. Cambridge: Harvard University Press, 1988.

Dickinson, H. T. *British Radicalism and the French Revolution 1789–1815*. Oxford: Blackwell, 1985.

Everest, Kelvin, ed. *Revolution in Writing: British Literary Responses to the*

    French Revolution. Milton Keynes: Open University Press, 1991.

Fletcher, Pauline, and John Murphy, eds. *Wordsworth in Context*. Lewisburg:
    Bucknell University Press, 1992.

Friedman, Barton. *Fabricating History: English Writers on the French
    Revolution*. Princeton: Princeton University Press, 1988.

Goodwin, Albert. *The Friends of Liberty: The English Democratic Movement in
    the Age of the French Revolution*. Cambridge: Harvard University Press,
    1979.

Hanley, Keith, and Raman Selden, eds. *Revolution and English Romanticism:
    Politics and Rhetoric*. London: Harvester Wheatsheaf; New York: St.
    Martin's, 1990.

Hirschman, A. O. *The Rhetoric of Reaction: Perversity, Futility, and Jeopardy*.
        Cambridge: Harvard University Press, 1991.

Hunt, Lynn. *Politics, Culture, and Class in the French Revolution*. Berkeley:
    University of California Press, 1984.

Izenberg, Gerald. *Impossible Individuality: Romanticism, Revolution, and the
    Origins of Modern Selfhood*. Princeton: Princeton University Press, 1992.

Johnston, Kenneth et al. *Romantic Revolutions: Criticism and Theory*.
    Bloomington: Indiana University Press, 1990.

Jones, Chris. *Radical Sensibility: Literature and Ideas in the 1790s*. London:
    Routledge, 1993.

Kadish, Doris Y. *Politicizing Gender: Narrative Strategies in the Aftermath of the
    French Revolution*. New Brunswick, N.J.: Rutgers University Press, 1991.

Kelly, Gary. *Revolutionary Feminism: The Mind and Career of Mary
    Wollstonecraft*. New York: St. Martin's, 1992.

Landes, Joan. *Women and the Public Sphere in the Age of the French Revolution*.
    Ithaca, N.Y.: Cornell University Press, 1988.

O'Brien, Conor Cruise. *The Great Melody: A Thematic Biography and
    Commented Anthology of Edmund Burke*. Chicago: University of Chicago
    Press, 1992.

Palmer, R. R. *The Age of Democratic Revolutions*. 2 vols. Princeton: Princeton
    University Press, 1959–64.

Paulson, Ronald. *Representations of Revolution 1789–1820*. New Haven: Yale
    University Press, 1983.

Philp, Mark, ed. *The French Revolution and British Popular Politics*. Cambridge:
    Cambridge University Press, 1991.

Prickett, Stephen. *England and the French Revolution*. London: Macmillan
    Education Ltd., 1989.

Roe, Nicholas. *The Politics of Nature: Wordsworth and Some Contemporaries*.
    New York: St. Martin's, 1992.

——. *Wordsworth and Coleridge: The Radical Years*. Oxford: Clarendon, 1988.

Schwoerer, Lois, ed. *The Revolution of 1688–1689: Changing Perspectives*.
    Cambridge: Cambridge University Press, 1992.

Smith, Olivia. *The Politics of Language 1791–1819*. Oxford: Oxford University

Press, 1984.

Thomas, D. O. *The Honest Mind: The Thought and Work of Richard Price.* Oxford: Clarendon, 1977.

Thompson, E. P. *The Making of the English Working Class.* New York: Random House, 1963.

Williams, Raymond. *Culture and Society: 1780–1950.* New York: Columbia University Press, 1960.

Yarington, Alison, and Kelvin Everest, eds. *Reflections of Revolution: Images of Romanticism.* London: Routledge, 1993.

Index

About the Contributors

David Bromwich (Ph.D., Yale University) has taught at Princeton University and presently teaches at Yale University. He is the author of numerous books and articles on William Hazlitt, Edmund Burke, political philosophy, and contemporary American education and culture.

Lisa Plummer Crafton (Ph.D., University of Tennessee) teaches at State University of West Georgia. She has published on William Wordsworth, William Blake, and Mary Wollstonecraft and is working on a study of Wordsworth's "The Brothers."

John Faulkner (Ph.D., Rutgers University) teaches at Ohio University at Lancaster. He has published on Burke's ideas about language and is presently working on a book-length study of Burke's *Reflections*.

Lowell T. Frye (Ph.D., Duke University) teaches at Hampden-Sydney College. He has published on Thomas Carlyle and Victorian literature, and on Rhetoric and Composition. He is presently working on a study of Carlyle's philosophy of history.

Jane Kromm (D.D., Harvard Divinity School; Ph.D., Emory University) teaches seventeenth-century and eighteenth-century European art history at State University of New York at Purchase. She has published on Hogarth and Goya and is presently working on a book *"Windowed Raggedness": Visual Thinking About Mental Disorders 1600–1900*.

Patricia Howell Michaelson (Ph.D., Northwestern University) has taught at Emory University and now teaches at the University of Texas-Dallas. She has published on Mary Wollstonecraft and on diaries of Quaker women in the eighteenth and nineteenth centuries.

Evan Radcliffe (Ph.D., Cornell University) teaches at Villanova University. He has most recently published articles on William Godwin and William Wordsworth and is working on a book manuscript on Godwin's political philosophy.

Paul Trolander (Ph.D., New York University) teaches at Berry College. He has published on the political effects of critical practice in the eighteenth century, on Adam Smith, and on eighteenth-century theories of eloquence.

ISBN 0-313-30496-3

9 780313 304965

HARDCOVER BAR CODE